Kingsley Amis

was born in South London in 192_ _ _ _ _ _ _ _ _ _ _ _ _
of London School and St John's College, Oxford. Between
1949 and 1963 he taught at the University College of
Swansea, Princeton University and Peterhouse, Cambridge.
He started his writing career as a poet, but it is for his novels
that he is best loved, for works including *Lucky Jim, Take a
Girl Like You, The Anti-Death League, Jake's Thing, Stanley
and the Women, The Old Devils, The Green Man,
Difficulties with Girls, The Folks That Live on the Hill* and
You Can't Do Both. The Old Devils won the Booker Prize for
Fiction in 1986.

His controversial *Memoirs* was published in 1991. Among his
other publications are *Rudyard Kipling and His World, The
Golden Age of Science Fiction, Collected Short Stories,
Collected Poems, The Amis Anthology: A Personal Choice of
English Verse* and *The Amis Story Anthology.*

Kingsley Amis was awarded the CBE in 1981 and knighted in
1990.

From the reviews of *The Biographer's Moustache*:

'A mischievous piece of work.'

JAMES WALTON, *Daily Telegraph*

'Amis's characters emerge with a truthful clarity. He knows
how to tell a story, and *The Biographer's Moustache* is as
well-structured as a dance.'

KATHY O'SHAUGHNESSY, *Literary Review*

'*The Biographer's Moustache* has some splendid and wholly
characteristic scenes and observations.'

ALLAN MASSIE, *The Scotsman*

KINGSLEY AMIS

The Biographer's Moustache

Flamingo
An Imprint of HarperCollinsPublishers

Flamingo
An Imprint of HarperCollins*Publishers*
77–85 Fulham Palace Road,
Hammersmith, London W6 8JB

Published by Flamingo 1996
9 8 7 6 5 4 3 2 1

First published in Great Britain by
Flamingo 1995

Author photograph by Snowdon

ISBN 0 00 654871 7

Set in Linotron Sabon by
Rowland Phototypesetting Ltd
Bury St Edmunds, Suffolk

Printed and bound in Great Britain by
Caledonian International Book Manufacturing Ltd, Glasgow

To Catharine and Tim Jaques

I

'Darling, who else is coming to luncheon?' asked Jimmie Fane. He spoke in a voice that had hardly altered since he was a young man half a century before, his full head of silvery-grey hair was carefully arranged and he sat up very straight in his brocaded chair.

'Sorry, darling, coming to what?' said Joanna, his wife, though she had heard.

Jimmie's already high voice rose a little higher. 'Darling, to *luncheon*. Surely the usual term for the usual meal taken in this country in the middle of the day.'

Joanna said in a slightly patient tone, 'Darling, luncheon doesn't mean the same as lunch any more, just food and people and wine and things, it means a great formal do like a City dinner with a toastmaster and speeches, you know, a, in fact *a* luncheon.'

'Oh dear, I wasn't thinking of anything remotely like that. I do hope you haven't arranged anything frightfully stuffy like that. You know I hate things like that.'

'Yes, I do, and I promise not to arrange anything frightfully stuffy ever if you'll help by calling things by their right names.'

'*Right* names? I will, I do. Like lunch in what one does and luncheon is what one does it at or with, or . . .'

'Was. Was what one did and what one used to –'

'Oh, was, was, was, I can't be expected to heed let alone follow these ephemeral fads of speech.'

Joanna Fane, now a thinnish woman in her early fifties who still showed considerable remains of earlier beauty, had once been famous for her clear blue-eyed gaze. Although no less clear than formerly, that gaze at the moment had begun to show some irritation. 'I thought you were a great one for words changing their meanings,' she said. 'Surely this is –'

'Darling, could I ask you politely not to lecture me about words? I think I may claim to know a little more about them than you.'

'Darling, I am married to you already and have been for years and years.'

'Well?'

'So there's no need for you to go on trying to impress me with your genius or anything else.'

For a moment Jimmie sat on without any movement, as if turned to stone. Then he shook slightly with laughter. 'Darling, my advice to you is to reconcile yourself to having married a very impressive man whose impressiveness has not been diminished by the passage of time, in fact if anything enhanced. I just am impressive, I have no need to try. But you still haven't answered the question I asked you just now, which was and is, who else is coming to ... wait for it ... *luncheon*,' he concluded, facetiously mouthing the word.

'I truly think I mentioned everyone,' she said without change of expression. 'As I said, it's only a small party.'

'You mentioned somebody I fancied I'd never heard of, some Scotch name would it have been?'

'Not Scott-Thompson?'

'Was it? Who is that, anyway?'

'I'm sure I said. Gordon Scott-Thompson is a literary journalist, freelance I think. He writes mostly for the *Sunday* –'

'Oh, a literary journalist. Should one have heard of him? I'm so terribly cut off these days.'

'I really don't know. Quite well thought of, I gather. He was at a party a couple of weeks ago. He said he'd got a proposition he wanted to put to you so I said he'd better come to lunch.

He must be about forty-one or -two. Not bad looking if it weren't for his moustache.'

'Have you told me all this before?'

Joanna hesitated. 'No,' she said.

'What's this proposition of his, do you know?'

'He wouldn't tell me, at least he didn't tell me.'

'He's not *queer*, I hope, the enterprising Mr Thompson? Just clearing the ground.'

'No. At least I shouldn't think so.'

'So many of them seem to be these days, especially the ones with moustaches. There must be some reason for it, I suppose. These days all that side of life is quite beyond me. These days I'm told the creatures have the impertinence to call themselves *gay*, thereby rendering unusable, thereby destroying a fine old English word with its roots deep in the language. You must have heard as much.'

'Yes, I had noticed. I don't think this chap's one of them, he had a rather pretty girl with him, Louise something, a few years younger. He asked if he could bring her along and I said he could.'

'Really.' What his wife had just revealed apparently alleviated any gloom that Jimmie had fallen into over the perhaps unrelated matters of Gordon Scott-Thompson and homosexuality. 'Good. What a good idea.'

'There's somebody now,' said Joanna as the doorbell sounded from downstairs. 'Have you seen to the wine?'

'Oh yes. And there's no actual need to respond to a possible arrival as if it might be that of your Uncle Arthur from Penge. Is my tie all right?'

'Oh, as usual it's all . . . Here.' She efficiently reduced the dark-purple knot from something the size and rough shape of a baby's fist to a smaller polyhedron. 'That's better but it's still not right. You're hopeless when it comes to tying ties.'

Jimmie said with pretended humility, 'I'm afraid I've never managed to learn,' and might have gone on to say something about the truly neat tying of ties being a body-servant's skill if Joanna had not been hurrying from the room. Instead he called after her, 'But then I've got you to look after me,' which was better anyway.'

2

'I shouldn't have thought he was your idea of fun at all,' said Louise. 'All those lords and ladies and butlers and what-not.'

'It was my impression I'm not meant to like fun anyway,' said Gordon Scott-Thompson seriously. 'As for lords and ladies and what-not, I can take them or leave them alone. It's up to him what he writes about anyway, within reason. There isn't any point getting hot under the collar about Hardy's peasants as such, before he does anything with them.'

'You do stick to the point, don't you, Gordon? It's a bit off-putting, you know. People don't necessarily like thinking what they're saying.'

'Blame it on my far-off education. Bad timing – another couple of years and the school I went to was comprehensivized out of existence. As it was they taught me how to read and write.'

'There you go again.'

Gordon had not been far off the mark about his being meant not to like fun. From time to time Louise certainly took that view and would often go on to say he would be well advised to keep that kind of attitude to himself; as he knew, she meant in his dealings with females. He thought she might have had a point there. He would never have said he knew a great deal about women, but he had noticed that one of the many ways in which they could be divided into two classes was along the lines of whether they did or did not show signs of wanting to remake their men to suit them better. According to him, Louise was one of those who did. As if in pursuit of some kind of symmetry, she had once told him he was obviously the sort of man who refused to compromise his standards when dealing with a woman. Though he had had enough sense (for once) not to say so, he interpreted this to mean he refused to palter with the truth or what he saw as the truth no matter what the company, what might be gained by answering any old rubbish a woman might talk with rubbish of his own, etc. He was intermittently aware of the repellent tendency of such an attitude.

Nevertheless, Gordon had had some success with women. He must have been, he felt, reasonably personable, otherwise people like Louise would not have considered being seen with him in public. Women interested him, too, though admittedly more as a series of individuals than, in the manner of his randier contemporaries, as one huge undifferentiated objective to be assaulted wherever it might show itself; after all, perhaps a man did that much better in this field for having a touch of the prig in his character. Even so, Gordon now and then felt dimly that he was missing or had missed something in life by not being permanently on full sexual alert.

There remained the question of his moustache. It was on his face now for a mixture of reasons, starting chronologically with dissatisfaction or boredom with his own unadorned looks as seen reflected in mirrors and such. His grandfather, his father's father, universally said to have been a striking-looking man, had worn a similar moustache all his adult life. Then he, Gordon, had remembered being secretly rather taken by how he had looked with just such a pencilled-in facial addition in a newspaper photograph. And he had since found it a useful talking point. Anyhow, there it was, establishing itself more firmly every day.

That morning Louise had come to his flat because it was a good point from which to set out for the Fanes' place near the river. She knew that the lodging across the landing from his own was occupied by a West Indian sound engineer called

Emmet Berry, and mentioned him conversationally to Gordon as the two were leaving.

'What's he like to have in the same house?' she asked.

'I hardly see him. He and I keep ourselves pretty much to ourselves.'

'Doesn't he make a lot of noise?'

'Nothing out of the way.'

'For a boogie, don't you mean? For a jig?'

'If you're telling me I believe in my heart or somewhere that black people make more than their fair share of noise, I'd have to say some of them probably do. But then some white people probably –'

'Yes, yes, yes. Christ, Gordon, why have you got to be so bloody *balanced* about everything under the sun? In your world it's always on the one hand this, but on the other hand that. I'm sorry, but the effect is most uncool.'

'You don't sound very sorry,' said Gordon mildly. 'I don't care that much what the effect is, and whatever it may be I thought everybody had stopped saying things were cool or uncool.'

'They had, but they're starting to again.'

In exchanges like this, he could never quite settle in his mind how far Louise was really ticking him off for being uncool and how far satirically recommending conduct calculated to go down well in a trend-crazed society like the present one. A bit of both, no doubt, unless that was him just being bloody balanced again. It was that kind of uncertainty that kept him and her in their separate establishments instead of moving in together somewhere. That and, he had thought more than once, a certain ambiguity in Louise's appearance, splendid, radiant, starlet-like at a short distance, slightly chubby, sometimes almost lumpish, when seen close to. Well, perhaps his moustache had a comparably unsettling effect on her.

'Here's our bus,' he said.

3

Quite soon afterwards, seven persons were gathered in the Fanes' first-floor sitting-room, a place of thick light-coloured rugs, glass-fronted bookcases and paintings and drawings from earlier in the century. Guests for lunch, or luncheon, consisted of an elderly boring peer of the realm and his elderly drunken wife, a lone man in his fifties who looked like a retired boxer but in fact helped to publish expensive books in Milan, and the relatively unknown Gordon Scott-Thompson and his girl-friend. That was anyway how Jimmie would have described her if left to himself, though he understood the contemporary world well enough to be aware that you were not supposed to call people things like that in it. The young couple, whether or not it was all right to call them that, had turned up not long after peer and wife, whom Jimmie instantly abandoned for the new arrivals.

'Come in, come in,' he cried as they were doing so, 'how absolutely splendid that you're here,' and he swept up to the girl and rested his hands on her shoulders. 'Oh dear, I knew your name as well as I know my own until half a minute ago but now it's completely vanished.' He removed his left hand to smooth his hair back, thereby drawing attention to its continuing abundance and distinguished coloration. 'Do help me out, there's a darling.'

'Louise Gardiner.'

'Louise,' echoed Jimmie, his right hand still on her shoulder. 'Does that mean you're French? If I may say so you don't look it.'

'I'm not. English all the way back as far as I know.'

8

'*Oh* I thought so. But the name did make me wonder for an instant.'

At Louise's side, Gordon admired the assurance of this while privately questioning some of its substance, and hoped he would be in as good shape when his turn to be seventy-six came round. At the same time he did rather wonder at what stage he might be expected to enter the conversation. His moment came after Jimmie had briefly wondered aloud whether there was such a thing as a characteristic English face without shifting his attention from Louise's.

'Do forgive me, you are . . . ?'

Gordon said, 'Gordon –'

'We haven't met, have we?'

'No, Mr Fane, but having read I think all your –'

'Come and be introduced.'

A drink, in the shape of a medium-sized glass of champagne, found its way into Gordon's hand after he had met two people called Lord and Lady Bagshot and just before meeting a latecomer in a high-necked sweater called Count somebody. The champagne tasted rather nasty to Gordon, but then champagne had never been his drink, and besides this sample of it could not in fact be nasty, because Jimmie Fane was known to be quite an authority on wines, had in the 1950s published a couple of books on the subject. Anyway, for the moment there was no alternative to be seen.

The view that Jimmie's drinks could never be nasty required some modification over lunch, or luncheon. The meal was taken in a room on the ground floor facing the street. Here on a sideboard were ranged three bottles of still wine, two whites and a red, all three with their labels facing the wall. They stayed where they were until the first course, a properly made vegetable soup, had come and gone. Then Jimmie went round the circular table pouring the white, his large and efficient right hand continuing to hide the label. As Gordon soon discovered, this wine, unchilled, was dry to the point of sharpness and, he

9

thought, not at all good with the well-done roast beef it was perhaps meant to help down. He drank sparingly of it. So did the other guests, except for the sweatered count, who from first to last had nothing to say of it or of anything else, but drained his glass at a swallow. Was he truly a count? It still seemed perfectly possible.

Lord Bagshot spoke up. 'What is this stuff we're drinking, Jimmie?'

'It comes from the prettiest little vineyard you ever saw, twenty miles or so south of the upper Loire.'

'M'm. It's only my opinion, I know, but it doesn't seem to me to go too well with this very nice beef.'

'I'm sorry to hear that.'

'I notice you're not drinking it.'

'No,' agreed Jimmie. Not quite surreptitiously but without attracting much attention, he had helped himself to some of the red wine and replaced the bottle on the sideboard behind him, its label still out of sight. 'The quack told me to avoid dry white wine with my acidulous stomach. Don't tell me you're in the same case, Basil, because if so . . .' His voice died away before he could reveal what he might do if so.

'No, I'm not,' admitted Lord Bagshot. He forbore from going on to say that, whether acidulous or not, a stomach was apt to welcome what must have been at least a tolerable claret more heartily than a tepid Muscadet with hot roast beef. All he did was push his barely tasted glass away from him, an action perhaps unnoticed by Jimmie, who at that moment was engaged in recharging his own.

Gordon had been placed between Louise and Lady Bagshot. Without trying he could think of plenty he wanted to say to Louise, but little of it seemed sayable then and there, and no amount of trying was ever going to suggest to him anything at all to say to Lady Bagshot, who had one of the largest faces he had ever seen surmounting a human neck and whose spectacles were in proportion. Not that she had the air of someone who wanted to be talked to, being quite satisfied with the companionship of a half-bottle of vodka stowed between times in a beaded woollen bag she kept within her direct reach. Before her stood an untouched bowl of cooling soup and a sparse plate of cooling beef. She was vigorously smoking cigarettes.

On her other side sat the count and beyond him Joanna Fane, who was giving him a full account of a visit to the opera paid perhaps earlier that week, perhaps a decade or two before. As he had been doing, the man nodded and smiled and now and then dilated his eyes sympathetically, drank and had his glass refilled. It might have been that he had had his tongue torn out by an indignant peasantry.

Many things might have been true of him without upsetting Gordon, who got conscientiously on with the task of sorting out impressions. The house, a few doors down from the King's Road towards the river, was only a room and a passage broad but it ran back some way, and no doubt fell into one or another upper category of posh people's praise like rather ravishing. Gordon could not have said much about things like lamp fittings and cutlery but he could tell they were expensive here without being either flashy or new. The ceilings had the look of having been the work of somebody in particular and over the sideboard there hung an oil painting of foreign parts that had a distinctly pricey appearance. Yes, but what about the couple who lived here?

A glance in Jimmie's direction showed him to be looking straight at Gordon. So did a second glance a moment later, with the increment that this time he was frowning slightly and evidently concentrating his attention on Gordon's moustache, until a great yawn supervened. Gordon could so vividly imagine Jimmie's high voice asking him to be a good chap and try not to stare in that extraordinary fashion that he lost no time in transferring his gaze to Joanna. She too proved to be looking back at him, while still telling the count about who might well have been, but fairly unexpectedly was not after all, to be seen in the opera-house bar. It occurred to Gordon to wonder what, if anything, the Fanes had said to each other about him and his possible intentions.

This wonderment returned in a sharpened form when the party had finished lunch and moved back to the sitting-room upstairs. Here Jimmie had seized him by the arm and borne him off in stagey style to a narrower extension where books of a more consistently solemn, leather-bound aspect were to be seen. Jimmie at once sat himself down on a comfortable-looking old-fashioned chair, did not invite Gordon to find a seat but made no perceptible objection when he did. After shutting his eyes and perhaps dozing for a few seconds he suddenly said to him,

'It's very nice of you to come over today and bring that enchanting little girl with you.'

'Oh, it's very –'

'Joanna, that's my wife, you know – Joanna tells me you've got a proposition you want to put to me.' Also suddenly, Jimmie reopened his eyes. 'I confess to you I'm all agog to hear what it can be.'

'Oh. Well, I was rereading *The Escaped Prisoner* the other day, and I thought –'

'Do tell me just what your proposition is, dear man.'

'All right. I'd like to try my hand at a long article or even a short book on you and your work. It's been eleven years since the –'

'Who would publish it?'

'If it ends up as an article I reckon I could get a couple of instalments into *The Westminster Review of Books*, they rather go in for length. If it extends to a book it would certainly be worth trying it on your old publisher right away. Somebody there seemed very interested when I mentioned the possibility.'

'I have to say I don't think many people today would want

to sit down and read a whole book about an old back number like me.'

'I don't think that's true, Mr Fane, and you're –'

'Jimmie, please.'

'Jimmie. I reckon you're due for a revival and I'm not the only one by a long chalk. Those novels aren't going to stay away for ever.'

'I haven't published a book of any sort since 1987, and that wasn't much better than a potboiler of snippets and cuttings.'

'Jimmie, you deserve to be back in the public eye and there are strong signs that you're moving in that direction or why would I, well . . .'

'Bother. Quite so. Yes, I suppose it might be taken as such a sign.'

This was not far out. Or it was a possible way of putting it. A way of putting it closer to Gordon's view of the matter would have been that, on the literary stock exchange, Fanes had been due for a recovery but for the moment could be snapped up cheap pending a strong reissue. He himself would have said he had no definite opinion of the quality of Jimmie's writing but saw clearly enough that as a figure of the prewar and wartime years and later, with an admittedly heterosexual but still conspicuous personal history, the old fellow could without undue difficulty be made the subject of a publishable set of articles or even a book. And now, or soon, was the time. What Gordon had been going to say was that it had been eleven years since the appearance of the last book on him. Just the right sort of interval.

Again Jimmie's attention seemed to focus for a moment on Gordon's moustache before diffusing itself. 'I imagine I can't stop you from publishing practically anything you like.'

Gordon nodded reflectively. 'No, in a sense that's true. But I hope to have your co-operation in this case.'

'Even if I give it you, what's to stop your writing and

publishing anything that comes into your head, however untrue or unpleasant?'

'Short of recourse to the law, you could stop me by refusing to let me quote more than the odd line from your works, which wouldn't be nearly enough for what I have in mind.'

'I think I see that,' said Jimmie. 'Of course.' Then he turned animated. 'Naturally, my dear chap, I've not the slightest reason in the world to suppose that any words of yours would be other than irreproachably veracious and well-mannered, I do assure you.'

'Well, that's a relief.' Gordon ventured a smile. 'Perhaps we can proceed to the next stage.'

'And what do you see as the next stage?'

'Well, just a thorough general chat, working out an approach. I'll need to do some thinking in the meantime, make a note or two.'

'You mean we should have a sort of preliminary discussion.'

'Exactly.'

'Very well. May I insist we conduct our discussion over *luncheon* somewhere?'

'That sounds like a good idea.'

'I do so adore being taken out to luncheon.'

'I'm glad to hear it,' said Gordon bravely.

'I'm sure you'll do me reasonably well, better than I did the Bagshots today.'

Gordon found this remark difficult to answer, so he merely nodded his head in a dependable manner.

'Perhaps I owe you a small explanation. When I was a young man, it used to be said of me, not only in jest, that when I wiped somebody's eye it stayed wiped. That unspeakable wine I offered was by way of getting back at Bagshot for the vile Peruvian red he gave us the last time we dined with him. He saw that all right, which was why he didn't make more of a fuss. Oh, and if you're worried about young Carlo, that count person, he doesn't care or notice what he drinks. Where he comes from one can't afford to.'

'I see.'

'I think now we might rejoin the others,' said Jimmie, rising to his feet. 'Give me a telephone call, will you?'

Gordon likewise rose. 'I will. I'll also send you my c.v.'

'Send me your what?'

'My c.v. My curriculum vitae.' He pronounced the first word like curriculum and the second like vee-tye.

'Your *what*?'

Gordon said it again and added, 'Meaning a dated account of what I've done and written if anything and where I've worked and such. So you'll have it by you, what there is of it.'

'Oh, presumably you mean a curriculum vitae,' said Jimmie, pronouncing the first word like curriculum and the second like vie-tee.

'Yes, if you prefer.'

'I do prefer if it's all the same to you. Since we're supposedly talking English rather than Latin or *Italian*. Yes I agree I know what you meant the first time but then one often infers as much from a grunt or a whinny and that's no argument for conducting one's discourse wholly or even partly in a series of approximations and lucky guesses. I hope you take my point?'

'Yes I do.' Gordon spoke with some warmth. He was relieved not to be called upon to repeat the phrase in its preferred pronunciation slowly after Jimmie.

'Good. Can I tempt you to a glass of port?'

'No thank you.'

'I think I'll let myself be tempted. I should give it up but I can't. No – cannot is false; I will not give it up.' Jimmie gave a smile that only the literal-minded would have hesitated to call charming. 'We'll have some fun with this business.'

'Indeed we will.'

The rest of the company had split into two, or two and a

half. The half was Lady Bagshot, who was sitting near but not with Joanna Fane and Louise and was conscientiously working her way through her half-bottle of vodka. Another drink like the one she had just poured herself would get her there with no more than a heeltap left over. Her current drink, as she took a mouthful, looked quite small beside the vastness of her face. By the window the still-vigilant count let Lord Bagshot go on telling him all about somebody's house, it might have been his own. Gordon went over to Louise and Joanna, who looked up expectantly.

'Well?' they both asked, and Joanna added, 'I've been hearing.'

'The answer's yes.'

'I knew it,' said Louise.

'Well I didn't,' said Joanna. 'Not his kind of thing at all. It's not that he doesn't like publicity, it's just that he likes to be in complete control of it and everything else. Do sit down.'

'I can't see Gordon letting anyone else control what he writes.'

'Time will show. What's he agreed to so far?'

'Lunch and a chat,' said Gordon.

'It'll be your lunch and his chat. Don't let him flannel you into taking him somewhere madly expensive like Woolton's or the Tripoli. Make it a little place you happen to know. Where is he now? Did he say where he was going?'

'To get himself a glass of port, I thought.'

'He'll be stretched out on his study couch and fast asleep and dreaming by now. Not a pretty sight.'

But if Jimmie was indeed asleep as his wife spoke he was very soon awake again and re-entering the sitting-room. Any port he carried back with him had come within him, a possibility that on recent form Gordon did not at all rule out. However that might have been, Jimmie seemed in elevated form and at once settled down next to Louise on the little padded couch with its vividly covered cushions and resumed the intimate-

16

revue style of their earlier meeting. Joanna cast her eye over Gordon to no purpose he could determine, but he evidently passed whatever muster it might have been. She said,

'I suppose you've written this sort of thing before.'

'About someone else, you mean. No, I haven't ever.'

'If you had, I was going to warn you you're up against something new this time. I was going to tip you off he's not like other people.'

Nobody is, thought Gordon rather dully, so this time he made what was meant to be a thoughtful face.

'You can't know very much about him.'

'Only his work.'

'His what? I thought you were going to write his biography.'

'That was the idea, or part of it.'

'Nearly all of it, surely. A catalogue of his principal publications and appointments would hardly get you on to the second page.'

'I hope to be digging a bit deeper than that.'

'If you do, watch out, as I said. You probably won't come to much actual harm, but parts of it won't be much fun if you do your job properly. You'd better let me talk to you about him to get a rounded picture.'

Gordon knew enough already about Jimmie to know too that he would be actively displeased with any really rounded picture, but he kept this reflection to himself, saying only, 'Does that mean I'm to take you out to lunch as well – on a different occasion, of course.'

'I expect it occurred to you that he'd do his damnedest to stop you printing the juicy bits. Maybe, but I think someone in your position ought at least to have some idea of what they are, don't you? And it's terribly nice of you to ask me to have lunch with you somewhere, if that's what you were doing, but it would be sure to get back to him, which might be embarrassing at this stage. So I'm afraid that's not on at the moment.'

'Oh.'

'But if we shared a crust one day when he's cavorting with his chums at Gray's, shared it here I mean, then that couldn't get back to him.'

'No.'

'In fact I can't see why it should get back to anybody, frankly.'

'Nor can I.'

'Give me a ring. Between half past eight and nine on a weekday morning is a good time.'

4

'Darling, what did you really make of that young man?'

'Not a lot, darling. Pleasant enough, rather conventional, anxious not to say the wrong thing. The very chap to be your biographer, darling.'

'It's to be literary too. A critical study of what I've written. I'm not sure he's up to that. For all I know he may be. I hope he's been properly educated. He says he'll send me what he calls his c.v. Fascinating. Do you fancy him?'

'Darling, please. With that moustache?'

'I'm sorry, darling, yes. It didn't look like hair at all.'

'More like something that's been turned on a lathe. Anyway he's about thirty years younger than me. What did you make of little Louise? I saw you firing on all cylinders.'

'Pretty as a picture but rather stodgy. Filling, like plum duff, you know. Do you think the noble lord enjoyed himself?'

'I shouldn't be surprised. He didn't care for being given wine he didn't care for.'

'I hope not. Now he knows how it feels.'

'I didn't care for that warm white stuff either.'

'Yes, I'm sorry, darling. I just couldn't think of a way of getting a decent drink into your glass.'

After a pause, Joanna said, 'Lady B sensibly brought her own tipple as usual.'

'I wonder when those two talked to each other last.'

'You can't really expect it of her. She talked to me a bit at one stage but she wasn't making much sense.'

'He might as well keep quiet too.'

'But both of them are positive conversational giants compared with Carlo.'

'These voluble Italians,' said Jimmie.

'Darling, I wish you'd have another go at him about his English. He gets about one word in twenty of what I say to him and one in a hundred of anybody else and apparently he can't say anything himself.'

'Not in English. His Italian's fluent enough.'

'Why doesn't he stay in Italy then? There can't be anything for him here.'

'Something to do with his tax, as I said. And he likes eating in friends' houses in London because he hasn't got to grapple with English as he'd have to in a restaurant.'

'Can't he go to an Italian restaurant? There are dozens all over London.'

'As I told you, he doesn't like Italian food.'

'But why do we keep asking him here? Actually I can tell you the answer to that. Because he keeps asking us to that palazzo place of his and we keep going there. After all, he is a count.'

'Well, if you must hark back to the primordial rudiments of everything,' said Jimmie in a weary tone.

'Hard luck on those youngsters, getting let in for two duds and one semi-dud.'

'Only duds conversationally.'

'Oh, you mean it's much more important that they've all got handles to their names?'

'That Scotchman and his bit of stuff would think so.'

'I can't see it cutting a single millimetre of ice with either him or her.'

5

'Well, what did you really make of that lot at lunch-time?' Gordon asked Louise.

'I wasn't particularly struck by any of them.'

'Not even by poor old Jimmie? He was doing his best, after all.'

'Doing his best to what?'

'Well, to make you feel at home or something of the sort.'

'If he'd wanted to do that he could have asked us to meet somebody a bit more interesting than his bloody lordship and his piss-artist elephant's-bum-faced four-eyed boiler of a wife. Oh, and that asshole of an Italian who never opened his mouth except to put food and drink into it. Not that I wanted him to talk. No, poor old Jimmie was showing me and you and Mrs Jimmie and possibly others that there was life in the old dog yet. Some hopes. By the look of him he hasn't had it up for half a century.'

'I reckoned he asked those people to impress us with his aristocratic connections.'

'Fancy that. Well, all I can say is he didn't impress me.' Louise spoke sulkily rather than with any heat.

'Nor me, actually.'

'If you're right about him wanting to impress us he's even more pathetic than I thought.'

'Yes, I think there is something rather pathetic about poor old Jimmie.'

'I don't mean that sort of pathetic. And you must be careful of poor old Jimmie. He's bad news.'

'I'm sorry I inflicted him and the rest of them on you.'

'That's all right, it was quite an interesting experience considered as an item of social anthropology. A chance to see the British class system in action.'

'You must mean in inaction. Decline from whatever it may once have been.'

'Christ, Gordon, after that display?'

'All . . . bangs and coloured lights. A hundred years ago, even up to 1939, the thing really had some teeth in it. There was an empire to run and a comparatively barbaric peasantry and proletariat to be kept down. What's left of either of them today? The, the remnants of that class system operate in the other direction. Dukes and what-not complain that their titles hold them back, get in the way of their careers in banking or photography or whatever it may be. The British class system, as you quaintly call it, is –'

'I know, it's dead, which up to a point is a good thing, but beyond that point isn't so good. Don't go on about all those dukes who can't get on in banking because they've admitted they're dukes unless you want me to burst out crying. But anyhow, please don't lecture at me.'

'I didn't mean to. But you must admit things have come to a pretty pass when you get someone like Jimmie Fane hobnobbing with an Italian count who never learnt to speak English. Even fifty years ago one wouldn't –'

'Fuck fifty years ago, and it's time you realized there's nothing I must do, all right.' Louise sighed and stretched. 'Except now I must be going and things like that.'

'Oh darling, do stay a little longer.'

Gordon got to his feet as Louise had done and grappled with her briefly in an amatory way, at the end of which she disengaged herself without hostility and telephoned for a minicab. Within a few minutes she was being borne away from his flat towards the rather more commodious one she shared with a girl associate. It might have mildly surprised the Fanes to hear that, although the younger couple had certainly done the deed of darkness together, as Jimmie sometimes expressed it, they actually lived apart. Whatever the merits of this arrangement, at times like the present he was more strongly aware of its drawbacks. He doubted if Louise ever felt like that. When the subject of literal cohabitation came up, which it seldom did now, she was liable to say something like she wanted to keep her independence. He had given up wondering what she meant by that and had never asked her how many other chaps she was keeping her independence from.

This apparent tolerance testified not to self-confidence but to unwillingness to imperil their present arrangement, which at times unlike the present suited him well enough. He asked himself occasionally whether he was suited to live with any woman at all. He had so lived in the past, up to and including the point of being married for nearly six years, not counting the interval between his wife's departure and their divorce. She had departed with a man who worked in a government office on something to do with pensions and who, according to report, was three or four inches shorter and substantially younger than he. These factors had not enhanced Gordon's self-esteem. His wife had once accused him of not knowing how to help a woman to feel pleased with life or even how to have a good time himself, and quite often and more succinctly of being hopeless. Perhaps he just had a low sex-drive. It was true, to be sure, that he thought or at any rate talked about sex less than his mates seemed to.

An internal twinge smartly followed by an eructation reminded him of the unpleasant wine he had earlier drunk and so of its provider. Someone had told him that Jimmie Fane was one of the most money-conscious buggers in London, but had not reckoned on a demonstration of this quality at his own table. Gordon wished more than ever that he had managed to get a glimpse of the label on that bottle of red. Moving now towards the corner where he kept his typewriter, he thought of what Jimmie's wife had intimated about the financial dangers of taking him out to lunch, but then she had probably been talking for effect, to impress him with how wild and free and not to be thought of as stuffy and middle-aged she was. However, discussing Jimmie with her was bound to have its points of interest.

Now, by the window that overlooked the gloomy suburban park, he put a sheet of inferior paper into his typewriter and got to work on roughing out his curriculum vie-tee for Jimmie. Experience led him to resist the impulse to get it over in one go and try for a fair copy straight off. Wincing with boredom, then, and x-ing out every other phrase, he set down the facts of his London birth, his sound but beyond all question non-posh schooling, his minimally creditable, non-Oxbridge college course and 'good' final grading. None of this, he felt, would impress or even interest any sentient being but it had to be there in its entirety. Couple of years' drudgery as sub-editor on *Barnsley Echo* or equivalent before lucky breakthrough to features desk, with special reference to culture, on London daily. Slow and limited ascent to books section on Sunday newspaper. Principal articles. Contributions to publications, to collections. First man to land on Mars 1995, on Titan 1996. The last entry would not survive retyping, but had been necessary to set down in order to ward off terminal coma. Something did that job, anyway, though far from having shown the least sign of private amusement he looked a little guilty at sinking into facetiousness, and hastily x-ed out the offending space fiction with the shift-key down.

Soon he was retyping. A word-processor would have been quicker and the result perhaps more imposing, but Gordon had not got one of his own. Too expensive, he would say, and he had a sort of access to a machine in the office provided he had a good enough story and could persuade the editor's secretary to let him use it. And this time there was the consideration that Jimmie would probably have learnt to tell apart a processor print-out and something run up on the old steam typewriter and, needless to say, would not have approved of anything in the former category. At the moment it was very likely not needful to say that he would have had no corresponding bias in favour of the latter. Having biases in favour of things, Gordon already suspected, was not something Jimmie was noted for, a trying characteristic in a biographee.

Challenged by somebody like Louise, Gordon would probably have stuck to self-interest, enlightened where possible, as by far his leading motive in writing about Jimmie. But in his mind he would freely admit that he hoped the result would do something more than advance his own career. He had not lied when he said earlier that he had recently reread *The Escaped Prisoner*, at least on the understanding that by 'reread' was meant something like 'read through to the end with some respect having several years ago looked at the thing and found it intolerably complacent.' The fuller text captured a youthful observation that the book was silent on critical issues like racial equality and equal rights for women. Well, that was roughly how he saw the matter in retrospect.

His transcription done, Gordon read through the page he had filled, trying to see what was there as a record of events and actions as well as a mere piece of typing with possible errors. Quite soon he stopped reading it and just checked it for literals. As a narrative of the better part of a lifetime it was undeniably thin, lacking in uplift. He now saw without difficulty that his original instinct had been right, and his personal history would not have been improved by including in it mention of the novel of his that had been rejected by fourteen publishers, even less of its successor that remained in rough draft if anywhere outside the mind of God. After some attempted clairvoyance, he pencilled a few words across the top of the sheet and got it ready for the post.

Having done so he felt committed to something, small as it might have been, and about time too.

6

The day came when Gordon was to take Jimmie Fane out to lunch. The morning of it he filled in at the offices of the Sunday newspaper he worked for. These had once been majestically sited in the area of Fleet Street, but rising costs had compelled a series of moves into humbler quarters, ending for the moment in a dockland semi-wilderness. The building was reachable, or nearly, by a water-bus service that was slow and uncomfortable but at least different from that of the ordinary land bus with its route through miles of houses in silent-screen disrepair apparently occupied by remnants of a dwarfish aboriginal race. Both alternatives had the quality of always seeming a little worse to experience than to remember. This time it was the water-bus that Gordon swore he would never use again. The weather was wet and he had to plod across a kind of mudflat between disembarking and reaching shelter.

'Nice of you to condescend to drop in on us,' said the books editor. Originally he had not much wanted to be books editor, but the then editorial editor, the Editor in fact, had not wanted him to be anything else. 'We appreciate immeasurably being spared some of your attention.' This man was now nearing sixty and called Desmond O'Leary, though he gave no other sign whatever of having to do with Ireland or any of its inhabitants, past and present. 'Everybody here understands that you have weightier calls on your time.' Whatever his origins, O'Leary looked like a kind of bird or lizard above the neck, having no hair at all to be seen on his head, though he was very ready with the assurance that he was like an ape everywhere else. 'All that we lesser mortals would beg from you in the foreseeable future is a thousand words on this latest piece of New England farmhouse guff, a round-up of female black American guff with some latitude as to space and, let's see, no, yes, whither the docudrama as seen on TV and film and what, if anything, is literary truth.' O'Leary laid bare and lit a smallish cigar of rectangular cross-section. 'Actually all I need from you more or less straight away is your next column piece and a word with Harry about our coverage of the Codex Prize. It looks like Latin America's turn this time round, much to my personal mortification. How did your lunch with JRP Fane go?'

'It's today.'

'Look, Gordon, when it comes to picking up the bill, mind you don't –'

'It's come to that already and I'm picking it up. He virtually made it a condition of coming out at all.'

'Oh did he? Clearly his hand has lost none of its cunning. Aristocratic sort of old sod, isn't he? I saw him at some party once and there was nobody there half grand enough for him.'

'He was quite willing to talk to me.'

'Ask yourself why. But what's the attraction as far as you're concerned? Not your cup of tea as a bloke or as a writer, I'd have thought. And he's what, he's passé, over and done with, gone for good, thing of the past, beyond revival even by you.' O'Leary stared over his half-glasses at Gordon. 'I happen to think you'd do the job about as well as anybody if it could be done, but it can't, as you'll see. Not worth the sweat.'

Gordon shrank from saying that O'Leary himself was something of a relic, specifically in the view he took of Fane's irrevocable departure as a literary figure. What he did say, no less truthfully, was, 'He may not be my kind of writer and he's obviously not my kind of man. That's an important part of what you called his attraction for me as a subject. I want to see how far I can –'

'Oh God, it's the challenge, is it, the fascination of what's

27

difficult and all that. Some old tit, even older and tittier than JRP Fane, anyway you remember he said when you've done something you can do, do something you can't. Wrong again. Do something you can do and then do something else you can do and never mind if it's the same thing. No virtue in trying what you find uncongenial because you find it uncongenial. You know that very well, or you would if you weren't still stuck in that bloody Scottish Presbyterianism you flatter yourself you've left far behind you. My own upbringing was – but it's a little early in the day to be bringing up bygones, I suppose. I shouldn't really have started on any of this. Sorry.'

'Oh, that's all right,' said Gordon, though he could see little enough to forgive, O'Leary having mostly stuck to his habitual friendly-jeering manner. Well, perhaps what he had said had fetched up a little nearer the bone than usual. 'In fact it's a nice change to be treated as an adult. Anyway, with your permission I mean to have a fair crack at showing how decent writing can overcome almost any prejudice in the reader, if that doesn't sound too pompous.'

Perhaps it did; whether it did or not, O'Leary seemed to pay it small heed. He said, 'I just hate to see a reasonably competent and successful journalist like yourself thinking it's about time he did something less perishable and throwing his talents away on a serious book. I wouldn't mind so much if you were going for something of your own, even a novel, but a critical biography, your phrase be it noted, of a prehistoric old sod like Fane, oh dear oh dear. Right, I've said too much already, not that any of it'll shake your determination to misuse your abilities. You know, Gordon, in this life it's important to recognize one's limitations. Mine extend as far as this desk and no further, not my first choice as you may have heard, which goes to show one can sometimes do with a bit of guidance in setting one's course. Now I mustn't be late for the Chairman's conference. He's become a degree or two less tolerable since he got that bloody knighthood, unless it's my imagination. Well, show me a pot of ointment and I'll show you a fly. Give me a call tea-time about the days of the week you'll be coming in to the office. Don't forget to talk to Harry before you go. And first thing in the morning will do for your column but no later.'

It had been arranged that, when the time came, Gordon as host-designate should call to collect guest at the Fane residence and he turned up there punctually, indeed with a couple of minutes to spare. A girl of about thirty answered his ring apparently clad in an excerpt from the Bayeux Tapestry. 'Yes?' she said loudly before he could speak. Her manner was unwelcoming.

'I've called to pick up Mr Fane.'

'What?'

'I'm taking him out to lunch.'

'Name?'

'Yes, meaning yes, I have a name, and if you ask me nicely I might tell you what it is.' That was something like what Gordon was tempted to say. But all he did say was his name in full.

'I'm terribly sorry but I've never heard of you.'

'I exist nevertheless,' Gordon actually did say this time. 'Will you kindly tell Mr Fane that I'm here as arranged with him on Monday this week?'

'Mr Fane is not here.'

'Oh, I'm sorry to hear that. Perhaps I could wait for him. May I come in for a minute?'

'Anything wrong, darling?' asked a new voice, new in this conversation but in other respects age-old. Gordon had spied its owner, or that person's head, sticking out of a nearby doorway inside the house a moment before. Now he was to be seen in full, striding up the hallway, a well-set-up man in a dark-grey suit and glasses. As he approached he repeated his question.

'I don't really know, darling,' answered the girl.

'M'm,' said the man. He came to a halt in front of Gordon,

at whom he still gazed while he said, 'Could this be the chap, do you think?'

'Well, he certainly looks and sounds like it.'

'M'm.'

Now the man took his glasses off his nose and put them folded into the top pocket of his suit. 'I think it might be better if you left, old man,' he said. 'No hard feelings.'

Gordon moved his arms a little way away from his sides and leant slightly forward, and things looked quite interesting for a moment, but then a distinctive high voice could be heard from the street.

'Ah, there you are, my dear fellow, I'm terribly sorry I wasn't here to greet you, I just popped out for some cat-food.'

'Never mind, Jimmie,' said Gordon, 'I've been well looked after.'

'Periwinkle's been taking care of you, has she? I'm afraid I'm absolutely hopeless at organizing things, especially people. Let's be off, shall we? I suppose I must have asked them along to give a . . . That's Oliver, my son-in-law, back there. I think you could hail this chap. Fancy painting a taxi *yellow*.'

When they had driven off, Gordon asked, 'She's your daughter, is she, Periwinkle?' He wanted to have it authoritatively confirmed that this was indeed a girl's name.

'Not a very friendly creature, I'm afraid, little Periwinkle.'

'She wasn't exactly welcoming me in just now. She seemed to think I was a tout or a hawker or something.'

'She must have got you mixed up with a sort of cadger kind of fellow from Bulgaria did he say, who's been hanging round the place for a day or two. She must have mistaken you for him.'

'How extraordinary.'

'Yes, different kettle of fish altogether. Horrible-looking broken-down sort of chap. It may seem an odd description of such a person, but what I believe is known nowadays as dead common.'

'Really,' said Gordon, remembering to make three syllables of it. He glanced surreptitiously down at his clothes.

'He did have a moustache rather like yours.'

'Perhaps that was what confused Periwinkle.'

'Of course, she's the child of my second marriage. She's a funny girl. I don't think she's ever kissed me of her own accord. The truth is she's a howling snob. I can't think where she gets that from, it must be from her mother. Between ourselves I've never greatly cared for young Oliver, what's he called, Turnbull I fancy. He's what they call upwardly mobile, or at any rate desirous of being so. He's also something in the City. Remind me. Just remind me where you're taking me if you would.'

'I thought —'

'And whatever you do don't please say it's a little place you happen to know.'

Since that was more or less exactly what he had been going to say, Gordon's reply was slow in coming. He was thrown off too by trying to remember where he had not long ago heard that very expression, and further still by wondering whether it was the form of words or the likely reality or both that was being interdicted. But in fact it was not at all long before he was saying gamely, 'Well, it is a rather small place and in the nature of things I do happen to know about it.'

'Yes yes, no doubt no doubt. What's it called again?'

'Cakebread's.'

'Really,' said Jimmie, far outdoing in all respects Gordon's pronunciation of the word. 'He's not an American, I hope, the valuable Cakebread?'

'Not as far as I know.'

'Nevertheless I prophesy that his establishment will be full of citizens of that great republic. Hiram and Mamie are just mad about little places they happen to know, yes sir.'

Jimmie's second sentence here was delivered in what was presumably intended as an American accent, though one that failed to recall any actually used within the nine million square kilometres of the Union. Gordon was at a loss for an answer, so he just smiled nervously.

'I'm sorry, dear boy, of course I adore Americans and feel at home with everything about them except the way they speak. I can never make out what their rules are for choosing between pronouncing every single syllable, as in tempo-rarily, and swallowing as much of a word as possible, as when Polonius tells Laertes, neither a bore nor a lender be.'

This time Gordon laughed nervously.

'You remember that Shakespeare wrote *borrower*, a word no American can pronounce. And all those glottal stops they put at the beginnings of words, as in Deutschland über alles. They're deeply German, you know, German to their fingernails. That awful Hunnish greeting that uses the bare name, so it's Tom, Dick, Harry, no hallo Tom, good morning Dick, give my love to your mother, Harry. German through and through. I wonder they don't all click their heels and wear monocles. Well, thank you for putting up with that harangue, dear boy. Of course, one wouldn't dream of letting a word of it reach an American ear, they're so desperately sensitive and nervous of being made fun of, haven't you found that?'

'I'm afraid I haven't noticed.'

'That's what they're like, I do assure you. Now. Where is Citizen Cakebread's eatery located?' This last brought a brief and perfunctory return to the Jimmie accent. '*Hopefully.*'

'A few doors off Edgware Road.'

'So we're nearly there.'

If Gordon had set out to tell the whole truth from the start he would have had to add something about not having visited the little place himself for some time, but he decided to keep this fact up his sleeve. In what he intermittently saw as the battle of the lunch, or his attempt to protect what he could of his disposable capital against luxurious Jimmie's ravages, the defence had made an encouraging start in the circumstances. Gordon's mind went back to Monday's telephone conversation. His ring had been answered by a voice he recognized with some relief as Joanna's.

'May I speak to Mr Fane, Jimmie Fane?'

'Oh, isn't that, isn't that Gordon? Are you calling him about that lunch you were going to give him? Right, I'll get him.'

Pause. 'Hallo, dear boy. Yes, of course I remember. I'm afraid I haven't really thought where. Oh, would you hold on just a minute?' Burble burble burble, soon translated without difficulty. 'Hallo? Er, it's kind of you to leave the choice of venue up to me, my dear fellow, but I rather think it's only fair that *you* should decide that question from your obviously more immediate knowledge than my, er . . .'

So, unexpectedly, it was not to be the Tripoli or Woolton's but the joint Gordon had on the spur of the moment recalled from a couple of lunches with Louise's predecessor. He was not a habitual luncher-out and Cakebread's, he thought, had been cheap and cheerful and not too bad. Thereafter his sense of adventure had taken over.

The taxi stopped outside somewhere that did not, at first glance, look much like the Cakebread's of Gordon's memory, though the name was to be seen in fluorescent tubing. Jimmie sprang athletically out on to the pavement and peered in through the glass door. In an abstracted state Gordon paid the cab-fare and joined him, or more truly followed him into the restaurant. For restaurant it was or had now become, neither cheap-looking nor particularly cheerful. Waiters in little striped waistcoats and bow ties darted to and fro where overalled girls had once moved more slowly, and the menu no longer appeared on a smudgy blackboard but between fat leather covers on every table. The noise was immense. Jimmie put on a good king-in-exile show, holding his distinguished white head high above the rabble, apologizing with gestures for accidental buffets inflicted on him by others. He and Gordon were shown to a table by a side wall and brought drinks.

'The industrious Mr Cakebread would appear to be prospering.'

'There have been considerable changes since I was last here,' Gordon shouted back. He felt he must immediately correct any mistaken impression that this was the kind of level on which he customarily refreshed himself in public.

'I shouldn't care to become an habitué here perhaps but it suits my mood at the moment.'

Gordon tried to look receptive.

'Last night I did something I hadn't done for what seems like simply decades and probably is quite a long time and dipped into one of those old novels of mine, not *The Escaped Prisoner* which you were kind enough to mention recently but another, no matter which for the present. And do you know it seemed to me, it seemed *not too bad*. A little wordy, a little clumsy, really rather embarrassingly clumsy here and there but on the whole *not too bad*. For the first time for many years I found it not inconceivable that I might one day return to the charge, try my hand at fiction once more. It was, I can't tell you, it was like being reminded of one's youth. And I've you or your advent in my life to thank for turning my thoughts in that direction. I see they offer natives here, meaning I take it oysters rather than cannibal islanders, offer them at what seems to me a ridiculously inflated price but I've long since given up trying to make any sense of such matters. Tell me, er, tell me, Gordon, from your past experience and your present information, do you imagine they would be of a respectable size or something falling a wee bit short of that?'

'I –'

'Because I know of very few minor disappointments as keen as that of expecting an oyster to fill the mouth in that agreeable way and then finding it just too small to do so, and this not once but a dozen times over. So to be on the safe side I think, yes, I think I'll order eighteen and then if the worst comes to the worst quantity will have to do duty for quality. Yes, I think that's the best solution in the circumstances.'

Holding his voice steady with an effort, Gordon said, 'I'm sure if we asked them nicely they'd fetch a couple of specimens to the table so that you could –'

'No no, dear boy, too much of a fuss and bother and certain to cause incalculable delay. Talking of which, they don't seem to be positively falling over themselves with anxiety to take our order, do they? Oh well, it gives us time to catch up with our reading.'

With that, Jimmie brought up an eyeglass on a fine silvery chain through which he proceeded to study the menu. Or to pretend to, to look effective while apparently so doing. Did it just happen that what he fancied turned out to be the most expensive dish to be had? Or had he quite consciously set out to sting his host as painfully as practicable? Or was his motive somewhere in the capacious territory between the two? In search of an answer, Gordon observed Jimmie's full-collared silk shirt and boldly clashing tie, side-parted silvery hair worn long for a man of his age, green-bordered handkerchief 'carelessly' pushed into jacket-sleeve, antique cuff-links. He would have observed the cut of the seasoned-looking dark suit if he had ever learnt to tell one sort of cut from another. Then Jimmie glanced up from the menu and round the room with an expression of tolerant superiority on his face that seemed to go with details of clothing and stuff. Old Jimmie Fane saw himself as an artist of a far-off time when artists were special people and looked special and of course ate lots of oysters. Any moment now he would be calling for a bottle of the Widow.

There were perhaps elements of the ridiculous in this picture, but Gordon felt no disposition to laugh, not even internally. He felt less like it than ever when a waistcoated waiter arrived and after appreciatively taking an order for eighteen natives asked what was to follow and got an inquiry from Jimmie about the available sizes of lobster. Gordon stopped listening for a while and did his best to put aside his copy of the menu. He swallowed the last of his gin and Campari – why had he ordered that? – and saw that after paying this bill he must simply go home and take to his bed and stay there until the end of the following week, when his monthly bit of salary would reach his bank. He would use the period of bodily inactivity to square his accounts with God and such matters.

Quite calm now, Gordon watched while Jimmie nodded approvingly at a bottle of no doubt expensive wine brought for his inspection, chewed an intervening mouthful of crust of bread, coughed thoroughly, drank fizzy mineral water, gulped a large mouthful of the wine poured out for him to try, followed it with more mineral water and after a short interval in which he sat stock-still, made a loudish noise that sounded like a kind of indrawn belch, but proved to be the first of a tremendously long and sort of well-entrenched series of hiccups. At first he stared at Gordon and held up his hand as if calling for a silence he failed to produce. Soon the waiter returned with a glass of still water and Jimmie sipped at it fast, slowly, from the right side of the glass, from the wrong side of the glass, to wash down any crumbs or other extraneous matter that might have been lingering in his throat, vaguely. Nothing happened, or rather he continued to emit belching sounds a dozen times a minute. Possibly these had acquired a new sonority, because now a partial silence did descend, though not on Jimmie. With the glass of water put aside, he pulled out a handkerchief, not the one tucked into his cuff, and stuffed it over his mouth, a manoeuvre that muffled his noises but failed to make them anywhere near inaudible.

Two managers, or perhaps one manager and one deputy manager, appeared and bent over Jimmie, partly screening him from view. Gordon found he was quite looking forward to the spectacle of the venerable artist swallowing his eighteen natives one by one between hiccups, but as yet no food, nothing further, had reached their table. Then Jimmie moved his face into sight. It had gone rather pale.

'Take me home,' he said tremulously, and clapped his handkerchief back just in time.

'There will be no charge for anything,' both managers said.

Gordon did not try to persuade Jimmie to stay. Watched by several of those near by they reached the street door and hurried through it to a corner past which taxis could be expected to cruise.

'Sorry I've made you miss your lunch,' Jimmie managed to say.

'That's all right, Jimmie. As a rule I just have a sandwich.'

After a minute or two watching for taxis Gordon felt a tap on his shoulder and turned to find Jimmie smiling at him in an almost spiritual way.

'There should be one along any minute.'

Jimmie was shaking his fine head. He looked now as if he was listening to heavenly music. He said nothing for the moment.

'My God,' said Gordon.

Now Jimmie nodded. 'They've gone. I've had these fits of the hiccups before and sometimes they just go away after a few minutes and don't come back. I wish I knew what I do to make them stop. Stopping trying to make them stop is what does it, perhaps. Let's get a move on – my appetite's come back with a rush. Ah, I think we're going to be all right. Yes, that's our chap, isn't it? Waiter!'

7

'Oysters and lobsters and some crêpes suzettes that were really quite well done. I'm afraid I rather over-indulged myself there. I seemed quite unable to stop eating them. Little Mr Thompson couldn't keep up with me. Well really, he didn't try, he said he'd had enough to eat.'

'Was it very expensive?' Joanna put a large dark Belgian-made chocolate into her mouth.

'What? I didn't do any sums and wasn't shown the bill. Perhaps it did cost a little by Mr T's standards. I must say, darling, it was really quite funny.' Jimmie produced a brief cracked laugh, an old man's laugh. 'He was *consternated* when he saw the place was slightly more what he no doubt calls up-market than he'd remembered. I only had to mention oysters to fill him with horror. He put on a great show of being frightfully concerned when I was having my hiccups but he couldn't hide his glee at the thought of not having to pay. And then when I recovered . . . well . . .'

'What did he have to eat himself?'

'I didn't notice much, I blush to admit. Some kind of soup, I fancy, and cheese or something. Why? I mean, should I have . . .'

'It sounds as if you chose the priciest dishes on the menu.'

'Not as such, they were what I fancied eating. Are you saying I should have lunched off a sardine and half a tomato out of consideration for Mr Thompson's pocket?'

'*No*, but you needn't have caned him as ruthlessly as you did. No doubt you managed to force down a bottle of wine or so?'

'Yes we did, but before you ask on behalf of your Uncle Arthur from Penge it was quite a decent Chablis but not even *premier cru.*'

'How many bottles?'

Speaking with less urbanity than before, Jimmie said, 'Darling, I can't think why we're having an inquisition. The answer to your latest question is one, one bottle.'

'Which you had most of.'

'If I did it was to save leaving half of it for the waiters to swill at their leisure. I don't think your precious Mr Thompson is used to wine. He'd obviously have felt more at home with a nice tankard of wallop.' Jimmie paused and eyed his wife. 'And if you ask me whether I drank any brandy I might get rather cross,' he said, giving the last word an old-fashioned pronunciation. 'To put your mind at rest I refrained, out of kindness not to my host not to myself. I'd had quite enough to eat and drink and I didn't want to run the risk of stirring my insides up. And I must say, darling, I find it a teeny bit boring of you to tell me I'm not to ask that fellow to take me where I want to go for luncheon and then when I manage to get a tolerable meal after all to haul me over the coals for eating and drinking what I fancied.'

'Well done,' said Joanna, looking for another chocolate but for the moment not settling on one. 'Your capacity for –'

'Oh, *what?*'

'I was going to say, your capacity for putting other people in the wrong seems if anything to increase from day to day.'

Immediately the telephone began to ring downstairs on the ground floor, there being from Jimmie's repeated prohibition only the one instrument in the house. On hearing it now he laid his hand energetically across his forehead like a figure in high drama expressing the ultimate dissatisfaction with fate. 'Oh, that damned contrivance, don't tell me it has no mind of its own, it knows just *when* to ring to cause the maximum . . . Well, I'm glad to hear that *some* faculty in me is increasing against the general trend. Answer that thing, would you, darling, there's a sweetheart, it's certain to be for you.'

But when Joanna came back again from downstairs soon afterwards she said, 'It's for you.'

'Oh God. I hope you –'

'The second Mrs Fane. She's hanging on.'

'That *bloody* woman. I thought I'd made it perfectly clear . . .'

Saying no more, Jimmie dashed from the room like somebody half his age. Joanna followed him as far as the door, then moved quietly to the stairhead. After a moment she heard a clink and a clash as Jimmie noisily rang off, and was sitting reading a fashion magazine and eating a chocolate on his return to the room.

8

'How sure are you there's a book in it?' asked Brian Harris a couple of mornings later.

Gordon Scott-Thompson answered without hesitation. 'Sure enough to sign a contract specifying a delivery date.'

'What delivery date have you in mind?'

'Oh, I haven't got as far as that yet. I'd need to think about it.'

'So think about it, my old Gordon. Anyway, you seem a good bit surer now than you were this time last week.'

'This time last week I hadn't talked to him much and I hadn't realized what a lot of stuff there was in the archives here for a start. You're going on as if you're a good bit keener on your side of the fence.'

'Yeah, we are, I think it's fair to say.'

Brian Harris used the plural pronoun out of no delusion of grandeur or of anything else but in general reference to the publishing firm in whose offices the two were sitting. His own office in these offices, partitioned off from them with man-high sheets of lavatory glass, had no special publishing look about them, except perhaps for the presence of rather more books than even a literate stockbroker, say, was likely to have installed where he worked. But then Brian Harris was not, in dress, hairstyle and accent, at all the kind of youngish fellow most people might have supposed to be a director of a publishing house, and a rather old-fashioned house at that, one that occasionally published works of literature.

'So you'll be commissioning a book on Jimmie Fane's life and works by me,' said Gordon now.

'Quite likely, yeah.'

'Under a contract.'

'I clock you,' said Brian, thoroughly scratching an armpit.

'With an advance.'

'I shouldn't be at all surprised, though of course that's off the record.'

'What about an advance on that advance?'

'You mean, you mean I go and give you some money, just like that?'

'Why not?'

'Why not, you want to know. Why is what I want to know, among other things.'

'I had to pay for this rather stiff lunch for the two of us.'

'You were telling me. I thought you were supposed to have an expense account on that paper.'

'Yes, that's right.'

'Well then.'

Gordon thought it would take too long to explain that his boss on the paper was opposed to the Fane project and might not look favourably on a submission for the refunding of expenses incurred in its furtherance. So he said, 'Louise has been spending money like water recently, my money.'

'What, without you there? Would a couple of hundred quid be any help?'

'Yes, it would. So you're paying me an advance on my advance after all.'

'I'll send it on to you. It'll be out of my own pocket actually, and before you say thanks a lot but no thanks it'll *actually* be the firm's money which I'm borrowing from them so when you pay me back I'll use what you give me to pay the firm back, and before you ask me just out of curiosity how I can be so sure you'll pay me back on the nail I'll say you're enough of a cunt to pay your own grandmother back if you had to cut your foot off to do it. I hope you understand I say that without the slimmest possible sliver of reluctant admiration or any crap like that. You don't deserve an expense account, you don't. On a paper that size?'

After giving a couple of upward nods in lieu of imprecations, the publisher recrossed his blue-clad legs on the hard chair he had pulled up to rest them on, and joined his hands behind his head. Uncharacteristically, he hesitated before speaking again. Gordon clearly had nothing to say for the moment.

'I told you we were thinking of reissuing some of the Fane works to coincide with your own effort.'

'Still only the novels?'

'At the moment. They seemed the obvious ones.'

'M'm. All of them at once, some then some later, or what? You hadn't decided when you and I talked before.'

'We still haven't. Most likely it'll be two at the time and then if they catch on the others the following season. Nothing fixed yet, though.'

'I'll be saying quite a bit about the novels. I'm going to feel, well, hampered, restricted, if some of them are still out of print.'

'I shouldn't let that worry you. After all, you'll be saying more than quite a bit about other items in the Fane story, I hope.'

'Such as?'

During these exchanges Brian had produced a small oblong tin with a green-and-goldish design on its lid. It proved to contain cigarette makings and their owner was soon demonstrating his skill with them. In this second pause Gordon fancied he could detect traces of actual embarrassment. He wondered a little what was to come.

Now Brian put between his lips a sort of cigarette of about the girth of a stout toothpick, and lit it. A faint narcotic odour became perceptible. 'Your book's going to have two kinds of stuff in it, call them critical and personal, what old Fane wrote and what he was or did. By definition, right? I'm sorry to say, but not all that sorry to say, more people are going to be interested in the second than the first. From what I know of you, my old Gordon, you're likely to be more interested in the first than the second. Fine. We'll work it out, we being you on one side and us on the other. For now I'd just like to ask you to remember that we're obviously very pleased when one of the heavy papers buys something out of one of our books to liven up its review section, and also, like you to remember too, none of them gives a toss about any of your critical or literary stuff. That's all for later. It has a bearing, but it's for later. What counts for the review editor is the personal angle, and Fane's on his fourth wife, okay? Now if you could let me have a specimen chapter and a synopsis by the end of next week we'll all be laughing. Nobody'll look at what you turn in, but they like to know it's there.'

Ten minutes later, Gordon was waiting for a bus in Baker Street. To do so was not at all pleasant on this autumn morning, but to go where he was going by Tube would have meant a longer walk at the distant end. He wished he could have dealt half as easily with the problem presented just now by Brian Harris, or more truly brought into the open by him. When Gordon had first thought of writing about Jimmie Fane he had had in mind a sort of working subtitle, something to be imagined as coming after the subject's name and a colon on the title-page, something no livelier or more inventive than Neglected Genius and not even to be committed to paper. Then as soon as he started looking to any purpose he had glimpsed something like Sexual Adventurer looming up on the other flank. Both phrases, he foresaw, would eventually seem appropriate in some measure, but he wanted to work all that out for himself, not be influenced by any pressure one way or the other. Well, there was one consolation, that the time for making up his mind about such matters was not yet.

These reflections lasted him till his bus came and he was climbing into it, at which point they were superseded or shoved out by a closer sight than before of the legs belonging to a girl of student age and general appearance just in front of him. It was not that the rest of her was specially attractive, nor even that the legs themselves were, it was simply that they did seem to extend a very long way upwards. No, he must mean he could see a very long way up them. How their owner stood the weather apparently wearing nothing between foot and crotch but a pair of tight tights was not his present concern. That was to do with Jimmie, had been suggested by thinking of Jimmie. Gordon settled himself in a seat from which he could see only the student's back view and only as far down as her shoulders and went on with the same line of thought.

Jimmie had presumably come to puberty in the late 1920s or early '30s, the golden age of the female leg, as was testified by many things, including films and mildly erotic calendar drawings of the period. By the 1940s, the decade of Gordon's own birth, the focus had shifted to the breasts and the pin-up, often emphasizing the nipples, which could not then be shown or seen in public. By 1960 anything went, or had started to go, and not long after that had come the golden age of everything or else nothing in particular. Gordon was just old enough to remember the departure of the brassiere along with its contents, and it happened to be no comfort to him among many others that behind all this the old female bottom had continued jogging along on its way undisturbed.

In a thin drizzle Gordon's bus made its way along Knightsbridge. He found that when he tried to call up an erogenous image of Louise in his mind he got little more than a blur. That might have been the result of defective sexuality on his part. Or more remotely of the kind of changes in socio-erotic history he had been trying to assemble. Or the fact that he was in a bus on a chilly, damp morning.

When the time came he got out into the middle of it. Not far to walk, though, towards the river but not all the way. To identify the house, ring its bell and wait called for no unusual powers. On the first floor above his head a window was opened, but by whom he could not see. The next moment a small metal object dropped through the air and tinkled on the pavement near by and the window slammed shut. The object proved to be a latchkey. While approaching and climbing the stairs within, Gordon called to mind his observations on legs and dates, but forgot them again on entering the first-floor front room and being greeted by the Hon. Mrs Jimmie Fane. He had reckoned that she was eleven or twelve years older than he, though he had to admit she looked less, today at any rate. She had on a snuff-coloured pullover with ribbing at neck and cuffs and a royal-blue skirt of smooth but non-shiny material. Apart from an unmemorable ring or two she was wearing no jewellery.

'Would you like a drink?' she asked Gordon.

The sort of drink that he would have liked was a cup of tea or coffee, but he felt he could not very well ask for such a thing here. 'It's a bit early in the day for me,' he said.

'It's a bit early in the day for anybody, but would you like one?'

'To be honest I'd rather not.'

'Fine, I'll keep you company and not have one too.' She smiled in a friendly way. 'Come and sit down. It's warmer up this end where the heating is. Jimmie went off to Gray's as advertised. He's lunching with a couple of earls and a marquis so he might as well be in Timbuctoo as far as we're concerned.'

Joanna smiled again. He thought to himself she had obviously been a very good-looking woman when younger. Then he thought his use of the pluperfect might look or sound ungallant, so he amended his first thought to signify that she was still a good-looking woman now, at that very moment. He could have sworn his expression had remained constant throughout this interior shift, but when she smiled for the third time it was not the same.

'Rather a waste from one point of view,' she said, 'don't you think?'

'How do you mean?'

'I gather he took a pretty flashy lunch off you the other day. I got him to let you choose the place but he didn't want to and you wouldn't have been able to influence what he ate and drank.'

'I survived.'

'Did you ever get the feeling he was choosing the expensive stuff on purpose, just because it was expensive?'

'Now you mention it, I did once or twice.'

'Good for you. But I don't think he was just enjoying the simple pleasure of getting somebody else to spend money on him, though perhaps one shouldn't put that past him in general. No, I think what he was doing was showing you who was master, coming out on top in a battle of wills. I'm sorry, Gordon, aren't you going to take notes?'

'I've a very good memory. As long as I write a few things down afterwards I'll be all right.'

'Did you write down how much that lunch cost you?'

'I didn't need to.'

'I can't help feeling I ought to reimburse you for what you had to cough up.'

'Don't worry about that, Joanna, I'll get it off expenses and anyhow I couldn't take your money.'

'How Scottish are you, darling?'

'M'm? Oh, only by descent. All my grandparents were born in London and I've no particular connections with Scotland. Why do you ask?'

'Oh, I just wondered. Look, er, isn't it time we got down to business? How are you on the early years of the great man?'

They quickly established between them that James Reginald Pruett Fane had been born in 1918 in Cheltenham, the son of the comfortably-off but not rich second son of a baronet who had made a study of country houses. JRPF had attended a small public school in Shropshire, where he had shown a precocious talent for painting in watercolour.

47

'Has any of that stuff survived?' asked Gordon.

'No. He renounced painting for ever when he went up to King's and made a bonfire of all his work, all he could lay his hands on anyway. He doesn't mind people knowing he used to paint but he's never tried to trace what he sold, not that there was much of it.'

At Cambridge 1936–39 JRPF had vocally supported the Nationalist side in the Spanish civil war, though he had not himself visited Spain at that time.

'Rather brave of him, wasn't it, coming out for Franco then?' asked Gordon.

'Not at Cambridge, at least among his mates, or the chaps he wanted to be his mates, you know, posh chaps. He was a bit of a Catholic then, or says he was.'

'But you mean he's renounced that too.'

'Just let himself lapse.'

Also at Cambridge JRPF had become known as a poet. In those still early days he had contributed to some of those journals and anthologies that were hostile or indifferent to the quasi-Marxist stance of contemporary poets in Oxford and elsewhere. His first volume had been published in 1939.

'What did he do in the war?' asked Gordon. 'I can't make out. His *Who's Who* entry just says he was in government service.'

'That's as much as he'll say when you ask him, all he's ever said to me anyway, he worked for the government. If it were somebody else that might mean he was to do with something hush-hush, so hush bloody hush in fact that he can't tell you about it fifty years after the event, and I did meet a queerish buffoon not so long ago who owned up to having helped to snatch a Nazi general in Crete but wouldn't say which one. But anyway I'd give a small sum to know what the old man's work for the government amounted to.'

Just before or just after saying that, Joanna had changed

position in her chair in a way that brought to notice her legs, which were enclosed in a pair of dark-blue stockings or tights that went well with her royal-blue skirt. Although not himself a great leg man, as indicated earlier, Gordon could see perfectly well that they were very good, shapely legs. It crossed his mind straight away that this fact was ultimately connected with Jimmie's preferences and their likely root in the period of his puberty. Other considerations could be deferred for later thinking over.

'I'll see what I can find out,' Gordon assured Joanna.

As his first wife JRPF had married the daughter of a newspaper owner in 1945. That wife had run away with an amateur jockey early in 1950. Later that same year he had got married a second time, to a less pretty girl who was also not all that well off but was a viscount's daughter. The 1960s had seen a third marriage, this time to the undoubtedly handsome daughter of a very rich commoner, and in 1975, at the age of fifty-seven, JRPF had married the then thirty-three-year-old Joanna, daughter of a very rich nobleman.

'If anybody wanted to be nasty about him,' said Joanna, who had supplied some of the details, 'they could say he hit the jackpot on his fourth try – money *and* pedigree, but that wouldn't be quite fair. All his wives, including me, have been the sort of people he mixed with socially, especially number three and me and I'm pretty sure he was pally with number two's brother at Cambridge. Perhaps he oughtn't to have gone around with nobs so much, but I can't see him downing his pint in the public bar because it's more real there or something. He knows I think he's a bit of a joke with his nobbery, but I got my nobbery as a sort of christening present, if you see what I mean.'

'M'm. *Who's Who* mentions one *s*. one *d*. by, er, number one and one *d*. by number two.'

'Number one took her descendants off and they haven't been seen for donkey's years. Number two's *d*. turns up occasionally, I'm sorry to say. Another thing I can't see him as is a proud father, caring father, anything father.'

Gordon waited a moment and said, 'Had you been married before?'

'Only once. He drank himself to death, but I may say he was already doing that when I came into his life. I didn't start him but I didn't stop him either, as you see. Talking of which, I don't think we'd be breaking any law of God or man if we had a drink after all that work.'

'I'd like to finish this lot first if you don't mind.'

'My, what a little stickler you are.'

'Just as well, perhaps.'

'Oh well, point taken.'

JRPF had been employed in the books department of the *Daily Post* from 1945, its literary editor 1949–63, James Cadwallader Evans Award 1961, Hon. DCL, Hove University 1978, FRSB 1980, Chairman, Carver Prize Committee 1981. Principal publns: three books of verse, *Collected Poems* 1970, six novels, last in 1965, two vols, on wine, etc., one vol. coll. journalism, etc.

'There's not much either of us could add to that,' said Joanna.

'Certainly nothing I can.'

'It's quite a complete list except for committees he's been on which he doesn't think are worth mentioning.'

'How can you be so sure?'

'I was his secretary at one time.'

'When was that?'

'Oh, I forget. Just the last *Who's Who* thing to do.'

Recreations: visiting churches in Tuscany and Umbria, good food, conversation.

'Anything to add to that?' asked Gordon.

'I'll say. And to subtract too. I'll tell you in a minute. Can we have that drink now?'

'I suppose so. I mean thank you, I'd love one.'

50

'What would you like? I have vodka, and tonic, and vodka and tonic.'

'I'd like vodka and tonic with not much vodka, if I may.'

'I don't see why you may not,' said Joanna, giggling a little with what sounded genuine amusement. She had got up and gone over to a costly-looking marble-topped chiffonier on which bottles and glasses stood.

'What's the joke?' Gordon had no desire to be told, but it was easy to see he was meant to ask something like that.

'Well, the way it was absolutely certain you'd ask for a small one if you got half a chance. Then . . .' Instead of continuing she came back and handed him his drink.

'Cheers. What was that last bit again?'

'Oh right. Italian churches, good food and conversation, wasn't it? I've never known him go near a church anywhere, though he might literally venture near an Italian one if it was next door to a kosher palazzo that had a proper duchessa in it he could chat up. His Italian's quite fluent, actually, and of course bits of Italy like Tuscany sound right, or did when he said that about himself. Yes – good food; he likes expensive food, as you well know, but that's about as far as it goes. I don't think he's much of a taste-buds man, do you? As for conversation, well yes, again on the understanding that the chaps he's conversing with are either rich or well-born, preferably both but if it has to be one or the other then give him rich every time. I suppose it sounds pretty awful of me to be saying some of that, and I suppose it is in a way, and I do think that side of him's a bit of a joke, but I don't . . . I don't feel superior to him or resent the way he goes on. I realize I might one day but as yet I don't. Now we'll just drink these up and give ourselves another small one and then we'll totter down and have something to eat. Mainly a chicken salad, which I'm afraid won't be very warming, but there's a pea soup to begin and I know you like soup.'

9

That evening Gordon noticed that Joanna's ultimately lenient attitude to Jimmie was not shared by Louise, or at least was not shared by her that evening. Earlier, starting about three-thirty when he got home, he had heroically beaten off drink-induced lassitude and written up his notes for that day. These had contained not only biographical details and dates but less starkly factual information, given over lunch, about Jimmie's dealings with such persons as priests and peers. Much of the latter material had not shown him in a particularly favourable light but the facts had gone into the notes anyway, regardless of whether Jimmie might sooner or later veto their publication. When Gordon had satisfactorily finished the job, he had brewed himself a very strong pot of tea and made the first of several unavailing attempts to telephone Louise, finally getting hold of her at seven-twenty or so.

She sounded full of beans. 'How did your lunch with Her Grace the Honourable Lady Joanna Fane FO go?'

'Oh, some quite funny bits. If you'll come out to dinner with me I'll tell you about them.'

'Can't do dinner this evening, I'm afraid.'

'Oh,' said Gordon, and added rather mechanically, 'Some other time, then.'

'But I am dying to hear. Are you going to be around later tonight?'

'I might be.' This time he spoke cautiously.

'So might I be. Start trying to ring me about a quarter to eleven.'

Then Louise disconnected and Gordon admitted to himself

he was quite glad in retrospect she had been booked for dinner, because in the heat of the moment, such as it had been, he had forgotten how hard up the great Jimmie lunch had currently left him. After some thought he heated up a tin of soup in his kitchen, not so nourishing it proved as the pea and ham concoction Joanna had fed him, but followed with cold sausages, which when smothered with mustard, spicy sauce and tomato ketchup turned out to be distinctly tastier than the chicken salad supplied earlier. To wash it all down he recklessly put away a nine-ounce can of a Dutch lager that, had he known it, had come second from bottom in a table of alcoholic strengths of imported beers in a recent Sunday-magazine survey. To offset these indulgences he read seriously in his copy of *The Escaped Prisoner*, Jimmie's first novel and by common consent his best, published in 1959.

Its story told of a young man, brought up in conventionally well-off and well-connected circumstances somewhere in the north of England, who had reacted against his upbringing to go and be a schoolteacher in the more proletarian parts adjacent to his native heath. As time went by he came to doubt the wisdom of having done so, found his new companions ignorant and coarse and his new girl trivial-minded and finally went back whence he had come. At the time and later there had been some disagreement whether the hero was to be thought of as having permanently escaped from the prison of working-class life or only temporarily from the patrician bondage to which he voluntarily returned. It surprised Gordon to find several of the posh characters effectively presented as disagreeable, even snobbish, and the story seemed to veer now and then between one interpretation and the other and back. He wondered if Jimmie might have had something to say on the matter and made a note to ask him about it some time.

The time was just after ten forty-five. Gordon telephoned Louise, who answered after two rings. She sounded distinctly less full of beans than when he had talked to her earlier, but

53

agreed that he should come and see her as soon as convenient.

'I'd only just that moment got in when you rang,' she told him as soon as he arrived.

'Sorry,' he said, feeling it was somehow required of him.

'I suppose you couldn't tell,' she grudgingly conceded.

Things had improved, but not much, by the time they were sitting in the area reached by her electric fire with mugs of hot decaffeinated coffee in their hands. When she asked him to tell about his midday dealings with Jimmie's wife it was not in the unguardedly friendly spirit she had shown before.

'What sort of line did she take?' Louise asked. 'Was she against the old monster, as she'd have to be to pass as a human being herself, or was she on the whole for him, trying to make out he wasn't too bad?'

'Well, just a minute. Even if she'd felt like it she wasn't going to denounce the man she'd been married to for twenty-odd years to a fellow she didn't know existed until just the other day. Be reasonable.'

'Gordon, I'm being reasonable. Jimmie sodding Fane is a, well, if not a monster then a monument of old-fashioned, passé class superiority and sheer snobbery. If his wife doesn't have the least inkling that that's what he is, then as I see it she's tarred with the same bloody brush.'

'Look, hold on, dear.' It had already occurred to Gordon that Louise's new-found hostility to Jimmie and all his works, as opposed to or further than a semi-genial rallying scepticism about poor old Jimmie, originated less in any kind of revision of the facts that in something that had happened in her own life. (Like having been stood up for dinner, it occurred to him later, though not then.) He said pacifically, 'She's got more than an inkling that old Jimmie's got a pretty stiff dose of the sort of prejudices you'd expect from somebody his age and, well, class, I suppose.'

'You suppose!' Louise answered at once and perhaps a shade predictably. 'If he's really out of the top drawer I don't see what you're doing writing about him in the first place, you being you, and if he's a phoney you just, you shouldn't, I mean you'll have to expose him in whatever you write about him, and you told me he can prevent you publishing what he doesn't like. That's unless you simply . . .' She shook her head about and made various impatient noises.

'He's the genuine article all right, uncle a baronet, went to school —'

'Spare me the sordid details, for Christ's sake. Well: it sounds to me . . .'

'Yes?'

'It sounds to me as though you've been won over.'

This challenge irritated Gordon, but he did his best to swallow any such feeling. 'Granted I'm to write something substantial about this chap,' he began, but got no further.

'You clearly grant it. I don't.'

They went on in their respective strains until an inadvertent lull brought the chance to say experimentally, casually too,

'Where's that flat-mate of yours this evening?'

'She's away,' said Louise in a tone that precluded further discussion of the matter.

He now asked, without much thought, 'Oh, where did you have dinner?'

This caused perceptible confusion. After hesitating for a full second, she said, 'Somewhere in Soho, I can't remember the name, I was taken there. Why, what of it?'

'Nothing of it, I was just trying to change the subject.'

'All right. You were going to tell me about lunch with her nibs. Especially the funny bits.'

He started on a pedestrian report of that event, thinking to himself meanwhile that to have failed to remember the name of a restaurant, any restaurant at any time, was most unlike Louise. Whatever she might now have been thinking to herself, she seemed not to be listening to what he said. Before he had managed to get to a funny bit she interrupted him.

'Did she make a pass at you? I don't mind if she did but I would love to know.'

'Nothing of that sort happened at all.'

'Because she was well and truly looking you over the day we were both there. Almost as if she was having trouble keeping her hands off you. I call that bloody cheek at her age.'

'She couldn't give me all that many years, and what do you mean, at her age? You make her sound about a hundred and ninety.'

'She's an old bag. An *old bag*.'

'On a purely objective, unemotional, factual plane, Louise, she's not, Joanna Fane is not an old bag. Middle-aged, if you like, if you must, but —'

When, not much later, Gordon was making his way out of Louise's flat in a sexually unsatisfied state, he was reflecting that what she had just said about having to make an early start in the morning might well have been true as well as decisive. Nevertheless he could not help feeling that he might not have been forced to leave in such an unceremonious fashion if he had handled things a little differently, if for example he had concurred at once with her view of the aged Joanna Fane. As he put the point to himself on his way home, when there was nobody to overhear, you could get it right, or you could get it away.

The telephone was ringing when he got back home, which circumstance made that place seem much less bleak and comfortless. 'Gordon Scott-Thompson,' he said into the instrument, wishing strongly for the moment that he had a less cumbrous name.

'Fane here,' said a recognizable high male voice. Its owner took some time to assure himself that he was connected whither he wished, but having done so he spoke quite freely. 'You will of course have dined,' he said.

'I'll have what? Oh yes, I've dined.'

'I too. Rather well, in fact, as perhaps you've already

inferred. I'm speaking from, where am I speaking from, yes, of course, I'm speaking from my club. There's been a slight difference of opinion here, not to say an argument, which you may be able to settle. Now. How would you, how do you pronounce T,I,S,S,U,E, as in the kind of paper?'

'Well, tissue, to rhyme with, er, miss-you, for instance.'

'I understand. Not like,' and here Jimmie paused for so long that Gordon thought he must have moved on elsewhere, perhaps in search of a taxi, until he came back on the line to say, 'Not like atishoo, the comic or fanciful representation of a sneeze. Just so. I'm greatly obliged to you, my dear Gordon, and good night.'

'Is that all?'

'Oh my dear fellow, I do hope I haven't got you out of bed, have I?'

'No no, I assure you. I was just wondering what the argument was about.'

But Jimmie had disconnected before Gordon had done more than start his second statement.

10

'I was just wondering what the argument was about,' said Gordon to Jimmie again. This time he said it not over the telephone but face to face or near enough, in the hall of Gray's club. Not wishing on the whole to have to go in search of Jimmie all over the building, which he had never visited before, Gordon had told the porter who was expecting him and had himself waited here in the hall.

At least he had hoped the fellow was the or a porter. There had been a moment of slight and wordless misunderstanding when, meeting some difficulty with the glass door from the street, Gordon had seen through the pane a man coming towards him who looked no older and was better dressed than he and whom he had briefly taken for a member of the club on his way out. From the change in this man's demeanour at Gordon's inquiring reference to Mr Fane, it was easy to guess that he for his part revised any first impression that the new-comer might have been some artisan or workman, arrived at the club to repair its dishwasher, say. All was quickly well, and no more than a couple of dukes or millionaires had put their heads round the corner to look him over when Jimmie himself arrived, full of total memory of who Gordon was and what he was doing there. After some irresolution on both sides Gordon had reminded him of the recent telephone-call.

'Oh good God *yes*,' said Jimmie amiably. 'I should have explained there and then but I didn't want to take up your time. I'd dined here, rather well as perhaps you inferred, and Johnnie Wessex and I and one or two others had got into some

58

sort of barney about language and pronunciation, a prime concern of mine as you must know, Gordon. I won't bore you
with an account of their rather unthinking points of view but
I was taking the line that the old natural way of speaking,
among reasonably well-educated and thoughtful people, was
being, how shall I put it, was becoming eroded by creeping
pedantry. Creeping pedantry,' he repeated, making no move
in the direction of the inner parts of the club where food and
drink were presumably to be found. 'Whenever I turn on the
wireless or the television I hear the announcer putting in glottal
stops in places where they've no business to be, they talk about
the *I R A*,' said Jimmie with a little explosion of breath before
the name of each letter, and I expect they call it the *R A F*,'
similarly enunciated, 'and in no time every English word that
begins with a vowel or vowel sound or looks as if it does will
begin with a confounded glottal stop. Have I told you all this
before, dear boy?'

Gordon hesitated. 'No,' he said. 'It's true you've mentioned
glottal stops before, but then they were part of an attack on
Americans.'

'*Americans?*'

'Yes. You said it went to show how German they were.'

'When was this supposed to be?'

'It was in the taxi on the way to Cakebread's. That restaurant.'

'An excellent place, let it be said.' Jimmie spoke strongly,
as if contesting disparagement. 'Excellent, what I had was
first-rate.'

'I'm glad you enjoyed it.'

'You did get my note thanking you for the occasion?'

'I must have done.'

'Oh dear, these days I'm quite capable of having forgotten
to post it. I'm afraid I've always been scatterbrained in such
regards and of course in recent years I've deteriorated even
from what I was. Which is not to say I make no sense any

longer. On the contrary, let me remind you that we were talking of pedantry in pronunciation and I was saying I come across it whenever I switch on any broadcasting device. Any moment now I expect to hear somebody talking about when-*ever* or how-*ever*. The traditional way of saying such words is I should have thought quite sufficiently comprehensible, don't you agree?'

'Yes,' said Gordon. He did agree. More than that, if Jimmie wanted to talk about ways of saying words it would have been impolitic and almost certainly useless to try and prevent him. On the other hand, something seemed to be needed to shift them from the kind of padded pews that, still in the hall, they had settled companionably down on. At that moment he caught sight of a youngish man, doubtless heir to a fortune or a marquisate or both, who had evidently come to peer at them. More to the point, he held a drink in his hand, a reasonably powerful-looking one, and it was not every day that Gordon felt he could do with a drink, but today was such a day. He swallowed furtively.

Jimmie had been going on, 'I take as part of the same undesirable phenomenon that it's becoming fashionable in ordinary speech, not just in song to give unstressed vowels their full value, not only Man*chest*er and *ob*server but, well, car*amel* and con*dom* and no doubt plenty of others. I say, would you fancy a drink perhaps?'

'Yes, I rather would.' Gordon tried to sound unequivocal without seeming to have no room for any other thought. 'What a good idea.'

'Oh. I'm terribly sorry, my dear fellow,' cried Jimmie, 'I do so clearly see that on a day like today you would be feeling in particular need of a wee tassie.'

Since the day was neither particularly cold nor rainy nor windy, in fact rather clement for the time of year, nor yet the notorious anniversary of the battle of Flodden, say, Gordon could not fully understand what was meant. He made a vague noise designed to show that there was no ill feeling on his side at least.

'How very thoughtless of me. We must repair that discreditable oversight with all speed.' Jimmie looked at his wristwatch, a piece that displayed its merit by being large rather than small. 'However it might be easier if I just rounded off this point while it's fresh in my mind. Fowler remarks somewhere that when reciting a sentence like, for instance, Hunt has hurt his head – m'm? – it's as important not to pronounce the initial H in has and his as it is to pronounce it in Hunt, hurt and head. Yet we hear trained actors bleating of their inamorata that they love *h*er and villains growling that they must kill *h*im. Years ago, much farther back than they remember, their ancestors decided to proclaim that they knew how to speak proper . . .'

As a conscientious but exhausted watchman might strive to keep awake, so Gordon fought to go on taking in what Jimmie was saying, and failed. He was beset by longing less for a drink than simply to be elsewhere, not necessarily far away, the next room would do, even at a pinch some unoccupied corner of this one, but it was not to be. What was to be took place quite soon after all.

'. . . not a very momentous sound-shift, but I think it is starting to happen,' said Jimmie. 'And now we simply must have that drink. You'd have got it earlier if you hadn't been so patient with me when I was going full tilt on my hobby-horse, or one of them. Ridiculous of me. Anyway, what will you have?'

They stood now in the bar, which was rather more like an immensely spacious and well-appointed cupboard than anything Gordon understood by a bar. He mentioned gin. Two elderly men had hurried out as they arrived; two others in dark suits studied them from some feet away. Or rather they seemed to be studying him, Gordon; in some puzzlement, as he thought. None the less, with his drink in his hand he felt bold enough to bring up tissue again.

'What? I'm sorry, I don't understand you.'

'Tissue,' said Gordon, pronouncing the word now in Jimmie's preferred style.

'Of course, of course.'

'We never quite got to what I was going to ask you just now.'

'Fire away when you're ready, then.'

'You remember my saying when you rang up that I pronounced the word to rhyme with miss-you? Well –'

'Oh yes, Johnnie Wessex had had the barefaced cheek to say he didn't believe any English person, anybody born in England pronounced T,I,S,S,U,E in any other way than the way he and I pronounced it. So then . . .'

'So then,' said Gordon, 'you thought of me as someone sufficiently far gone in creeping pedantry to pronounce the wretched word in what we'll call my way, and that was enough to enable you to win your argument with Johnnie Wessex.'

Gordon would have said he had pitched the foregoing at a tolerably low level, though would have had to admit that his tone when uttering the name Johnnie Wessex had not carried a favourable view of that nobleman. It seemed at least that he had spoken nevertheless loudly or warmly enough to cause the nearby elderly men to look sharply at him and then at each other before doing a fast shuffle out of the room. The barman glanced up from a list he was checking through, but only for a moment. Jimmie seemed a little troubled or vexed, though in no way conscience-stricken. He said,

'I suppose all of us speak much as those around us do, or used to early in our lives. But I suggest that's enough on the subject. Well, Gordon, have you made a start on your book about me? Good God, how pompous that sounds.'

'I've been reading through your works and making notes which I'll be using later. In the meantime I'll be asking you the odd question about your earlier life, as something occurs to me if that's all right. I don't want to subject you to long interrogation sessions like a —'

'My dear boy, you may ask me any question you think proper at any time within reason and I'll answer it. I've thought about it and I can see no virtue in my making things difficult for you. If I find I've told you too much and want you to take out something I don't want made public, I'll tell you when I come to it in your manuscript. Oh, and I'm making some notes of my own which I'll pass on to you in due course, as they say.'

'Very good; fine; agreed. Here's a question to be going on with. When you met —'

'I think if you don't mind we'll finish these and proceed to luncheon. They turn somewhat reproachful if one arrives at what they consider to be an inopportune hour. In fact I'd have suggested to you that we should go straight in to where one eats if it didn't sound such a dismal notion, and a mean one. Sounds a mean idea? Nay, it is. Are you ready?'

They mounted a single turn of the fine staircase and went through a sort of outer dining-room into a sort of inner dining-room beyond it. Both were full of men in suits vigorously talking, eating and drinking. Several of them looked up at Gordon as he went by, making him feel like a spy in an old-fashioned film. Jimmie led the way to a vacant table laid for four near the back of the room. They had hardly settled into their chairs before two additional men in suits came out of the middle distance and took the spare seats at the table. Jimmie introduced them as Bobbie something and Tommie something else, both these surnames denoting some county or other portion of the land area of the British Isles. Gordon was unsure at the time, and was never able to establish afterwards, whether these two arrivals had been invited or had invited themselves. They treated Jimmie as their host throughout, but what with one thing and another there was no certain indication there.

'So this is the great man's biographer, Tommie,' said Bobbie, and Tommie nodded and smiled. Both of them continued to look Gordon over in a considering and also greedy fashion, as if they had half a mind to eat him later. 'You mustn't mind us,' Bobbie went on, 'but you are called Gordon, aren't you, I mean that is right, I hope?'

'Gordon Scott-Thompson.'

'How do you do. I mean it is marvellous that you're here, isn't it, Tommie?'

'You're very young, aren't you, to be taking on a demanding job like writing Jimmie's life?'

They were so friendly, or at least were smiling at him and at each other so much, that Gordon found it hard not to go along with them. Jimmie gave no lead, showed no more sign of being disconcerted than of being gratified at their presence. For the moment Gordon could see no alternative to reciting dull facts about himself, dull to him at least, though Bobbie and Tommie listened in seeming fascination. This phase lasted until a man too active-looking and speedy in his movements not to be a club servant appeared and gave out menus, a service unremarked by any of the three club members present. His own menu, Gordon saw, had no prices on it, no doubt to remind him that he could choose whatever he fancied – fancy that! And fancy another thing, already becoming clear, that Jimmie was going to have to pick up the bill for all four lunches, including the wine, which Bobbie and Tommie were now engaged in vociferously choosing from the list. Gordon told himself that what prevented him from ordering oysters followed by lobster, and so tit-for-tatting Jimmie, was not any form of compunction but simple dislike of those dishes. But when his preludial slice of melon arrived in front of him and he started on it under Bobbie's observant eye, he had to admit internally that the real deterrent had been the prospect of that eye turned on his unpractised attempts to deal with oysters and such.

The meal progressed without resort to violence. The conversation between Jimmie, Bobbie and Tommie was mostly about the doings or condition of men referred to only by names similarly terminated. So Gordon had to say little and had little to say. He had meant to take the opportunity of seeing how far Jimmie had meant what he said about answering questions, but that now seemed to be ruled out. Tommie and Bobbie were chattering away with Jimmie nineteen to the dozen, as if they had lost interest in the fourth member of the party, but something in their occasional glances or his imagination suggested that they would come back to him when they felt like it. Both were drinking what he would have thought of as a fair amount of wine.

His moment came. The three others shared a sort of end-of-chapter laugh and collectively turned towards Gordon, who started to concentrate on sitting still in his chair. Both Bobbie and Tommie showed a friendly curiosity, though it struck him as a little excessive too. Jimmie was more non-committal, as if he was being told by Lord Bagshot about a delightful little place for lunch in the hills above Rome, now unfortunately closed down. At last Tommie said,

'Well, Gordon – it is Gordon, isn't it? – you haven't had much to say for yourself for the last half-hour or so, have you?'

Gordon made gestures indicating that that was indeed the case.

'I don't suppose you know very many of the people we were talking about just now. Not very polite of us, I'm afraid. Perhaps never even heard of most of 'em, eh?'

'I have heard of the Prince of Wales.' Gordon tried to push all expression out of his voice. 'Not many others, it's true to say.'

A single yelp or bark of laughter broke from Bobbie, who had just refilled his own glass and Tommie's, vigorously waving away with his free hand the proffered attention of a servant. Jimmie raised his eyebrows in a further demonstration of impartiality. Tommie pressed on.

'Yes, it was rather naughty of us to go on chinwagging about our cronies in that fashion, but Jimmie here is always bursting to hear the latest gossip, and we don't seem to see him as often as all that.'

'Oh, that's all right,' said Gordon.

For a moment Tommie looked at him in a new way, one accompanied by a small frown of puzzlement. 'Didn't we meet at Henley a year or two ago? Or was it, er, you know, Cowes?'

'I've never been to either place.'

'M'm. I must be mistaken. You may remember my saying when we met just now, Gordon, how young you seemed, I meant young to have taken on the job of writing up the life and works of an old josser like Jimmie here — I should add hastily that I'm a good year older than him. Anyway, I know I said something of the sort.'

'Yes, you did.'

'Well, it strikes me now, how shall I put it . . .' Tommie spoke with a short silence between each phrase and the next and Gordon fancied that Bobbie started listening with heightened intensity. 'I don't know whether . . . of course I should have explained that I only heard about this . . . this *project* of yours a short while ago, just before you . . .'

'I merely happened to mention it in passing,' said Jimmie, as one who exculpates himself.

'I haven't had time to . . . think very deeply about what's involved, or . . .'

'Get along with you,' said Bobbie, with some roughness in his tone as well as his words. 'What did you say to me as soon as Jimmie had told us a little about our young friend here?'

'I don't think we need actually . . .'

'What did you actually *say*? Come on, Tommie old bean.'

'All right, I said something to the effect that his earlier life, his background, Gordon's background probably hadn't often brought him into contact with the kind of people Jimmie had been, well, brought into contact with.'

Tommie made to face Gordon again, but Bobbie broke in. 'All right, as you say. All right. If you feel you somehow ought to water it down, all right.'

'I was simply –'

'All right, all right.'

Now Tommie did say something to Gordon. 'It's quite straightforward. Obviously you and Jimmie have had different sorts of upbringing and, and life. Nothing mysterious about it.'

'No,' said Gordon. 'Nothing mysterious at all.'

Aware that Bobbie looked like breaking in again, Tommie hurried on. 'What I'm getting at, what we're getting at is just that you can't, you wouldn't want to write any sort of book on Jimmie without, er, seeing him in the company of the people and the kind of society he grew up in and has, well, been in ever since, and it's not the same as the kind you grew up in, am I right?'

'Or don't you think things like that matter?' Bobbie immediately said to Gordon.

'Oh, do shut up, Bobbie,' said Tommie in a weary, pleading tone.

'I certainly think things like that matter.' There Gordon spoke the truth, but kept to himself his next thought, which had to do with whether the things in question ought to matter as much as they did. Aloud, he said, 'But I also think that the *difference* between Jimmie's background and my background should give me an advantage when I write about him. It, I mean the difference'll give me perspective, make me more of a detached observer.'

Bobbie nodded his shiny bald head. 'Yes. Yes, well we'll have to wait and see, shan't we?'

'Yes, you will have to wait and see,' Jimmie said to him. 'For what it's worth, and it must be worth something, I consider Gordon to be ideally suited to write my biography, which perhaps I omitted to tell you will be a critical biography, in other words it'll incorporate full discussions of my works. I use the simple future tense because the die is already cast. One of the purposes of his presence today is run over with me the publisher's contract, which if you'll forgive us we'll now go and do.' Jimmie rose from the table. 'What fun to bump into you and have this delightful chat.'

Good wishes to wives and families were speedily exchanged. Gordon and Jimmie were half way to the door when Bobbie called Jimmie back. From where he was, Gordon had no difficulty seeing what followed as some sort of apology being offered (by Bobbie) and some sort of reassurance supplied (by Jimmie). It took only a few seconds.

'Poor Bobbie is really the most frightful snob,' Jimmie explained to Gordon as they sat in an otherwise empty corner of the lounge, or whatever it might have been called. 'I've known it to show itself before when he's had a couple of glasses of good claret at luncheon. It must come of being the youngest son of an earl. Nice enough fellow on the whole, and thought a great deal of in this club. Now I suppose it's inescapable that we two really and truly go over that contract? Thank God, what a relief, I hate contracts, yes of course you can tell me the gist of it. But before you do that I've got a question to ask you, if I may.'

'Of course, Jimmie,' said Gordon, who himself had not been looking forward to having to communicate a clause-by-clause exposition of the aforesaid document. 'A couple of dozen if you feel like it.'

'Just one will do for the moment.'

'Let's have it.'

'How do you pronounce O,F,T,E,N? Sounding the T or not?'

68

II

Gordon sat in the corner of his room, by the window from which he could have surveyed the grey apparently deserted park had he wanted to. He was not at the moment using his typewriter, instead vigilantly reading through a sheaf of rough typescript headed Early Years. This was not a title he held in much esteem or affection, but there was plenty of time to come up with something more deserving. The dissatisfied frown he kept reverting to as he read was produced by contents rather than heading. Jimmie Fane's early years, primeval, indeed ante-natal years, were well documented, those relating to his family rather than himself. In Gordon's world a family started when somebody got married and stopped again when that person died, by which time his or her descendants would probably have originated another family or two. In Jimmie's a family evidently went back in history through the male line like the house of Saxe-Coburg-Gotha and further, fetching up in times like the early seventeenth century and places like Barra and Normandy. Gordon had got all that in Jimmie's case. The trouble was he had got in the kind of profuse detail that would have been all right at the opening of an 800-page study but seemed top-heavy for the kind of 180- or at most 200-page book he had been modestly contemplating. And yet the stuff was so *good*, so factual, so much the sort of thing people liked or expected in biographies. Was it? How did he know?

Shifting in his chair, Gordon feverishly attacked an itch that had started in his right eye as if it meant to eject it forthwith on to his cheek. The itch itself vanished at once but left a powerful stinging sensation behind. He thought of making himself another cup of coffee, looked at his notes less attentively than before, tried without success to heave a great all-encompassing yawn. His vision went misty with the effort of it. Then he picked up the telephone and punched buttons.

'Is it possible to speak to . . . Oh, hallo, it's Gordon here, Gordon Scott-Thompson, Gordon the . . . Yes. You said it was all right to ring you between . . . Good. Look, I've got a bit bogged down in the first chapter, with . . . Yes, I know, but I want to get it right before I press on. Well, I don't really fancy asking him unless I have to. Well, it would be marvellous if you . . . When? I mean what sort of time?'

Out in the street it was less damp than the day before but colder. Wishing he had been drunk, Gordon got on a bus apparently reserved for winners and runners-up in some pan-European repulsiveness contest. Successions of coughs, sneezes and nose-blowings could be heard above or through the sounds of traffic and an Oriental observer was holding a handkerchief over his mouth and nostrils. When Gordon eventually got off the bus he turned to his left at the first opportunity and walked a short distance, turned another corner and was soon pushing a bell-push. With the advantage of knowing what to expect he actually caught the latchkey this time when it was dropped in his direction.

'You're a bit later than when you came before,' said Joanna Fane, 'so what about a drink now? It's the sort of day for one.'

'It certainly is. I'd love a drink.'

'A small one as before?'

'Not necessarily.'

'You're getting the idea.' When Joanna had come back from the chiffonier with a vodka and tonic in each hand, she said, 'I gather you were put through the hoops recently at Gray's. What happened exactly?'

'What did Jimmie tell you?'

'Let's hear your version.'

Gordon started to oblige. Before long he was saying, 'He looked at me, Bobbie looked at me in a funny way when we were introduced.'

'What sort of funny way?'

'Sort of . . .' Gordon let his mouth hang open and his eyelids droop. 'As though he'd come over very tired all of a sudden.'

'I can just see him.' Joanna giggled slightly. 'You're quite good. I know that look of Bobbie's. What did he say?'

'I remember he wanted to know if I had a double-barrelled surname, and I said I supposed I had, and he asked if it had a hyphen in it, and I said again I supposed so, and that was more or less it.'

'What did he say then?'

'I don't know, I've forgotten. Anyway, that was it, end of conversation about my name. I'm not sure just what he was getting at, I mean he was obviously –'

'I am. He was wondering whether to ask you if you knew there are only seven families in the British Isles or anyway England and Scotland that can actually claim the right to use the hyphen.'

'Families,' said Gordon with strong but vague feeling.

'I heard him use the thing once on a chap who could trace his ancestry back to Henry VII.'

'Whenever he happened to feel like it.'

'If he didn't go that far Bobbie must have decided to let you down lightly. In a good mood for some reason.'

'Snakes alive.'

'Darling, sorry I mean Gordon – Gordon, poor Bobbie seems to have got under your skin rather.'

'Well, it was where he was trying to get. And what's this poor-Bobbie bit?'

'You don't seem to mind it so much when Jimmie gets grand. Of course I agree compared with Bobbie young Jimmie's a raging egalitarian. After all, he married me, didn't he?'

'M'm? What does that show?'

'My folks aren't nearly as grand as his folks. Trade, you know. Groceries.'

'Oh God. Anyway, I still can't decide whether he'd asked Bobbie and his mate along or they turned up under their own steam. Any ideas?'

'Not from here. You never quite know where you are with Jimmie. Bobbie's a much simpler, more straightforward sort of chap, though I agree that doesn't make him a nicer chap, or a nice chap at all.'

'Did I mention that when Jimmie and I were on our way out, Bobbie called him back to apologize to him? I was too far away to hear what they said.'

'I'm not. I hope you don't mind me talking like that. No, what Bobbie said was, I'm sorry if you think I leant a bit on that double-barrelled young bounder you brought along, and Jimmie said, That's all right, Bobbie, he has worse to put up with any Saturday down the Mile End Road.'

Gordon scratched his jaw. 'Do you think that's altogether fair to him, to Jimmie, that is? I realize you've known him longer than I have.'

'Maybe, maybe not. You know, darling, I think you're some-times a bit carried away by fairness.'

'You'd find plenty of unfairness down the Mile End Road any day of the week.'

'Oh, you've actually been there a couple of times, have you? You are the most –'

'If things in that neighbourhood are at all the way I imagine them to be.'

'You know something, I don't think Bobbie would have been as hard on you as he was, not that he seems to have been hard on you much by his standards. You should hear him tell an American the score.'

'If what? He wouldn't have been so hard on me if what?'

'Sorry, it's actually but for, not if. Bobbie might have been nicer to you than he was but for your moustache.'

'Oh. I hadn't thought of that.'

'There's nothing much wrong with it when you're sort of ordinary, but when you smile it makes you look terribly ingratiating. Jumped-up, almost.'

'Oh,' said Gordon again. 'I didn't know that I did much smiling.'

'You don't. It's time I got us both another drink.'

Once or twice since arriving, Gordon had wondered whether the first drink he had seen Joanna drinking was not in fact her first but her second or even third. It was well enough known in his world that married ladies no longer in the springtime of their youth sometimes tended, if they had not much to do in the house, no visible children and an often-absent husband, to drink out of hours. Watching her trim figure at the far end of the room efficiently engaged, he thought the characterization less than fair to her. Today she was principally wearing a high-collared carmine blouse and a short leather skirt, not very short but short enough to allow a fair showing of leg. The room was pleasantly warm. He thought in the second place that she was looking better, even indeed slightly younger, than he had first supposed. He assured himself with some emphasis that any such improvement was objective, or at least derived from a more refined view of her, less hasty and negligent than before. What he saw was actually *there*

Joanna came back with the fresh drinks. One of her shirt-sleeves had become unbuttoned and he saw the faint hairs on her forearm.

'Where's Jimmie today?' he asked when she was settled in a dull-green cushiony chair near him.

'He's in Cambridge, having lunch with the Master or the Warden of somewhere in college. He does manage to get some strange people to give him lunch.'

'I didn't think they put on that sort of lunch in colleges any more.'

'All right, it was just going to be drinks beforehand and then lunch somewhere else. Don't be so bloody *literal*, Thompson, or whatever your name is.'

'Sorry. Anyway cheers, Joanna.' Gordon raised his glass briefly.

'I was thinking about your moustache while I was over there sawing away at that lemon.'

'And?'

'I decided you ought to shave it off. What induced you to grow it anyway? It's not as if you're short or round-shouldered or anything like that.'

'I suppose you could say it goes back in time to when somebody told me I had a boring face.'

'A female somebody, I presume. Come on, darling, she was only trying to get a rise out of you.'

'I'd been thinking rather along those lines myself, but I didn't actually start growing it until –'

'I've heard exactly the right amount about your moustache. There's only one thing about it that still interests me, and that's got to do with what some other female it must have been a long time ago like before the first war or even earlier said that being kissed by a man without a moustache was like having to eat a boiled egg without salt.'

The ensuing pause was quite brief, but it was long enough for several thoughts, if the word could be stretched so that it included mere inchoate scraps of fancy, to pass through his head at a brisk trot. Joanna's attitude to him from the first had been leading up to this point, or to a point like this. He must have been responding without knowing it, or more likely without admitting it to himself, taking misplaced pride in his own objectivity. Several remarks, several glances of hers swam towards memory and vanished. Part of his mind, a part that possessed an unusually efficient security system, had no doubt been steering him to this same point, but whatever it was that had propelled him into coming here this morning had left him unaware of the fact until now. Even vaguer intimations, touch-

74

ing on Joanna's looks and how they struck him, together with much else, he unhandily shoved out of range. The only certainty was what he had to do next. But exactly how was he to do that with a gap of several feet between them? At that moment she got out of the green chair and strolled towards a window or a picture or a bookcase, so there was no difficulty at all.

He found he was so strung up that he failed to notice what she was like to kiss, but he was aware of considerable pressure against his moustache.

'I see what the lady meant,' said Joanna. 'I don't say I go all the way with her, but I see what she meant. Mind you, she must have said what she said when moustaches were the rule rather than the exception – Winston Churchill had one in his younger days. They're a bit thin on the ground these days, moustaches, except among queers they say, one doesn't like to think what they see in them. I expect you trim yours a good deal, don't you?'

'Now and then.' Gordon's head was in a whirl. By this time he was back in his original seat without any clear idea of how he had got there.

'Perhaps you put something on it to sort of hold it together.'
'No.'

'It struck me as very dense. You know, close packed. I'm sorry, darling, I mean Gordon, I realize I'm the one that's supposed to know exactly what to do, in fact I thought I did until a moment ago, nice line in patter, then I suddenly got nervous. Whatever you may think I don't make a habit of this sort of thing.'

'Neither do I,' said Gordon. 'I'd better tell you I mean the whole thing, not just this sort. But you'd probably guessed that already.' When she made no reply he went on, 'I hope I haven't put you off or anything.'

'Absolutely not, I promise you faithfully.' She took his hand and squeezed it.

'Louise doesn't really care for my moustache. She doesn't mind the way it looks so much, but she says it chafes her face. Makes it sore if she's not careful.'

'No doubt she's had more extensive experience of it than I have at this stage, but I think I see what this lady means too.'

'So . . . some things are just as well. We couldn't have had you looking all inflamed round the mouth when Jimmie gets back from Cambridge.' Gordon felt quite daring as he said this.

'Oh, he wouldn't notice a thing like that, probably wouldn't even see it.'

'How do you mean?'

'Well, he doesn't like wearing glasses.'

'Oh. But surely at his age he has to have them for reading.'

'Of course, but that's all right because they're reading-glasses, ones you put on and take off again, not like wearing them all the time in the ordinary way. Only old people and Jews have to do that. He had very good sight when the two of us started life together, but I doubt if he sees much more than what things are now.'

'Are you telling me he's never had a good look at my moustache?'

Joanna laughed a lot when he said that, especially perhaps at its note of real mortification. After kissing him rather noisily on the cheek she said, 'I'd better start lunch.'

'Do you cook everything here yourself?'

'I sometimes boil an egg or two at breakfast-time and do some toast for myself in the afternoon, otherwise nothing. Mrs Sargent does the meals. She's the one that starts and finishes lunch, but she likes me to be there to see her start.'

Left to himself, Gordon thought over what had taken place and what it might mean. He soon found himself quite unable to decide whether he had started an affair or received the equivalent of a very friendly pat on the head. Both alternatives seemed to him extraordinary and also somehow fraught with difficulty, but then what might have been called the sexual side of life had always seemed like that to him. In his case, though he had good reason to believe it was not only in his case, the strong childhood feeling had persisted that what men and women were supposed to get up to together could not really be true, or if true after all was not the whole story. He had of course grown up or learnt better since those early days, but the whole thing was still apt to strike him as, well, extraordinary, peculiar, curious, odd. Not so many years earlier he would have said to himself it was bizarre too. Eventually he might be able to knock another adjective or two off his list. One day, perhaps, the last of them would go and all that would become part of life instead of an image in a distorting mirror. Being able to foresee that state of affairs might mean he was growing up, unless of course it was nothing more than a premonition of growing old. He picked up his glass; there was not enough liquor left in it to be worth the effort of drinking, but he swallowed it just the same.

Would it have been true to say that all this extraordinary, odd etc. stuff was merely the product of inexperience, un-familiarity, that and no more, as an Eskimo might still feel some disorientation on even his third tiger-shoot? If true, an unenlivening truth. As he quite often did, he let his mind run back over his sexual career, an exercise that took him only a short time. On this occasion, however, it reminded him of his years in the married state and suggested to him what he sometimes thought to himself under a different heading, namely that he had actually found out very little about his wife during the years they had spent together, painfully, shamefully little. She had been pro-him and a very nice girl at the start, and not nearly so pro-him but still quite a nice girl at the end, and that was about it. Well, it was over for good.

Gordon continued his brief recapitulation or roll-call. Quite soon he realized, or saw as he had seen before, that although he had done what his grandfather would have called committing adultery a number of times, the wronged husband had in both cases been at some distance, living with another woman or further off still, with a bloke. What would have been a third irregularity had suffered abrupt cancellation when the absent one had unexpectedly come out of the gaol he had been locked up in for a boldly executed insurance fraud. A wronged husband seldom more than a few miles away, often only feet away, would be a horse of a different colour. Gordon was not at all sure he would be able to face up to that one.

If indeed there was going to be anything that required to be faced up to. That, whatever the rights and wrongs of the matter, was the first consideration, if not the first morally then first in point of time. And here it came in the very tangible shape of the Hon. Joanna Fane, back from witnessing the start of the lunch. One look at her and the rights and wrongs of the matter disappeared. Perhaps they had never been very prominent. Gordon stood up and the two embraced.

'I'm sorry, darling,' she said, and sounded it. 'The trouble is . . . But tell me, you do want to go on with this, do you? I mean now's the time to say if you don't.'

'Of course I do,' he said warmly. He said it because he could not have faced saying anything different, and he said it warmly to cover any flicker of indecision he might have felt.

'Oh marvellous.' After a few moments she said, 'Can we sit down?'

'All right.'

'The thing is, now darling you're not to laugh at me, but the thing is, I don't really fancy, you know, going all the way in this house. I don't feel right about it.'

'I see.'

'I doubt very much if you do, with the information at your disposal. Do you mind terribly if we have another drink?'

'Just a small one for me.'

'Don't you know you're supposed to say thank you when

78

somebody offers you a drink?' she asked, looking not so much older than he as senior to him.

'Sorry, I didn't mean to be rude. Thank you, I'd love a drink.'

'That's more like it.' Now she did smile. 'Thank you for not throwing a sulk.'

When it came it was not a very small drink but Gordon sipped at it anyway.

'Now darling,' said Joanna, 'the chap before you, there haven't been many as I told you, but there was a chap before you, and he and I were running a bit behind the clock one afternoon, and Jimmie was back a bit early from his lunch, and he didn't catch us but he came closer to it than I cared for. He could have guessed, he didn't say anything but he doesn't say everything, as you know. So whether he guessed or not, I made up my mind, from then on absolutely no hanky-panky on the premises. That's *these* premises; other premises are other premises. I'll tell you the rest of the story another time. Never mind, do you like rissoles?'

'What? It rather depends on the rissole. Sometimes –'

'They do vary a lot, obviously. Mr Tucker round the corner here makes his own and they're *out of this world* darling. Anyway they're what's in store for us.'

With several of Mr Tucker's rissoles and some curious but acceptable soggy peas under his belt, plus a couple of glasses of severely ordinary red wine, Gordon finally left the house. He was also the beneficiary of some information about Jimmie's earlier years that would at any rate give him something to follow up for the next few available mornings. When he got back to his flat he sat himself down in a large chair with his outdoor clothes still on and made exhausted-sounding noises for a time, though he would not have said he was physically exhausted. Then he made himself a cup of tea, moving very delicately about as he did so as if fearful of disturbing somebody old or ill. After he had drunk the tea he looked for and found a pair of scissors and took them into his bathroom, where he unwrapped the safety razor and packet of blades he had bought on his way home, dropping the wrapper tidily into the waste-bin. Then he set to work with scissors and razor. Fifteen or so rather painful minutes later his moustache, having hidden a rectangular portion of his face for nearly eleven years, was no more. He was far from sure that he liked the change but found he could no longer remember why he had had any time for the previous state of his upper lip, and anyway the thing was done now.

12

'Gordon,' said Jimmie with a smile, 'you've shaved off your moustache.'

'Is it an improvement?'

'An *immense* improvement, dear boy. Oh confound it, how dreadfully tactless of me to imply that your erstwhile appearance could ever have been *immensely* improved. Let's agree to call it a definite, *manifest* improvement, shall we?'

'Fine with me.' Gordon smiled back. He had got over his momentary feeling of disappointment, or irritation, to find what he still liked to think of as a wondrous metamorphosis so unceremoniously penetrated. 'I'm glad you welcome the change.'

'You look younger, more optimistic, altogether less . . . what shall I say, less gangling, more sophisticated perhaps is what I mean.'

Noises of moderate pleasure came from Gordon. He knew Jimmie well enough by now to be in no doubt that what he had been going to call his new appearance, before balking in the nick of time, was less *common*. Oh well, it took all sorts to make a world, thought Gordon to himself.

The two were standing, Gordon having just arrived, in what Jimmie called his writing-room. There was indeed to be seen there an oblong table bearing blank sheets of blotting-paper, equally blank sheets of foolscap paper that somebody might well write on one day, a pen-tray of amber glass containing pens or penholders with steel or perhaps gold nibs but with an unused look, and an elaborate painted china inkstand which it was possible to doubt had ever featured any actual ink. It was

81

hardly necessary for Jimmie to assert that he wrote whatever he wrote, much or little, in pen and ink, in longhand. But Gordon looked on the array with indulgence; although as he sometimes said he was not much of a writer, he was enough of one to understand the importance of such forms of sympathetic magic as an aid to getting blood out of a stone and forcing the words to flow or, more often, especially in prospect, ooze.

Jimmie seemed to sense that, after an initial mild sensation, Gordon might have welcomed a move to other topics than his newly seen absence of moustache. Accordingly he continued to focus on it, uttering variants on his surprise and pleasure at the transformation, soon insisting that Joanna should be shown it without further ado. This took place in such a way that for a short but appreciable moment she failed to recognize Gordon and for longer than that evidently thought it was no great matter.

'He looks altogether different,' Jimmie kept saying, turning from one to the other of them. 'Younger, to start with.'

'I suppose it did have a sort of old-fashioned association, that moustache,' conceded Joanna. She was so far from making any other concessions that Gordon began to worry slightly lest Jimmie should notice a peculiar constraint of manner in her. But he gave no immediate sign of having noticed anything. Soon the two men returned to the writing-room, where Jimmie lost no time in saying,

'I hope my lady wife [an expression, thought Gordon, mischievously designed] is proving useful to you in your researches, dear boy.'

Forewarned by Joanna at their last meeting, Gordon found it easy enough to field that one, but he filed it too while he was about it. He made some affirmative reply. Jimmie went on,

'She's a very observant girl, always was. She knows me as well as I know myself, if not better in some respects. I'm afraid she thinks I'm a hopeless old snob. Well now, what's on the agenda this morning?'

'Well, if it's all right with you, I thought something along those very lines. Class distinction and all that, your views on the subject. These days it pretty well has to come up in anything I might write about you.'

Jimmie's face took on an expression of overdone and also somehow proletarian dismay. Gordon was emboldened to drop into his efficient television-cockney.

'Tell me, Mr Fane, what do you understand by a snob and would you say you were one yourself?'

'The relevant article in the *Concise Oxford Dictionary*, 1964 edition,' said Jimmie in a slightly better version of the same, 'talks about exaggerated respect for wealth and social position. I'm sorry,' he continued in his customary high posh tones, 'but if I keep that voice up for more than a few seconds I find my jaws start aching. I can't imagine how some people go on like that all their lives. Anyway, er, I'd say unrepentantly that by that reckoning I am indeed a snob, except for the qualification *exaggerated* respect. So it seems that in the view of the diction-ary I'm not a snob after all, since the respect *I* feel for wealth and social position, far from being in the least exaggerated, strikes me as by any reasonable standards perfectly proper.' Jimmie started to go on but burst out laughing instead. After a moment he did go on, saying, 'I'm sorry, my dear, but one result of the removal of your facial hair has been to lay open your expression to the public gaze. Oh dear, how ill-mannered of me to laugh.' At this point he started laughing again, though with less abandon.

'What expression did you see just then?' Gordon spoke in a thoroughly controlled voice.

'Oh, a mixture. An abundant, not to say a heady mixture. I suppose the chief ingredients were disbelief, consternation, shock and, let it be said, amusement. Good for you, Mr Scott-Thompson.' Jimmie delivered the last half-dozen words in his

TV accent, but changed back to say, 'Hadn't you better turn on that gadget of yours, what's it called?'

'This? A tape-recorder. It's been on ever since we came up here. I hope you don't mind it too much.'

'Oh no no no, not a bit, not a bit.'

Jimmie made it sound as if the tape-recorder had been a typification of the modern age (initiated 1960, 1939, 1914 or earlier date) and to be accepted without fuss as equally inevitable. He sat in his high-backed chair, which might have figured in a Victorian cartoon as a self-evidently 'writer's' chair, and looked expectant, but went on without being prompted.

'I agree there are snobs and snobs,' he said in his smoothest tones, 'I'll even go so far as to grant that there are snobs and snobs *and snobs*. But it's quite proper that the original use of the word, and the first sense given in the *Concise Oxford*, refers merely to a person of low birth or social position. Nothing about respect for wealth and rank and so on, exaggerated or not. But that is surely unnecessary. It goes without saying that the lower orders, as we see whenever we are unlucky enough to catch sight of a popular journal, have at any rate an inexhaustible interest in the doings of the rich and well-born. What is less often remarked is that alongside the plebs' noisy satisfaction at the disgrace or ruin of one of their betters, that that feeling of triumph is accompanied by something not far from its opposite, bitter disappointment at a moral failure to observe the highest standards. I say, am I expected to go on all the morning about this topic, fascinating as it may well be?'

'As long as you like,' said Gordon. 'Just you carry on. It's a fresh tape.'

'But do you want to hear?'

'Everything you've said so far I can use, Jimmie.'

'You don't say so. Very well. Now where was I? Oh yes. Enough of the toiling masses for the moment. Ascending in the social scale, but tactfully not specifying how far, we come to people like yourself, my dear fellow. You wouldn't say, would you, that you were free of all feeling about your social betters as a group?'

'I . . .' Gordon hesitated.

'*All* feeling includes what I believe goes by the name of negative feeling, such as dislike, disapproval, disgust, impatience, resentment, et cetera, both inward-looking and outward-looking. In other words, more numerous but better words, you may feel impatient with yourself for liking or disliking lords and ladies as well as simply impatient with lords and ladies. It all counts provided it's say lords and ladies *as a group*. Now, would you say you were free of *all* such feeling?'

'Certainly not,' said Gordon without demur.

'Excellent. Nobody is, nobody in these islands at least, unless he's either a . . . I beg your pardon, unless he *or she* is either a moron or a monster, and by the way I know for a fact that I'm not a moron. Now I've mentioned me I might as well go on with me, it'll only take a moment. Also like everybody else one ever hears about who isn't insane I prefer the society of my own kind, but I must tell you that that seems to me a rather lame self-exculpation, hardly better than an excuse. So I'll just say of myself that I like people of wealth and rank *as a group*, they're the people I want to mix with and have as friends and live among and live with and marry and whose language I speak and understand, and as to *why* in the sense of why do I prefer such people to others I say who knows, who cares, I was born among them or it's something I got from my grandfather, just as another fellow's revolutionary zeal can no doubt be put down to something he got from his grandmother. And as to, as to . . .', said Jimmie, more in earnest than Gordon had ever seen him, 'as to what do I see in the kind of people I prefer, I see first individuality, and I know, I know from experience there's a great deal of uniformity too but not everywhere and in many cases, in most cases not very deep, unlike what could be said of other social groups. Where does English eccentricity belong? In the English upper class or classes.

Individuality, then, and freedom, not only freedom to live any-where and go anywhere and so on, which is very important, but freedom of thought. The upper class is the only class whose members don't care a tuppenny damn what anyone thinks of them. Oh very well, also true of the plebs, no doubt, but I'm obviously not going to set about cultivating their society, partly because I happen to prefer claret to lager and Royal Ascot to the Cup Final and all that. Wooh, that'll do for the moment, if you don't mind too terribly.'

Gordon stopped his recorder and said, 'I suppose you must have said some of that before.'

'In bits, perhaps, not end to end, and less elegantly expressed.'

'I see.'

'You'll be able to use it, I trust.'

'It'll need very little in the way of trimming and tidying up.'

'I'm delighted you think so.'

'Is there anything more you'd like to say on the subject? Or on any other subject?'

'Just a final word, perhaps. Yes, all right, I'm ready. Aren't you going to actuate that device again?'

'If you want it on the record what you're going to say.'

'Why not? I can always strike it out later, as you observed. Ready? Here we go, then. Lastly, there's nothing wrong with being a snob, in moderation of course. In fact as dear Evelyn remarked more than once in my hearing, he puts it in the mouth of one of his characters but he was fond of offering the comment himself, being a snob is surely the most sensible thing to be. It was for him, certainly, as his books show with their wonderful command of social nuances such as a snob is specially fitted to register. And I feel my own novels on their inferior level would suffer if the snob's eye and ear and *nose* were somehow to be removed from them. So yes, I'm a snob and jolly good luck to me I say. It does seem to be a way of winning the Muse's favour.'

'Is that all?' said Gordon after a pause. 'For now, I mean.'

'I think so, don't you? Should I come up with anything more on the topic I'll make a note of it if you think that'll do, dear boy.'

'Of course. Jimmie, may I ask you a question?'

'Nothing too intimate, I hope.'

'That's really up to you to decide, but I doubt it.'

'Okay, shoot, as they say in the cinema.'

'Since you and I obviously come from let's call it quite different social groups,' said Gordon steadily, 'what possessed you, I mean what was in your mind when you agreed to not merely let me write something about you and gave it your blessing but so to speak accepted me as your official while-you're-alive biographer and you've already told me so much about yourself.'

'Oh dear, that's quite a question if that's what it is, but very roughly I thought whatever you as a, as an outsider might say would carry much more weight than anything an associate of mine or a son of such might. Be more fun to read too. Sufficient? If so perhaps I may ask you a question in return.'

'Let's have it, Jimmie.'

'Are you having an affair with my wife?'

Until a second or so earlier, Gordon would have expected to be asked how he pronounced CONTROVERSY or IDEAL, but a warning flash from somewhere enabled him to say 'No' even more readily than when asked some minutes before whether he considered himself free of *all* class feeling.

'*Oh*, what a relief, and I hope you won't mind my supplementary asking if you have any strong or firm intention of trying to bring about such an association.'

Gordon had hardly had time to say No to that too before Jimmie's words rode over him.

'. . . because I would strongly advise against any such embroilment on the grounds of, how shall I put it, what about incompatibility, intended as a description neither vague nor, I hope, obnoxious. Rightly or wrongly, and if I had to choose I should probably plump for rightly, a large and unchangeable part of each one of us is decided for us by the circumstances of our birth and the environment, to use the word correctly for once, in which we did the first part of our growing up. The chance of overcoming an initial disparity here between individuals depends on the temperature of the feelings involved. If it's low, as in the case of a writer and his biographer, the result may be a fruitful and amusing relationship; if it's high, even for a short time, the result will inevitably be dissatisfaction, reproach, recrimination, misunderstanding, bitterness, mutual contempt and above all embarrassment on both sides. I won't go on, I don't think I need to. Here, I say, er, I say, this thing is still listening to everything I'm telling you, isn't it? I notice its little red light is on.'

'Don't worry,' said Gordon, pressing the On-Off button. The light went out.

'Oh I'm not *worrying*, dear boy, I doubt if you'll want to *use* this last chunk for anything. I merely dislike the thought of wasting all that wax or whatever it may be.'

'I can blot it out if I want to by recording something else over the top.'

'That must be absolutely marvellous for you.'

'It has its uses.'

13

But of course Gordon did not at all want to blot out that last chunk. He even wrote down a fair approximation to Jimmie's following couple of remarks as soon as he got home that afternoon. This done, he took out of his recorder a nearly full tape of Jimmie's later account of his first year at Cambridge and put this on one side to go over and type up later. For the moment, but not only for the moment, what most interested Gordon was the gradation in Jimmie's tone of voice from the half-humorous self-deprecation of his opening remarks on snobbery, through the seeming objectivity of their middle reaches, finally to something almost defiant, even strident, by the close. So at any rate Gordon remembered what he had heard that morning. Now he settled down in his working corner and started to play back the earlier tape from the beginning.

She knows me as well as I know myself, if not better in some respects. Private joke.

The relevant article . . . Yes, very good accent. ?Maybe disturbingly good, tending to indicate close attention to how people sound as well as what they say. Not borne out by dialogue in his novels. What about Hunt hurting his head etc.?

I'm sorry, how ill-mannered of me to laugh and what followed. Observant. Compare preceding note.

Ascending in the social scale [from the plebs], *but tactfully not specifying how far, we come to people like yourself, my dear fellow.* NB *fellow* also has force of 'one of same class' (*COD*). But no malice here. Laughing and inviting me to laugh with him at expense of pompous sociologists et al.

Now, would you say you were free of all such feeling? Still no malice.

Excellent ... I happen to prefer claret to lager and Royal Ascot to the Cup Final and all that. It's during this speech that his *tone*, actual tone of voice, changes in the direction of personal animosity (?deliberate). Compare *tone* to remarks that follow:

if you don't mind too terribly

less elegantly expressed (but even so a bloody sight more elegantly expressed than the likes of me could manage)

You'll be able to use it, I trust (slight but appreciable stress on *you*)

and finally ... *if you think that'll do, dear boy.* Similar stress on *you* but also compare and contrast the *tone* of this use of *dear boy* with earlier uses.

Not to mention the alas-not-taped couple of remarks he, Gordon, had jotted down on returning here.

That first session had in fact closed with a sort of addendum from Jimmie:

Just one thing I forgot to say but now remember – when I said that about the upper class having the freedom of not minding what anyone else thinks of them, perhaps you noticed, I meant to say or should have said too that this enables us to be free of envy, and that is a rare and priceless virtue or a rare and priceless gift, whichever you will, in our country as it is today. As she is today.

Gordon stopped his tape and listened to the silence, complete for the moment without passing vehicles. It occurred to him now to wonder again what Jimmie had had in mind when he made his lady-wife remark, noticeable enough at the time, since then perhaps unfairly overlooked. Surely it was on the tape. Yes.

I hope my lady wife is proving useful to you in your researches, dear boy.

M'm. After three or four replayings Gordon was as sure as

he could be that Jimmie's purpose there had been, if anything more than conversational, just to assure him that his chats with Joanna were no secret from anybody. His own guilty conscience had had a distorting effect there. M'm.

But later . . . In a few seconds Jimmie's recorded voice was asking him if he had *any strong or firm intention of trying to bring about such an association* with Joanna. At that point he pressed the Record button, said at his normal pitch and speed, 'As a matter of fact that will be the sole object of my endeavours until it and the association itself are consummated, you stuck-up old fart,' pressed Play and heard Jimmie's voice placidly saying, *a description neither vague nor, I hope, obnoxious.* Off. By way of completing this section, Gordon laughed loudly and in a jeering fashion at his tape-recorder for a short time.

Feeling sufficiently charged up by now he went to the telephone, intending to ring Louise, but his own instrument chirruped at him before he could get that far. 'You're another,' he said to it and picked up the handset. 'Hallo,' he said. What he heard was not quite silence, more like a distant someone of indeterminate sex trying to shout through an efficient gag. When things failed to improve he disconnected and punched Louise's number. Engaged. He swore mildly and hung up again and again his own telephone trilled.

'Hallo,' he said into it with some impatience.

'Is that Mr Scott-Thompson?' asked an elderly female voice pleasantly. 'My name is Madge Walker. You won't know me, but I used to be friendly with Jimmie Fane. I heard you were writing an article or perhaps a book about Jimmie and his earlier life, is that correct?'

'Yes, that's broadly correct.'

'Ah, so my information is accurate.'

'May I ask who gave it you, Mrs or is it Miss Walker?'

'Mrs. Oh, it was just somebody I know. Well, now I'm sure I have the right person perhaps I can tell you that many years ago I used to know Jimmie quite well, and I was wondering whether you might like to hear something from me about those days. I'm an old lady now but my mind is clear and my memory is excellent.'

'I'd appreciate that very much, Mrs Walker, that would be most interesting.' And it really might be. It might equally be that Mrs Walker was little or nothing but an enterprising old blatherer, but that was a risk that had to be run. 'When can we meet?'

'So you haven't yet sent your pages to the printer? Good. Well, perhaps you'd like to come round here, Mr Scott-Thompson. There's only me and my husband and I'm afraid I don't find it very easy to get about any more. I could give you tea.'

'That sounds delightful if it wouldn't be too much trouble for you. Whereabouts are you?'

The answer to this question took little for granted beyond a knowledge of where and what London was. Victoria, for instance, not to be confused with the sovereign of that name, turned out to refer to a district as well as a railway station and one readily accessible by bus and underground train. Gordon listened and made a grunt of comprehension or reassurance. He felt indulgent about the whole rigmarole, reflecting that before it set in Mrs Walker had come to the point with commendable speed. He further reflected that her parents at least must have been born while that incarnate Victoria was still firmly enthroned.

'Pearson Gardens is first on the right and number 14 is down on your left.' Mrs Walker withheld any data about where 14 came in relation to other numerals. 'We're on the first floor. Our name's on the bell-push. Walker.'

'When would you like me to come, Mrs Walker?'

'We're free this very afternoon, but I expect that's a little soon for you.'

Gordon considered, but only for a moment. 'Not a bit. What a good idea. Thank you.'

'Perhaps you'd like to arrive between a quarter and half past four.'

Gordon managed to turn up and ring the appropriate bell at 14 Pearson Gardens just after four twenty-two. A voice spoke to him out of the wall, he answered it, found his way into the house and mounted stairs to the first floor. Here he was welcomed by somebody who was indeed an old lady and to spare, though she was dressed more like a character in a pageant, with a purple tabard and a sort of shiny apron, an outfit recalling to Gordon that of the girl Periwinkle. Mrs Walker had streaked grey hair cut in a short bell with fringe and altogether looked unusual but not ridiculous. Her manner was friendly without being confident.

'Let me take your coat,' she said. 'Then come and meet the captain.'

The captain had not been captain of anything substantial for a long time. He was generic retired officer above the waist, including ancient good looks and a dark pullover covered lower down by a blanket. This hid details of what exactly he sat on and discouraged curiosity on the point. He gave Gordon a sunny smile.

'Alec, this is Mr Scott-Thompson, who's come to have tea with us.'

Extending his right hand to be shaken and making with his left a mimed apology for not rising, Alec gave no sign of having heard or listened. This and something in the way he carried his head made Gordon think he must be very deaf, though no doubt he expected to be spoken to at suitable times like the present. So Gordon smiled back at him and told him, he hoped without mouthing any of it, that he was very glad to meet him. Alec nodded amiably and motioned him to a chair.

'If you don't mind I think I'll go and bring the tea in now,' said Mrs Walker. 'Get it out of the way.'

As soon as she had gone, Alec picked up a newspaper that had been lying on the floor beside him and held it in front of his face. Around them was a rather small room full of small ornaments but pictures of a size or two larger, including several photographs of superannuated-looking warships that indicated which of the services Alec had risen to the rank of captain in. Such matters apart, the decor reminded Gordon of his father's parents' sitting-room in Bromley in the 1950s, but perhaps belonged even further back, like the houses whose outsides he had seen on his way down Pearson Gardens. He had got no further than that when Mrs Walker started bringing in the tea, a meal that had no doubt been in a high state of readiness at his arrival. First she took Alec a plate of mouthful-sized jam sandwiches and a blue mug of tea or other hot liquid. Gordon saw this as invalid-style service and was mildly surprised to find the other portions similarly organized instead of being the doily-napkin affair he had half expected. But on reflection it was no wonder that things were as they were.

'Perhaps I should tell you, Mr Scott-Thompson, that my husband is not just hard of hearing but more or less totally deaf,' said Madge Walker. 'The only reason I don't simply say he's totally deaf is that, when he watches the television as he does in the evenings, he puts on a pair of earphones with the volume turned up as far as it'll go and perhaps he gets something from that, though I'm very doubtful about how much. Nine years ago he was no more than a little hard of hearing, not bad at all for a man in his late seventies, then it all went in a matter of eight or ten weeks, and he was as he is now.'

Perhaps Alec had somehow caught the drift of this, because he looked over and said in a remarkably normal tone, 'Lovely sandwiches, darling. Thank you very much.'

'Glad you enjoyed them, darling. Would you like some more tea?'

'When you're a moment, darling,' said Alec, and picked up his newspaper. His wife presumably had a moment just then, because she went over immediately and recharged his mug.

'There's only the one question I'm going to ask him at that

point,' she explained to Gordon, 'so he knows what to say. It would have been just the same if you hadn't been here. But I expect you see that.'

'Yes, I think I do.'

'We know a very nice fellow, from Yorkshire I think it is, who comes in every morning to see to him. He's awfully strong, which is a big help because Alec's not a light weight. That's usually all that's necessary, but then of course you never know. You just have to have lots of hot water and so on and lots of spare doodahs, if you see what I mean, but I don't suppose for a minute you want me to tell you all this, do you?'

'Yes, I do, I want to hear.'

'Bless you, and have you got a shorter name I can call you by? Well, Gordon, I think that's about as much as I need actually tell you, though I expect you'll have guessed quite a lot. Now tell me, how's Jimmie? Is he all right, is he well?'

'I saw him this morning and he was fine, as regards health that is.'

'That's all I want to know. No it's not, it's just all I feel I can ask you about him for the moment. I'm still very fond of Jimmie, you know, after all these years and everything that happened. He's the sort of man one stays fond of. I sometimes wish I could see him again, but then he's obviously changed a great deal since the time when I knew him. I saw a photograph of him at some dinner a little while ago and I should hardly have recognized him, but I'd still like to see him.'

'How many years is it since . . .'

'Since I knew him. Oh, a great many. During the war and just afterwards, long before you were born or thought of, Gordon. Long before I met the captain, even.'

'What did he do, that's Jimmie, what did he do in the war?'

'I think I'd sooner leave it till another time to tell you anything more about him. I shouldn't feel quite comfortable, going on discussing him in front of this one. Yes, I know he's stone deaf, but I still shouldn't feel comfortable. It's silly of me, of course, but I always remember a story we were told at school about a lady with a blind husband and she misbehaved with a servant chap in front of the blind man and the gods gave him back his sight then and there and it was absolutely terrible for the three people. I know it's just a story and probably only an allegory and it's hopeless of me, but, well . . .'

'I understand, but when would be a good time to have a chat?'

'Any evening after seven-thirty. I've put him to bed by then and I'm here, in this room, by myself. Could you possibly ring me on the day you're coming? Don't go just yet, Gordon, there's a dear. Stay and tell me about your whatever it is you're writing.'

Gordon did as requested. One point of minor interest emerged when he happened to ask Madge Walker again how she had come to hear of his Jimmie project.

'A neighbour told me, she's called Margaret Bardwell, not that that'll mean anything to you I expect. She told me she saw something in one of the papers about somebody called something Scott-Thompson writing something about JRP Fane, and she knows I used to—'

'No no, don't go on. I just didn't know that little bit of news was out yet.'

'Gordon dear, what do they call it when somebody lets the papers into a secret or one of them?'

'You mean somebody leaked it?'

'*Yes*. Well, I shouldn't be in the least surprised if it was Jimmie who *leaked* this himself. It would be just his style.'

14

When Gordon left the Walkers' flat not long afterwards he
was in thoughtful mood. Part of the thoughtfulness centred on
the question of where he had recently come across something
similar to Madge Walker's scruples about discussing Jimmie
in her husband's admittedly unknowing presence. He was no
more than half way to his bus-stop when the question was
answered from inside his head: the similarity lay in Joanna's
scruples about, well, letting him get on top of her in the house
she shared with her husband. A large part of his thoughtfulness
disappeared with that recognition, leaving only the mild problem whether women were sometimes visited by a desire to
spread things over, to defer action, to keep matters in suspense
as long as possible with the object of attracting attention to
themselves. Not for the first time ever, Gordon felt for a
moment he was on the threshold of an important discovery
about women, before it slipped away from him and left him in
his everyday condition of puzzlement and unsatisfied curiosity.

Dusk had descended early, giving the air a watery look and
feel and a deep yellow quality to the lights of shops and
vehicles. Ordinary passers-by seemed charged with por-
tentousness. It was one of those times when a sudden transfer-
ence to some completely different order of existence became
easy to imagine as possible or even imminent. Gordon's bus
came and he boarded it. From his seat by a window he could
see along the pavement and take in the way lights of all sorts
were reflected in the fallen rain, but he could not recapture
how he had felt a moment before, when he had been out there
himself.

What he could do and needed to do was more thinking about Joanna and, as it now struck him, her rather curious behaviour in leaving it to him to arrange their next and presumably decisive meeting. When he left her after the rissole lunch she had talked without pause till they were on the doorstep, then said something hurried and unemphatic that he remembered or had interpreted as a directive to get in touch or keep in touch with her, then retreated. Looking out of the bus window, he suddenly asked himself whether the whole thing might not have been part of a cunning scheme of Joanna's to detach him from her or allow him to detach himself as painlessly as possible. That could still not be ruled out, but between then and now Jimmie's statement on snobbery had intervened and he, Gordon, had inserted on the tape his historic declaration of intent with regard to the wife of the stuck-up old fart. That intent he would pursue as far as he could. The next moment it occurred to him that if he stayed in his present bus instead of changing, he could get off it not far from the Fane residence. Suppose there was nobody in. He would think about that when and if.

Somebody was in: Jimmie, screwing up his eyes, staring in puzzlement for a short space before breaking into carefree laughter. He was wearing a dark suit and collar and tie, but then he always was, presumably never sure when some ducal or baronial summons to luncheon would suddenly take him haring off to Gray's club. 'Ah, it's the young man with no moustache,' he said, and waved to Gordon to come in, still laughing.

'I was just passing. I'm afraid I can only stay a minute.'

'I'm delighted to hear it, because I have to go out shortly myself, and I presume it is me you've come to see.'

'Yes of course.'

'A most unpleasant evening, isn't it? We have time for one drink at any rate, so your brief visit won't be entirely wasted.'

A culinary noise came from the kitchen as they filed past it to the stairs. On the floor above there was no sight or sound of anyone but themselves. Jimmie drove him into the green chair in a room he was coming to recognize as familiar and asked him what he would like to drink. Gordon asked for Scotch, not out of any real preference except for the exclusion of Albanian absinthe, Venezuelan vermouth or kindred liquors that might have been lined up for unexpected or even expected guests.

'Ice?'

'Yes please. And a splash of soda if you have it,' said Gordon with an unappreciated boldness, as one would normally have settled for no addition.

'So what have you been up to since we parted?' asked Jimmie quite soon.

'Nothing much. I've been to see an old friend of yours called Madge Walker.'

Instead of the display of, say, friendly interest or even blankness that might have been expected, Jimmie raised his hand in a self-defensive gesture and a look of genuine horror passed across his face. He said with some apparent difficulty, 'Oh that, that old . . . bag.'

'She seemed quite old, certainly. She told me she'd known you in your younger days.'

'I suppose that is literally true.'

'During the war and just after it, she said.'

'Have you come here simply to tell me that, dear boy?'

'Well . . .' It was the sort of question Gordon had hoped not to be asked. To say yes to it, though truthful, would have raised difficulties, but then devising an alternative was not straightforward either. Luckily there was something else that Jimmie wanted to know, perhaps more urgently.

'How did you find out about her? Who told you?'

'She found out about me. Apparently –'

'She would. She always had ways of finding things out. A

marvellous nose for information. How did she say she heard, as a matter of interest?'

'She said a neighbour saw it in the paper, probably some diary.'

'Yes, again that's the kind of thing she would say. Well, it might even be true as far as it goes. Tell me now if you will, what sort of style was she living in? You say you went to see her.'

'Yes.' Gordon found it quite easy to answer this question, putting in a couple of surmises of his own to eke out his report.

Jimmie had been nodding his head thoughtfully. 'Did she try to get money off you?' he asked. 'I say, I'm terribly sorry about all these questions. It's just . . .' He mimed helplessness.

'That's all right, Jimmie. No, she didn't try to get money off me.'

'No, of course, that'll come next time, that's if you go back there. She's not poor, you know, she's, she's just close-fisted.'

'What she and Alec had didn't strike me as close-fisted, more just the result of being hard up. Though it's true she mentioned some Yorkshireman who comes in every day to look after him.'

'There you are, costs the earth, that kind of thing, as you must have noticed yourself. No, she's not poor. Anyway, dear Gordon, I strongly advise you against having anything more to do with this exceedingly dubious creature. Obviously I can't stop you, I do realize that, but in both our interests I do, I *do* want to make it *difficult*, as difficult as I can. I warn you most seriously and in the most educated way that to get to know her any better would be to involve yourself in a highly danger- ous and disagreeable web of intrigue and lies and deception and, what can I say, something I escaped from by the skin of my teeth. She'll hit your pocket too if she can. Now I think it only fair to warn you that I won't be able to give my sanction to any account of my life and doings that contains material supplied by Mrs, what is it, Mrs Madge Walker. I'm sorry to be so uncompromising but I do feel rather strongly on the matter and I am so convinced I should put you on your guard. Well.'

After a short pause, during which he folded his hands and stared down at the rug, Jimmie went on in a quieter, less impetuous tone than just before, 'I really beg your pardon for that . . . exhibition. That's not quite the word, I'm afraid, with its implications of display and insincerity, but, well, I mean I hope you'll give me credit for sincerity, I'm just sorry I let myself be carried away.'

'That's all right, Jimmie.'

'Now put my mind at rest if you will, dear boy, and tell me you'll have nothing more to do with that dreadful woman, that's if you've come to a decision yet.'

'I certainly have no intention of seeing her again.'

'It would be an insult to ask you to promise that, so I won't.'

'All right, I'll just swear that nothing she could say or do would induce me to go near her.'

'Oh, you don't know what a relief it is to me to hear you say that. Oh dear, I regret to say I must be off,' said Jimmie, giving himself a real treat with his pronunciation of the last word. 'I'm late already. Are you coming?'

Both men were on their feet when the door opened and Joanna appeared in the room. She was dressed for the evening but not, or not yet, for the outdoors. She and Gordon greeted each other cheerfully enough.

'Gordon and I are just on our way, darling,' said Jimmie.

'I didn't know you knew the Parkinsons,' Joanna said to Gordon in some surprise.

'Whether he does or not I assumed, er, Gordon was homeward bound.'

'Correct,' said Gordon.

'Oh but you can't go now when I've barely set eyes on you.'

'I think I'd better be off if you don't mind.'

'Stay and have a quick drink with me before you go.'

Gordon looked at his watch without seeing what time it was. 'Ten minutes, then,' he said with a sort of smile.

'I'm afraid I must say good-bye and leave,' said Jimmie, and did as he said.

As soon as he was out of the sitting-room, Joanna set about preparing drinks for Gordon and herself. She had just finished doing so when they heard the sounds of Jimmie's departure from the house. She waited a little longer, then came over and put her arms round Gordon and kissed him heartily on the mouth. As well as liking this in and for itself, Gordon was pleased to be assured that nothing important had changed, that he and she were indeed going to get up to some of what she had recently called hanky-panky some time in the near future, though probably not on these present premises. But at the moment he found it hard to think about the future, or to want to.

'Good,' she said, having perhaps just been over some of the same ground as he had. 'But I'm afraid that'll have to be all for the moment.'

'Where are the Parkinsons?'

'Five doors down. Even so it's a rotten night. Some prince of the blood must be slated to appear there.'

'He won't be back then, will he? I'm merely accumulating information about him.'

'I can promise you it wouldn't be in the least uncharacteristic of him to find he'd come out without a handkerchief and make a quick return foray for one. So in the general interest you'd better put that drink down in something like six minutes from now and then smartly bugger off.'

'Do you think you could bear to come to my flat? It's not very nice really, but it's all right, and at least nobody ever comes there.'

'Darling, I don't think you have any idea of how much nicer you look with that moustache out of the way. Completely different. Well no, not *completely* obviously, just very. Remarkably.'

'Let me give you the address.'

'You look younger and sort of half a size larger, though I can't think how that's come about.'

'You'd better write it down.'

'No I hadn't, darling, I'll lose the bit of paper and you never know where it might turn up. You'll have to say it to me.'

'You'll forget it.'

'No I won't. Say it to me twice over slowly and I'll remember it, I promise.'

'All right,' he said, doing his best to sound cheerful and confident, and recited as asked.

'There,' she said after repeating it, and went on, 'Drink your drink. It's thanks to me you've got it.'

This too he did, or started to. 'But it's thanks to him I got the first one. He came straight out and asked me what I'd have. Surely that's unusual.'

'Not as unusual as you might think. He reckoned you wouldn't be staying, and he goes in for being lavish in short controlled bursts. Or he may simply have forgotten to screw you. He's mean all right, but that's all a matter of policy. By instinct he's quite a generous old bastard. I'd better not go any further along that track or you'll start wondering whether I'm going to remember that address. Which by the way I have every confidence in my ability to do. No darling, not now.

'Knock the rest of that back and get out of here unless you want to find James Reginald Pruett Fane tapping you on the shoulder, so to speak.'

For the third time in a row Gordon did as he was told and nothing more of significance, except perhaps to inform Joanna that he would telephone her at a suitably early hour the next morning. On his way home by bus he tried to describe to himself how he felt at the prospect of starting an affair, which it now looked as if he was really going to do, with Joanna and an older woman and a married woman and Jimmie's wife and the Hon. Joanna Fane and the female who was married to the author of *The Escaped Prisoner* and no doubt other aspects. Some of the ones listed must have prevented him at the time from seeing what he now saw clearly, that he had taken a fancy to her the moment he set eyes on her for the first time. He knew further that he must have the equivalent of a serious talk with himself about what he was getting into, no question about it, and yet he could by no means imagine what such a talk-equivalent would be like. The rain ran down the outsides of the bus windows and here he was feeling like a man who had written a masterpiece and just remembered he had fatally mugged somebody in Basingstoke.

As soon as he had reached his flat, before even taking off his raincoat, he went to the telephone and arranged with Madge Walker to come to Pearson Gardens the following evening. He was buggered, he thought, if he was going to be told what to do and what not to do by any stuck-up old fart.

15

For Gordon, there were two things about the next morning that differentiated it from others, one thing that happened and one that failed to happen. The one that happened was the arrival by post of a xeroxed press-cutting accompanied by a printed slip that brought him the compliments of Brian Harris. The cutting was from the diary of an up-market daily newspaper and stated clearly enough that Gordon, with his name only slightly misspelt, was at work on an authorized critical biography of JRP Fane. The diarist added that the choice of biographer had raised some snooty eyebrows in certain circles not a hundred miles from Gray's club, without particularizing further. Irony of uncertain direction lurked here and there in the paragraph, but that was standard. Anyway, Madge Walker had not needed any special nose for information or web of intrigue to find out about Gordon and what he was up to.

The second thing, the one that failed to happen, started when he started to try to ring Joanna and went on with more of the same. The number was or seemed to be continuously engaged. There were various insignificant possibilities that would have explained this state of affairs, but he found it hard to shake off the suspicion that Joanna had decided he was not a good idea after all. The thought of this displeased him so much that he lost any capacity he might have had to estimate its likelihood. He punched the number for the sixth or seventh time. Engaged. What was he to do? If a grown-up man would have shrugged his shoulders and got on with some work, then that only went to show he was, as he had suspected before more than once, not a grown-up man. He crossed to the window.

Last night's rain had cleared up and there was pale but bright sunshine in which even the vile park looked all right. He had to go out.

Not very long afterwards Gordon was in a bus, yet another bus as it appeared to him, consigning him to yet more of his life spent in surroundings he had not created nor even wished for and was permitted to leave only at certain predetermined points. One of these came up eventually and with some exertion he left the bus at a corner where he had alighted before, or so he soon discovered. Was he drunk? Not at this hour of the day, and probably not in any case. He was telling himself so and exciting some credence when he took in the fact that the tall elderly man in whose steps he had been treading for some while was in fact Jimmie Fane, returning home perhaps with a purchase of cat-food. At once all faith in the questions he had run up to justify his presence if needed, questions any old biographee would be dying to answer, entirely collapsed. He would ask Jimmie, 'What decided you against becoming an academic?' and Jimmie would reply, 'I thought I told you not to start fucking my wife or [how had it gone?] trying to bring about such an association.' If it came to fisticuffs . . .

Gordon soon halted on the pavement, doing so in diminuendo style in case Jimmie, a bare twenty yards ahead and known to be short-sighted, should notice a sudden change of noise-level and swing belligerently round. Only a few yards off, Gordon saw a small side-turning, no more than an alley, and dodged into it. Then, this time telling himself from two incompatible points of view not to be a fool, he peered in the direction he had been going and saw Jimmie just started on a very life-like imitation of a man unself-consciously opening the front door of his house and presently shutting it after him. Finally, against the possibility that Jimmie might suddenly reappear in the street and look back the way he had come, Gordon hunched his shoulders and limped off round the corner.

Once there he relaxed and tried moderately hard to remember what he had been intending to do if he had had untrammelled access to the Fane house. Abandoning this line of inquiry for lack of evidence, he found he was forced back on the one about what he was getting into, or thought he was getting into, a pair of questions or more likely a single one that seemed to become more and more rhetorical with every recurrence. No doubt, but there were good or at any rate strong reasons, to do with chivalry and lust, why he was buggered if he was going to bow out at this stage. By now he was on another bus still, which he got off again a short walk from the St James's Library. Once there he telephoned the literary department of the Sunday paper he worked for, though it would have been fair to say he had not worked very hard for it lately. Desmond O'Leary was not in the office and nobody who was present seemed to have any clear idea of when and why he, Gordon, would be required to turn up there; still, it would look good to have telephoned. Most of the remaining hours of daylight he spent not quite profitlessly looking through the books on the open shelves of the library in search of reminiscential material relating to old Jimmie Fane. When evening had come he climbed on board an after all further bus and was carried like the wind, with none of the delays he might have been resigned to expecting, to a point where another short walk took him to the flat occupied by the Walkers. In fact he arrived at the building a few seconds before the agreed hour, just when a neurotically precise or something-like-that person would have got there. Nothing daunted, Gordon at once rang the bell and was admitted as before to the first-floor flat.

Alec Walker was not to be seen, though it was clear very soon that his absence was due not to death or kidnapping but to more temporary displacement to the bedroom. Madge Walker was present, however. She had dropped her medieval-persuasion get-up in favour of a more orthodox jumper and dark skirt, though the orthodoxy was one of Gordon's parents' day or a couple of days before that. A polished-wood brooch in the form of a letter M was pinned below her shoulder and she had made her face up just a little, not enough to alarm him. Her manner was still friendly but no more assured than when he had first met her. He for his part tried to behave as if he dropped in on her at about this time two or three evenings a week, easing himself with a contented sigh into the chair he had sat in before.

'I hope you like whisky,' said Madge, producing an unopened half-bottle of Scotch.

'Ah. Just a small one for me if I may. Lovely.'

'Would you like some ice, Gordon? It's no trouble, I'd have got some cubes out ready, only I didn't want them to start melting.'

'No really, I prefer it without. With just a little of that water. That's fine, marvellous. Aren't you going to have one?'

'Later on I might. Cheerio.'

'Cheerio.'

It was at this early stage that Gordon started thoroughly disbelieving Jimmie's account of Madge Walker as a dangerous and-or dreadful woman at the centre of a web of deception and lies. Nor did he set about changing his mind back again at any point in what she went on to tell him about Alec and their life together past and present. When the talk shifted to Jimmie, Gordon put himself on alert.

'Yes, I must have asked him three or four times what he was doing in the war,' said Madge, 'but he wouldn't give me so much as a hint. Just said he was working for the government, well that was no help at all, everybody was working for the government in those days. He didn't like being asked about it and once he got quite cross and made me promise not to ask him again.'

'And did you?'

'No, I'd promised. That's not to say I wasn't strongly tempted from time to time or stopped wondering.'

This exchange had the effect of reminding Gordon that not so long ago he had sort of promised Jimmie not to see Madge again. Certainly he had sworn that there was nothing she could say or do that would have led him to go near her in the future, but he was in the clear there, having himself initiated their present meeting. In the clear technically, maybe. There was also the consideration that to imply so strongly that promises were unbreakable, even ones made to Jimmie, was no doubt the sort of thing said by women at the centre of webs of this or that. But Gordon could not see that either of these points counted for much compared with his recent feeling that Madge's version of events was to be trusted.

'How did you first meet Jimmie? — but before you answer, do you mind if I use this contraption?'

'What is it?'

'It's a tape-recorder. I've got a good memory but without this I'd have to keep writing things down and stopping and starting.'

'I see. At least I think I do. Nobody will be able to hear what it says, will they? Hear what I say, I mean.'

'Not without your specific written permission.'

'That's a relief. I can see I'll have to trust you, Gordon, but I'm sure I can do that. Very well. I'd better come closer, hadn't I?'

'No need, it can hear you from where you are. Right, tape running.'

It emerged that, their fathers having been at school together, Madge had first met Jimmie before the war, when both were in their teens, but they were never close friends, let alone anything more, until 1943. By that time she was married to her first husband, a well-to-do young Peruvian who had volunteered for the RAF.

'Yes, he was really quite well off,' said Madge, 'and quite charming, good at parties and so forth, and he danced like a dream, but he was a horrid little man really. They have llamas in Peru, you know, and I used to wonder whether that had any sort of bearing on what he wanted to do to me, or rather me to do to him. But I didn't have to hang about wondering for very long because I ran into Jimmie again, and I lost no time in scampering off with him and ditching nasty little Flight Lieutenant Padilla. I can't tell you how wonderful Jimmie was in those days, I couldn't understand why every girl who met him didn't fall head over heels in love with him. Just the way he *talked* . . .'

One subject he evidently disliked talking about, in addition to what he was doing in the war, was marriage. Jimmie's taciturnity on the matter was neither here nor there for quite a while, because the only marriage of any concern was Madge's to Padilla. When this eventually ceased, however, after a rather long interval by present-day standards, the question of marriage between Jimmie and Madge seemed to become more immediate. At least it had to her.

'I can only tell you what happened,' said Madge to Gordon. 'The chap I really got on with like a house on fire was Flight Lieutenant Paso-Doble's papa. He was a proper South American hidalgo of the old school, such an old school that I rather suspected him of having wanted to run off with me himself, though of course he was far too much of a gent to put any such thought into words. But what he did do was insist that the Flight Loot should go on paying his wife, i.e. me, the same very decent allowance as before while the marriage technically lasted. A matter of family honour, you know. But the instant marriage ended so did allowance, like *that*, in fact wham!'

'Which presumably had some effect on your relationship with Jimmie,' said Gordon.

'And how!'

It was really not very funny to hear how Jimmie had quite suddenly become remote, uncommunicative, with intervals of exaggerated warmth and intimacy, and not funny at all to be told about their final parting. The fact of its taking place had been no great surprise to Madge, though, as she pointed out now, even fully expected nasty things lose none of their nastiness for that. And what she had not expected by a long chalk was Jimmie's method of intimating to her that their romance was at an end.

'We'd arranged to meet for a cocktail in the bar at the Tripoli,' said Madge. 'It wasn't as madly expensive then as I gather it is these days, but it still wasn't cheap. I remember I got there a few minutes early, so I ordered a drink, a White Lady it was, and settled down to wait for Jimmie, he was never one for turning up on the dot. Look, I hope you don't mind, Gordon dear, but before I go on I think I'll just go and see if the captain wants anything. I usually pop in on him about this time. The nice man who lives upstairs fixed up what he called an intercom between the bedroom and here, but Alec would never teach himself to use it. I shan't be very long. Help yourself to some more whisky.'

She went out. Gordon switched off his recorder, left the bottle as it was and heard Madge's voice and Alec's from where the bedroom presumably was. The serenity with which she had told her tale so far had been total, never deviating into forced vivacity or any other kind and seeming likely to remain. Well, the events happened fifty years before.

'All squared away,' she said when she came back. 'You have to hand it to the captain, never a word of complaint. Now where had I got to?'

'You'd just ordered a White Lady in the bar at the Tripoli,' said Gordon, switching his recorder on again.

Madge gave it an unfriendly glance. 'Have we got to have that thing on?'

'It saves trouble, that's all.'

'Would you mind very much if we didn't have it on for the next bit?'

'If you'd rather.' He pressed the On-Off button to signify Off.

'I expect you're thinking I'm just a silly old woman but I can't help feeling it's like another person listening to what I say. It's ridiculous, I know.'

'No, I understand. Please carry on when you're ready.'

'Thank you, dear Gordon. Well, you'll have guessed that Jimmie didn't turn up that time. I tumbled to it fairly soonish, I suppose, what with one thing and another, though I'd embarked on another White Lady by that time. I felt a bit of a fool quite frankly, sitting there exactly like somebody who'd been stood up, either that or a cruising tart who hadn't clicked. Anyway it wasn't as bad as it might have been, because I had just enough money on me to pay for the drinks and get myself home. I made myself some scrambled eggs on toast and listened to some awful clever play on the wireless where everybody in it was meant to be dead and then I went to bed and slept not too badly at all. You see it wasn't the first time he hadn't turned up like that. But then he didn't telephone first thing in the morning to apologize and sort of explain and suggest another date.

'Then when after a couple of days I'd still heard nothing somebody rang me up and told me Jimmie'd been dining at the Ritz that very same night, we worked it out, and what he'd been at was a kind of unofficial engagement party where the centre of attraction was him, naturally, and a lady called Betty Brown, the daughter of that newspaper-owner chap, who was giving the party. I didn't see Jimmie after that for years, not till about 1950 or even later. The former Miss Brown had left him by then and I was having a lovely time with another gentleman, so you see the world had moved on quite a way since the evening Jimmie and I were supposed to meet in the bar at the Tripoli.'

'Did he ever say why he hadn't let you know beforehand, I mean try and apologize or say he was sorry or anything like that? I mean . . .'

'It's *all right* darling, it was all those years ago and I must have told you I'm still very fond of him. Well, I suppose it might be more accurate to say I've been very fond of him for a very long time, because I certainly wasn't very fond of him when I understood what had happened or when he rang me up for a chat and for a few months afterwards. Yes, he rang me up eight days from the evening he'd handed me the frozen mitt, which also happened to be the day his engagement had been announced in *The Times* – he'd considerately given me time to get over any feelings of surprise or disappointment I might have had. He explained in that special high I-will-not-be-interrupted voice of his that he'd deliberately chosen a sudden and, what word did he use, emphatic, an emphatic method of breaking it off, or letting me know it was broken off, the idea behind that having been to impress on me, to leave me in no doubt whatever that we had parted for good.'

'And breaking your date and keeping you in suspense for a bit had all helped.'

'Some of that might have seemed remiss of him, but really it was hardly to be expected in the nature of things that it would take so long before some third party came along and, er, filled me in.'

At no point in her recital had Madge's tone deviated from what might have been expected of an interested and reasonably neutral friend of the participants, however clear it might have been that her sympathies on the whole lay with one side rather than the other. Gordon waited to see if there was anything more to come. When nothing did he asked Madge about the last time she had seen Jimmie.

'It must be five or six years since he came to this very flat, I thought about it a lot but I've never been able to decide what he came for.'

'But it was after the captain . . .'

'Became more or less as he is now. Oh yes. Why?'

'I just thought Jimmie might have weighed in, or offered to.'

'Weighed in? You mean stumped up, do you? Financially?'

Gordon nodded his head in some embarrassment. 'Sorry, I didn't mean to poke my nose into any of your —'

'You're not, I promise you, and anything you say won't go any further. It's kind of you to think about us like that but really and truly there's no need to. Alec and I have both got a bit of money, not very much but then we don't need much. I saw you looking at that whisky-bottle and perhaps you were saying to yourself a half's all they can afford, but no, it's more a whole one would have been an extravagance, and we certainly can't afford to go in for any of that.'

'What about your Yorkshireman? That sort of fellow doesn't come cheap.'

'Young Coop, he's called Cooper actually, he's honestly quite reasonable, and he does more than he has to now and then and nothing's too much trouble, he's here every morning at ten on the dot and it's just let me know if there's anything special for me today Mrs Walker, I can't do the accent. I've got very fond of young Coop. He's taken away a lot of my worry about going before Alec does.'

A moment later Gordon said, 'We've come quite a long way from Jimmie.'

'Haven't we just, and perhaps you've been thinking after some of the things I've told you I might be too proud to touch a penny of Jimmie's money, and perhaps I ought to be but I'm afraid I'm not. So for the sake of my immortal soul it may be just as well the situation is shall we say unlikely to arise.'

After another pause Gordon said, 'Could I have a spot more whisky?'

'Sure thing, baby. A small one with a dash of water. I don't see why I shouldn't join you for once in a blue moon.'

'You do that small thing.'

'You betcha sweet life. Here's how!'

He could not quite bring himself to say anything back, but gave a great cheek-involving wink as he raised his glass.

'There's more to tell you about Jimmie if you want to hear

it,' said Madge. 'To do with his literary career and all that.'

'Yes, I do want to hear.'

She put her glass down and smiled at him. 'You can turn your tape-recorder thing on now if you like.'

Later, at his work-table, Gordon found that he remembered almost word for word what he had been told about the evening of the great stand-up and its sequel, or lack of one. He had said truthfully that his memory was good, but it had never before been as good as this. In the morning or even sooner he would very likely find he had started to forget. Within seconds he had begun typing on a fresh sheet of paper:

M in Tripoli bar waiting for J who didn't show. Feels a bit of a fool, her predicament obvious, has just enough cash to pay for 2 drinks and get home. No word from J. 'After a couple of days' someone [who? if it matters] rings up and tells her J been at Ritz on evening when

At this point Gordon stopped, read through what he had typed and sat and thought for a time. Then he took the piece of paper out of his typewriter and crumpled it into a ball which he dropped into the waste-bin. He was far from clear in his mind why he did this, but it had something to do with not wanting to deceive old Madge. Not, he had told himself, that old Madge would have been at all taken aback to hear he had done his best to get round her recording ban, but she might have been disappointed in him or, to use a phrase he associated with his childhood, surprised at him. When he put this to himself it sounded very much as if he had decided without any real qualification to believe her story and reject Jimmie's portrayal of her. Well, so he should.

And yet . . . He had indeed started disbelieving the Jimmie version soon after setting eyes on Madge for the second time, and he had seen no subsequent reason to modify this disbelief. Nevertheless Jimmie had shown abundant signs of holding a low general opinion of persons at the Scott-Thompson social level and Madge had shown none. And she was a woman, however old, and her version of events, the picture of a woman abandoned by a ruthlessly self-seeking lover, made a clear appeal to sentiment, however sugary. All true enough. And yet . . .

Gordon had obviously had no inkling of such moral-emotional difficulties when he first formed a serious intention of writing something like a book about JRP Fane and his works. It was undeniable that they, the difficulties, made the project more interesting, but all the same he wished quite heartily that they had never arisen. He was most relieved when a mate telephoned with the suggestion of a couple of halves of Callow's best bitter at the pub on the far side of the park.

16

'Have you been living here long?' asked Joanna.

'Nearly two years. I know it's not very nice but it's not really supposed to be.'

'What is it supposed to be?'

'Well,' said Gordon, 'it's quite near the middle for the price, and there's a good bus and Tube service, and anyway I'm usually out a lot of the time.'

'No, I can't see you giving any lunch- and dinner-parties, and anyway if I found myself living here I'd certainly be out a lot of the time, and I suppose you meant it's cheap for what you get. Darling, I'm not sure how to put this, but could you lay your hand on your heart and say you think it's quite . . . cheap . . . *enough*?'

'Joanna, why are you so cross? What have I done, or have you just thought of something?'

'Christ, do you see? You men are all the same, said the contessa. Actually she wasn't so far out, if she'd said you're all either As or Bs she'd have got it right to an inch. Shut up, I was going to tell you anyway, one lot it never crosses their minds they could be anything but right the whole time, like no names no pack-drill, and the other lot are always moaning and apologizing and asking where they went wrong. You get half a mark for daring to ask if I've had second thoughts – no, you did.'

'Which you haven't.'

'No, not quite, but don't you ever ask me what you've done again, and don't pretend you don't know what I mean. And no, I wouldn't like a cup of tea, there's never a right time for

117

that as far as I'm concerned.' She sat up. 'I must say in fairness to it the place is quite warm. Is that you or the landlord or whoever it is?'

'I suppose what there is of it is me.'

Without saying any more she got out of bed and left the room. As she did so he got a goodish look at her naked back view, not quite as good as he would perhaps have liked but good enough to lend some support to the belief he had more than once heard expressed, that of ladies of more mature years the part below the neck retained the look of youth longer than that above. Joanna had given Gordon his first close experience of such a person and he was relieved and delighted that things seemed to have gone well, and hoped he had not felt or shown too much vulgar triumph at having carried off the situation. He knew without minding that it was beyond him to have felt and shown none.

He looked back now, with much less nonchalance than he had felt at the time, to learning that the telephone chez Fane had been off the hook yesterday through inadvertence, incompetence, lordly and crappy failure on Jimmie's part to see the handset was properly back on its rest after a chat with some Ascot-frequenting property tycoon. Without actually starting to strip as soon as the door of the flat was fairly shut behind her, she had shown no signs of wanting to have a serious talk with him about what they were getting into or indeed any kind of talk about anything. In one way or perhaps in more than one he had welcomed this, but felt at the same time that such thoroughgoing avoidance of inessentials rather lowered the tone of the occasion. A different type of man might have resented any implication that he was being what such a man would very likely have called used. If this thought had occurred to Gordon he might have felt flattered instead, toned up by the notion that at least one female considered him worth using. Very soon the rush of event and action had swept away all such thoughts and most others too. But the point had returned to his mind and stuck there, so firmly that he had tried to think of a safe way of bringing it up. But as it happened Joanna had soon moved not far from it herself.

'One terrific advantage of an adulterous affair is that it cuts down the preliminaries, not necessarily out but down. I mean if a chap kisses the lady of the manor and she responds, well they're away unless she's having him on, but you don't have to be married to have a chap on, as perhaps you've noticed yourself. It's funny, though, how seldom people mention the what, the time-saving side-effect of adultery. They probably think it's bad form in some way. You know I've often thought it's a big selling-point of queerdom they never seem to go on about that it gets jolly near cutting *out* the preliminaries. But after all, there are limits. You wouldn't have to hanker after a French dinner or a dozen red roses to feel a bit let down by just getting your bottom pinched.'

Gordon had got about as far as this in playing over what had earlier been done and said when Joanna came back into the room and, not at all in the slow-motion tempo he would have voted for if consulted, got into bed beside him.

'I hope I didn't give you the impression I was seriously dissatisfied with the appointments in this of course one would call it a flat,' she said quite close to his ear.

'I can see it has its shortcomings.'

'We won't dwell on those, though as my old headmistress might have put it I do think you might find it helpful in future to consider softening the austerities of the decor with a few pictures, reproductions thereof of course, and while we're on that sort of point, old boy, get those suitcases of yours out of sight unless you're letting it be known that you mean to be off first thing in the morning at the latest.'

'Sorry.'

'And don't say sorry unless you really are sorry and don't mind sounding it, and even then you're better off not saying it.'

'I see.' Gordon thought it best not to say he was nearly sure she had said it to him illegitimately more than once.

'And that's another one I'd contemplate dropping from my phrase-book if I were you, darling. It's a sort of short cut on the cheap to sounding knowing and experienced.'

'You're not leaving me much it is all right to say.'

'Let's get up and go out and have lunch somewhere.'

'Is it a good idea, you and me being seen having lunch? Somewhere?'

'More than a good idea – necessary. Everybody knows by now you're on the scene and will expect us to go round together a certain amount, it would be pretty odd if we didn't. And it isn't as if you've still got your moustache.'

'What difference would it make if it was still there?'

'Think about it.'

'I didn't tell you, did I, Jimmie warned me against having what he called an association with you.'

'What, on the grounds that you might find me a lousy screw?'

'Er, no, on the grounds that we come, that's you and I come from different classes.'

'I say, did he actually put it in those words?'

'Not much, he preferred to talk about social groups and the rich and well-born and the toiling masses and the plebs and so on.'

'And that was the clincher, what? You need not answer that question. Wow, I knew he was a cunning old bugger, but that takes the biscuit.'

'You mean warning me off you for being . . .'

'Exactly, darling. The cunning old bugger. But I wonder *why.*'

'Thank you for coming,' he said when they were in the sitting-room about to leave. He had not said it before to anybody in these circumstances, and thought it quite witty although unlikely to be original.

Joanna ignored it, however. Her eye fell on a tumbler with

water and some nascent daffodils in it. 'Do you usually have that sort of thing hanging round the place?' she asked him. 'Fresh flowers?'

'No, I don't bother usually, but I thought today was special.'

'Just as well I noticed. I mean I suppose they are there because of me or am I making a complete idiot of myself?'

'No, they're there because of you.'

'I nearly missed them. Why didn't you put them in the bedroom?'

'I was going to, but then I thought that might be a bit forward.'

She seized him round the neck and held on to him tight without kissing him. After a moment she said, 'A hug says more than a fuck any day. They've been trying to din that into us for years. Without getting through.'

'Who? Who've been dinning it or whatever it is?'

'I don't know. We'll go to Woolton's and I'm paying and just you bloody well shut up, I want my sort of lunch. Let's go.'

'Will they have a table there if we just walk in?'

'They will for me.'

With however much hidden reluctance, they did. It was Gordon's first visit to Woolton's, reopened the previous year, he remembered someone saying, after a long period in limbo. Its interior, reached after a complicated descent, had the look of being originally designed for some other purpose than serving meals, as a hangar for non-rigid airships, perhaps, or a film-set of vaguely science-fictional tendency. He and Joanna were shown to their table, the furthest of all from the entrance, by a succession of dauntingly beautiful, disdainfully polite girls, all of them in heavy make-up and showing as much leg as practicable. A similar girl provided an authentic pre-war touch by bearing a cigarette-tray mounted on a yellow silk sling round her bare shoulders. Gordon blessed his own foresight in having had a pee before coming out: he would not lightly have faced a journey to the gents and back in a place like this. The surrounding noise was like a hundred Jimmies all insisting on being heard.

'Would you like to pretend to be paying or shall I just pay?' asked Joanna when they were sitting down. 'Think before you answer.'

He thought. 'You just pay,' he said.

'Is there anybody you know here?'

'Only you.'

'You haven't had anything like a proper look round yet.'

'I don't need one. I'm not saying that in any carping spirit. This just isn't my kind of joint at all but that doesn't mean I disapprove of it.'

'It would have meant exactly that if you'd kept your moustache.'

'At a time like this I quite wish I had. By the way I'm not trying to be funny.'

'That's a relief.'

'I keep being afraid they'll all suddenly see through me and throw me out.'

'I remember thinking the same sort of thing about this sort of eatery when I was seventeen.'

'How did you get over it? My God, listen to me.'

'Two large Dry Martini cocktails straight up with a twist and don't forget the gin,' said Joanna to a waiter behind Gordon. 'It's best to be on the safe side and stress the gin,' she explained to Gordon. 'Otherwise they're liable to give you plain vermouth these days.'

'What do they think we are?'

'It's just that you've never been a part of this kind of set-up, just treated it as something to hear about and once in a blue moon look at. You'll have to be at home in it for however long we've got. You can still think and say nasty things about it if you're anything like me.'

'Does Jimmie come here a lot?'

'Christ no, I doubt if he's ever put his head inside the door. Far too loud and vulgar and brassy and flashy. And full of Americans.'

'I've already heard dozens of people talking in here but not one in an American accent,' said Gordon.

'Metaphorical Americans. Americans in the sight of God.'

'Why Americans?'

'I suppose ultimately because they've never asked his permission to exist. He says they think they know everything but all they really know is how to rope a steer.'

'Some of us don't even know that much.'

'If he ever goes near a real American he's afraid he'll be frightfully rich and he, I mean Jimmie, he won't know how to deal with him.'

'So much for freedom from envy,' said Gordon. 'Sorry, but can we stay on Jimmie for a bit? According to you he warned me to keep my paws off you in such a way as to have the opposite effect, is that right?'

'Well, it did strike me as a characteristic Fanean move.'

Gordon cogitated. 'Does that mean he really wanted me to go back to Madge Walker and get her full story and believe the lot?'

'Oh no, the way you told it it seemed to me as if he really wanted you to have nothing more to do with the lady and to not believe anything she might have told you. He was being sincere, if that's not a too absurdly incongruous expression to apply to him. Consistency of approach is not a Fanean trait. Only devotion to self-interest is. And don't tell me that applies to everybody.'

At that point the drinks arrived. It was instantly clear to Gordon that to thank the waiter, as opposed to saying thank-you to him in a preoccupied way, was not done at this kind of dive, so he did it extra hard and stoutly never mind how much of a prat and a scholarship boy it made him feel. That was not difficult because for all his would-be bright talk since coming here, his mind had been more than half full of something else, to do with how pleased he felt about Joanna and at how things had gone between them. He was only disappointed that there seemed no way of telling her so, any more than he had ever in the past found it possible to convey things like that in any direct way or even, for all he knew, indirectly. In any case, he was new here.

'Do you mind if we talk a little more about Madge?' he asked.

She said with a remnant of irritation, 'I've never met her and I know next to nothing about her.'

'But you must have heard this and that.'

'I suppose so.'

'Do you mind telling me what you've heard?'

'Why do you want to know?'

'I'm not going to let you have it verbatim, but Madge gave me a long circumstantial account of how, well, how ruthlessly and humiliatingly Jimmie dropped her when he got the chance of marrying somebody rich.'

'Not only rich, be it said. Old man Brown, the girl's father, had a lot of influence and he used some of it to get Jimmie jobs and stuff of that kind. As regards ruthlessness and so on, that sounds like standard Jimmie behaviour. In this case something like that might have been justified, partly anyway. Apparently she was a bit of a clinging vine. There was a bit of a sort of collective sigh of relief when he dropped her. That's his side of it at least.'

'So you think Madge was exaggerating,' said Gordon flatly.

'Not consciously, perhaps, after all it's a long time ago. And Jimmie must have been piling it on in what he said to you, but then he always does when he's making that kind of point.'

'Which leads to the conclusion that the truth lies somewhere in the middle.'

'I thought that was where it's usually meant to lie. Don't look so fed up, darling, what do you care, you're not the recording angel, you're just trying to write a book that'll make you and the publisher a spot of cash and in the second place advance your reputation and with a bit of luck old Jimmie's as well, right?'

'Well . . . yes, that too, but any kind of book, that's to say any book with purported facts in it has got to get those facts right as far as possible.'

'How far's that in this case, only two witnesses who disagree, and something that happened fifty years ago? You've already gone as far as can be expected.'

'Maybe. But there might be other surviving witnesses. I don't know there aren't.'

'Darling, assuming you have a bit of luck and find out what really happened and it turns out to be even slightly damaging to Jimmie, can you see him letting you print it?'

'Very likely not. But I'll know.' He drained his glass.

'Oh, Christ, we've got Mr Valiant-for-sodding-Truth to deal with, have we? I see you're not a Scot for nothing.'

'Scotsmen are notorious for being on the make, don't forget. Newspaper editors are prepared to pay quite a lot for a scandalous story about an upper-crust figure like Jimmie Fane.'

'Bravely spoken, but it's not on. He's not prominent enough and it's much too long ago and it wouldn't be scandalous, just discreditable. Surely you see that.'

Gordon made a large internal effort. 'You're probably right, but I would just like to know out of curiosity. I've made it sound more important than it is. Let's forget it and have another drink. If that's all right with you.'

For a moment he thought he had left it too late as she stared at him intensely and yet without definable expression. He felt an equally nondescript qualm. Then she smiled, with a faint tremor at one corner of her mouth. The waiter came and was duly despatched. Gordon wanted to say something apologetic but prevented himself. She did say something about the restaurant and the way she said it brought him a vague though timely warning about what it must feel like to have served her a Dry Martini cocktail that deviated from the perpendicular or had in it an insufficiently contorted twist. Thinking this distracted him from taking on board what she actually said, but he endured that with resolution.

The menu proved to consist mainly of uninformative, sometimes cryptic entries apparently in English for the most part with a few enigmas in some other tongue or tongues. Gordon felt like going through the whole lot asking the waiter in a loud slow voice for clarifications, but realized that to start with he was about fifty years too young to play that game. So, doing his best now not to impersonate a schoolboy taken out for a special treat in a grown-up restaurant, he brilliantly got Joanna to order for him. Then he felt a part of his insides give a sort of lurch as his second Dry Martini cocktail (with gin) took possession of him, and he reckoned he could take on anything short of a prince of the blood royal or a head of government without turning a hair. When his first course arrived, irregular strips of mummified chicken enlivened with half-melted peanut butter poured over it, he fell on it with avidity.

They had some wine, some red wine which evidently only the man who brought it was allowed to pour. After he had poured some of it for the second time Joanna said to Gordon,

'I've been meaning to ask you, what do you actually think of old JRP Fane's works? Are they any good according to you? All this time you've never said.'

'No, well for the moment let's leave it at they naturally have their points of interest.'

'Yes, naturally I see that, darling. In fact I think anybody at all could see that, but you're supposed to be writing an entire book about them and their author. You surely feel there's more to them and him than just points of interest.'

'I hope to find out how much more there is to be said in the course of writing the book.'

'But you must have thought that they, the works, were seriously underrated as part of the idea of writing about them at all. Or seriously overrated, but it wouldn't have been that.'

'It won't make much difference to Jimmie whatever I thought to start with.'

'But it makes a difference to you, to what you are, whether you're somebody with real ideas and enthusiasm or just a, well, a Scotsman on the make. Of course Jimmie always tells me I don't understand these things.'

Joanna's voice slackened. She had the look of somebody who has said more than enough, or perhaps less than enough, less than intended. Gordon was not sure which, but either way he felt grateful.

17

Gordon's parents lived near the western edge of London, in the belt of postal districts in double figures. The house they now occupied was not the one Gordon had lived in from babyhood to university age, but was only a couple of miles from that primeval and gravely undersized relic, as it had appeared to him on the very few occasions he had happened to go past it. Most weeks he spent an evening with the old people, eating with them either at their table or, less often, at a nearby Italian restaurant, where he habitually did the paying. Whichever it was to be, he would turn up at the house in the first place. So he came to be ringing its bell shortly before seven o'clock in the evening of that same day.

Habit died hard: he found he was bracing himself against some expected onslaught before he realized that any such need had passed with the belated passing of the snarling, squealing Jack Russell terrier Jip, so named by his father after Dora's dog in *David Copperfield*. Gordon's mother had not greatly cared for Jip and quite likely had vetoed the introduction of any successor. It was she who came to the door now, dressed up for most things short of a Buckingham Palace garden-party.

'Hallo, Mum, how are you?'

'Gordon!' she said as if in surprise, embracing him a little more fervidly than he wanted.

'I thought you might like this.' He gave her a small plastic pot with a yellow-and-orange primula blooming in it. 'The girl said it would plant out all right.'

'Oh, you really shouldn't, dear.'

'Only 99p, and you won't be getting anything so extravagant next time.'

Now an idea seemed to strike his mother. 'Come into the warm,' she said.

In the warm already were Gordon's father and his young sister Gillian. Both of them greeted him affectionately and showed pleasure when they saw what he had brought them, a packet of fags and a couple of flimsy pink-bordered handkerchiefs. Scott-Thompson senior looked like an elderly businessman who was still sufficiently active but, being a retired schoolmaster, was neither of those things, Gillian, in jeans and with fresh-from-the-curlers hair, looked like the teenager she was, though she bore no signs of drug addiction or other bodily harm. She, the late fruit of her parents' embraces, was no trouble and never had been any but on a notional level to those who really cared for music. Nobody under that roof did, so the offensive sounds she caused to be made there aroused no intrinsic objection, and she kept their volume down.

She had slipped away to set some such sounds going overhead when Gordon placed himself opposite his father. Public-library copies of the works of Anthony Burgess and William Golding were on display. Mr Scott-Thompson visually alluded to them as a kind of prelude to what would inevitably have been a full exposition of their authors' merits and possible demerits. Experience showed Gordon that to plead he had not read the books in question would make little difference. His only hope of forestalling talk of coruscating genius and mythic passion was to plunge in with a suitably elevated topic of his own choice.

'I expect you saw that statement in the paper about Arts Council grants to the opera and the symphony orchestras,' he said.

Luckily his father forbore from asking him whose statement and what paper. His comment was, 'No doubt those fellows are moaning about not having a penny to bless themselves with.'

'The costs of that sort of thing are shooting up all the time,' said Gordon.

'It beats me why people can't be expected to pay the economic price of their seats.'

'A city like London has got to have more than one ballet company.'

'They'll happily fork out hundreds of pounds in a restaurant.'

'Without a subsidy, lots of things we take for granted would simply disappear.'

'Why should a taxpayer in Bolton help to finance somebody's evening out in Hampstead?'

They were happily settled now till supper. Both father and son, especially son, refrained from asking a comparatively radical question like how many times they had been over that same ground before. Mrs Scott-Thompson kept out of their way for the time being. If challenged to account for why she did so, she might well have said something about there having to be a time in the evening for men's talk, a description of it both the men concerned would have assented to, though not in the same tone of voice.

As supper-time approached, Scott-Thompson senior produced two small wine-glasses into which he poured dry sherry. More exactly, it was superannuated dry sherry that had started to lose its savour after being opened a fortnight before and by now, without having gone off, had lost nearly all of it. The old man, who had been almost deprived of his senses of smell and taste as a result of a street accident shortly after his retirement, was doubtless unaware of any change. Gordon sipped with pretended relish. Without wanting to come here any oftener than he did, he felt comfortable and secure in the small room among furniture he remembered from his childhood. Indeed, nothing more than the modestly sized television set, which he had only ever known his sister to watch, was in that sense unfamiliar. Probably some of the hundreds of books on the shelves were not many years older, but unlike his father he took no account of them.

Gillian came and announced the meal, not catching Gordon's eye as she did so. That was normal: though on good terms, the two had never been close, as perhaps they could not have expected to be, having grown up quite separately. This evening, to nobody's surprise, the main attraction at the table was shepherd's pie. As always, Mrs Scott-Thompson had browned the top layer of mashed potatoes to just the required degree of crispness and had got the proportion of sliced onions right too. Spicy brown sauce and bottled mild ale complemented the dish, with apple pie and fresh Cheddar and biscuits to follow, as always.

Through most of the meal, Gordon's mother kept up a flow of information about relatives and neighbours barely known even by name to him. He had heard it said that small-talk became in time, perhaps was from scratch, the foundation of a successful marriage. Either his mother supplied enough talk of that kind for two, since his father had none of his own, or the pair of them provided an exception, an undoubtedly successful marriage nearly fifty years old between one party who wondered if Ted and Laura would be going to Frinton again this August and another party who showed an enduring interest in the social function of art in a democracy. Both themes were tenaciously pursued, but the Frinton one had pauses between paragraphs. After one of them Gordon's mother said to him,

'How have you been getting on with writing your book about that man, what's his name, you did say.'

'JRP Fane,' said Mr Scott-Thompson. 'A typical product of –'

'I've become a sort of friend of the family,' said Gordon, not very accurately, he knew, but at least promptly. He hurried on, 'His wife used to be his secretary and she's got some really quite interesting stuff about his early career when he was still

131

principally a poet though I suppose these days he's thought of as a novelist though again . . .' He proceeded to give a not very coherent, but at least long, account of Jimmie's career as a whole, not just its early part. Not unexpectedly, Mrs Scott-Thompson's interest in what her son was saying began to fall off at about the point when Mr's began to quicken. Some quirk of training or temperament had seen to it that he never interrupted anyone who was actually talking or pausing for breath. At the same time he had silent ways of indicating that he wanted to say something, notably by making unambitious faces. Just then, for instance, as a summary of the sixth novel and its publishing history showed signs of drawing to a close, he parted his jaws and began fluttering his eyelashes behind the massive multifocal glasses he wore.

'Is that all?' he asked when silence had fallen.

'It's all for now.' For a brief moment Gordon luxuriated in the self-admiration he felt at the quality and precision of what he must be carrying in his head about Jimmie and his output.

'You told me before you started work that you meant to write a critical biography of your subject.'

'Yes.'

'In other words you'll be offering critical judgements as well as descriptive accounts.'

'Yes,' said Gordon again.

'When we last discussed the matter you told me you'd set out to read all Mr Fane's books, not a protracted enterprise I should have thought.'

'No, I've managed to at least run my eye over just about every volume he's published.'

'I can't say I have. I've had to be content with what the library round the corner had or could get, but I've managed quite well considering. Having nothing else to do I read what I did read more, more concentratedly than perhaps you've had time for as yet.'

'I shouldn't be surprised.' Gordon vainly searched his

memory for some remarkable but hitherto undisclosed fact about Jimmie, the sort that might interest Gillian, whatever that was, or distract his father, if there had been any such thing.

'I thought it might amuse you to hear very briefly what I made of what I read,' said Scott-Thompson senior, his tone and his choice of words both hinting lightly that something like irony was somewhere present in his remark.

'Of course,' said Gordon rather helplessly.

'The poems are the product of skill and a genuine feeling for language rather than anything that could be called emotion. I think you'll understand what I mean by a phrase like, how shall I put it, they have nothing to say, as read from . . . the standpoint . . . of the present time. Or am I talking nonsense?'

'Not as I see it.'

'The fiction, the novels, there's skill there too. But all that has dated to a degree the poems have not. When we say a work of literature has dated, we don't mean merely that it shows signs of its period and so we keep reading about horses and carts instead of cars and lorries or some men put brilliantine on their hair or even that people hazard or flourish an utterance instead of just saying something. No, we mean if it seems to a contemporary reader silly or affected or absurd or embarrassing or laughable, the work has failed to survive the passage of time and the associated changes of fashion. All Mr Fane's novels seem to me to suffer some degree of damage from this fault, the first two or three and especially the first one, *The Escaped Prisoner*, being touched by it least, as isn't surprising. I'm afraid all this must seem rather obvious to you, Gordon.'

'Well, it can't be said too often.' Actually Gordon thought different, that it had indeed just been said once too often. Far from seeming to him obvious, let alone mistaken, his father's judgement was very much the conclusion he was himself approaching, with the same exceptions or partial exceptions made. With a hazy idea of gaining time, he said, 'But tell me, why do you say it's not surprising the early Fane books have dated least?'

'Well, perhaps all I really mean is they're better than the later ones, which is certainly not in the least surprising. After all, a man can put everything he has into his first novel, everything he's seen or thought up to that point, but into his second only what he hasn't put into his first, or so at least he's likely to feel. A writer, almost any writer but Shakespeare, has only a limited number of things to say and he's going to get them said as soon as he gets a chance. Auden is an example in point. If you pursue, Gordon, if you take that sort of line on this chap and what he's written I'm afraid he's not going to be very pleased with you. If he's anything like other creative people he imagines, however ludicrously, that his later productions are at least as interesting and as worth-while as his earlier ones and doesn't like to hear that contradicted. Imagine what Mendelssohn would have said if you'd told him the best thing he'd ever written was his *Midsummer Night's Dream* music.'

Gillian surprised Gordon very slightly by saying, 'Is that what you think yourself, Dad?'

'Not being a musician I'm afraid I'm not qualified to say, my love, but I understand it's by no means an uncommon view in this century.' Mr Scott-Thompson turned back to his son. 'I feel perhaps I went on rather a long time about what we mean when we say a work of literature has dated and the rest of it. For one reason and another I don't often get a chance to discuss matters of that sort. That thing about Mendelssohn was the sheerest self-indulgence, based on a remark I once overheard in the common-room.'

Again very mildly, not emphatically, Gordon felt such points would better have been left to be inferred rather than openly stated. But he sympathized with his father and, as often before, wished for a moment that they met more often.

'I quite thought you two would have finished your talk about books before we sat down to supper,' said Mrs Scott-Thompson genially, 'but there you go still chattering away like a couple of magpies.'

'I'm afraid it was mostly me,' her husband admitted. 'I never find it easy to talk about somebody who writes or wrote books without, well, talking about books, his books at least.'

'Of course, I quite see that. But the way you do it, I've said to you before, it does rather tend to shut other people out.'

'Oh, I'm sorry to hear it, my dear, I promise you I don't purposely talk in any special way, certainly not one intended to exclude anybody.'

'No, really, I'm sure you don't mean it. I was just sort of apologizing for not joining in much myself. I'm afraid Gillian and I haven't had the sort of education you need to have if you're going to go in for literary theory.'

At no time in that brief exchange, not even in her last remark, had Gordon's mother allowed any hint of malice or sarcasm to colour her tone. Theory, sometimes particularized as now, more often left unadorned, had become her favourite description of the kind of thought and talk she found impenetrable or unprofitable or, an earlier favourite, heavy. It was as near as she ever came to recognizing what differentiated herself from her husband, whom Gordon had never known to suggest any simpler way of contrasting the two of them. Only a stranger to the house could have suspected that tonight might have been the night for plainer speaking.

With the question of (literary) theory left behind, Gordon's mother said to him, 'You haven't had much to tell us about Mrs Fane, have you? I can't help feeling a little bit inquisitive about her. According to your father she's years younger than her husband.'

Gordon went into that kind of thing. His mother gave every sign of listening, though he thought the inquisitiveness she had mentioned was more a matter of what she should declare than of what she felt. Just as well if so, he also thought. At the same time he was aware that Gillian was paying closer attention than usual to what he was saying, in other words closer than minimal. Really? How much closer? He found himself unable to dislodge from his mind the fancy that his sister was on to him, at least that something about his look had suggested to her that his interest in the Hon. Mrs Fane went beyond what was strictly proper. As he talked inexactly of Joanna's clothes and dinner-parties he did his best to concentrate on his own negative feats like not blushing or knocking the cruet over. He was doing well at that when Gillian spoke for perhaps the third time since sitting down to supper.

'Would you call Mrs Fane attractive?' she asked.

He had just shoved a spoonful of apple pie into his mouth, so was off the hook for a couple of seconds. In this interval he decided that a show of uncertainty was the thing to be avoided here, and accordingly said with ready emphasis, 'In fact she's almost exactly twenty-five years younger than old Jimmie, but that still puts her somewhere in her middle fifties, so in a way I can't really tell. Even so, I can see she's taken good care of herself over the years.'

'I'll bet she has. There's nothing like never having had to lift a finger to boil an egg for keeping the signs of age at bay. *And* massages and facials and moisturizing creams galore, I'll be bound. A woman of that class, no wonder she's well preserved.'

Gordon heard this contribution of his father's with mixed feelings. It was good to be offered a way out of having to say just how attractive he found the wife of the subject of his biography. On the other hand he had been led up this side-track too often in the past to be able to look forward to anything in the least unexpected along its course. So he put on a considering face.

Having muttered, rather mechanically, 'Now then, Dad,' Mrs Scott-Thompson said to her son, 'I saw somewhere that

Mrs Fane was one of the great English beauties of the 1960s period.'

'Oh yes, everybody seems to agree she used to be absolutely gorgeous and she's still got a marvellous pair of . . .'

'Sorry, dear?'

One moment, Gordon thought to himself, he had been nowhere near where he was now, and the next here he was. He said in a matter-of-fact tone, 'Blue eyes.'

Across the table from him, Gillian let out a great snort which merged into a brief coughing-fit over some biscuit-crumbs.

'It's not at all surprising,' Scott-Thompson senior pursued, 'that such a person should possess lasting good looks. Things like that go to the highest bidder as a matter of course. You may say that's just a piece of flippancy or easy cynicism, but I don't think you would if you'd seen as much of the other end of the scale as I have. I remember when I was about your age going up to Dundee to visit my Uncle David and Auntie Grace, you must have met them, they're both long dead now, and where they lived there was no chance at all, no prospect of encountering a woman over forty, over thirty-five, who retained any handsomeness she might once have possessed. Up there, women of that age looked like old women, dragged down by years of childbearing and housework and getting all the family washing done in the copper on a cold dark Monday morning and then putting it through the mangle with just the wee daughter giving a hand till she had to be got off to school. And then ironing on the Tuesday depending on the weather. Ah, you don't keep your pretty looks for long when you've got that to cope with week in week out and nothing to look forward to bar more of the same as far ahead as you can see.'

Gordon had no doubt of the genuineness of his father's emotion in recalling or assembling this picture. What he felt he could not drive away, was a slight doubt of the genuineness, or at least the universality, of the picture. In his experience human beings were good at avoiding unpleasant things if they could and making the best of them if not. 'It's just as well that Mum's generation was spared all that,' he said after a pause. His mum, though pleasant enough to look upon, had not had much in the way of handsomeness to lose, but he avoided glancing at her. A trifle annoyingly, his father now said, 'Of course, I admit I was laying it on rather thick just now about how life used to be for the underprivileged. If things were ever as bad as that they've got much better since those days, there's no use pretending they haven't.'

Mrs Scott-Thompson's expression showed some relief. It had looked to her as though her husband was fully set on the other of his two unwelcome courses, the pursuit not of what she meant by theory but of class. Now it seemed as if he had voluntarily drawn back from contemplation of a world of pri- meval misery and impoverishment, a world she did not recog- nize as anything real in her own life, or that of any forebear of hers, but which presumably meant something important to him. That was the sort of way she might have put matters to herself when on her best behaviour, like this evening. At other times she might have described what he had been saying as schoolmaster talk, a phrase she might have found hard to clar- ify but one instantly acceptable to her contemporaries, includ- ing some who had never had even a figurative schoolmaster in the family.

Her husband perhaps felt he had drawn back too far from his original portrayal of proletarian life in the past. At any rate, he made some meditative noises while he took off his glasses and cleaned and polished them. Then he said, 'Mind you, the position at what we'll call the better-off end of the scale hasn't changed. The poor aren't as poor as they used to be but the rich aren't any less rich. Far from it. They may have changed a little in their composition and they've certainly developed some new forms of extravagance, like the people they think of as the lower orders, who seem to get rid of most of their spare cash on foreign holidays, preferably in places like Florida where King Mammon rules, and secondarily on magazines and videos and the like that celebrate the doings of ... of the people I very much hope they don't regard as their betters in any literal sense.'

With his closing words Mr Scott-Thompson betrayed a mild complacency, no doubt at having said what he had said, and particularly at having brought its long final sentence to a successful conclusion. The quick glance he sent his wife and son, though, showed something different. At such times it was hard to shake off a feeling that he knew how he seemed or sounded to the rest of the human race, if not precisely then much more so than appeared at other times. Gordon could not think of any useful reply to make to this last lot, so he made none. Over a cup of instant coffee, his father went on soon enough.

'I know you too well, old chap, to imagine you took on the Fane job of work with the least intention of ingratiating yourself with Fane himself and his circle and the others you might run into, what we used to call social climbing. No, of course you had no such thought in your head when you started. But now you're some way into the business – I'm sure you won't take it amiss if I just remind you of the dangers of letting your good nature run away with you so far that your judgement is distorted. I've learnt how responsive you are to kind and sympathetic treatment such as you tell me you've been getting from Fane and his wife and so on, but don't get confused, don't mistake charm for decency. Fane and all he stands for belongs to a different world from yours and you know what I think of that different world, however pleasant some of its individual inhabitants may be. Don't let yourself be circumscribed by what I say, well you wouldn't, I'm well aware of that, just cast a cold look on what you're writing about is all I ask.'

Gordon looked over at his mother and sister, happily

engaged it seemed in discussing some female topic like holidays or money. He said, 'It sounds to me as though you're telling me I'd better give old Jimmie Fane's stuff some pretty hard treatment.'

'That too,' said his father.

18

The next morning Gordon awoke with an entire dream in his head, entire in the sense that it was complete in itself but also that he knew the answers to all questions that could possibly be asked about it. But in the very moment, in the very act of starting to contemplate it, something in his mind started to take it away from him, something that kept pace with his accelerating efforts to remember, until all of it was gone for ever. There must have been a woman in it somewhere, he thought, but could not think who, and within a moment even the participation in it of any such character had become doubtful. Enough.

He reasoned that nothing much was to be expected of a day that began with getting up, but got up nevertheless. While waiting for the midget gas-stove to heat his egg-water he was startled, as he always was, by the imperious twitter of his telephone.

'Gordon Scott-Thompson.'

'Hallo darling,' said Joanna's voice. 'It's me. Are you alone?'

'Hallo darling. Of course I'm alone.'

'Listen darling, Jimmie's remembered he's got a meeting of his Rupert Brooke committee thing so I could come and see you after all, that's if you still want me to.'

'Of course I still want you to.'

'You don't sound particularly keen. Do say if something else has come up.'

'Don't be ridiculous. Hang on a minute, something's boiling over.' Nothing actually was, though it was true that the egg-saucepan might have done if left to itself much longer. After pottering about for a moment or two, he went back to the telephone and said loudly into it, 'What time shall I expect you?'

That did the trick. Over his breakfast egg and two slices of toast, eaten in the sitting-room so as not to be in the kitchen, Gordon reflected on the brief telephone conversation. On the face of it Joanna had really wondered whether he might really not have wanted her to come to his flat that morning to make love and had anticipated or sort of finessed this by suggesting as much before he could. He saw that this spoke either of a distressing condition of insecurity or of a desire to bugger him about or a mixture of both. And her reasons were to do with her being either upper-class or a woman or a mixture of both. Enough! No more thought, he thought, not for a bit.

But then soon afterwards he was back in his bedroom wondering about the sheets. This would be the third time Joanna lay in this bed, the first time between sheets both clean and fresh, the second between sheets fully clean enough to satisfy a normal person but not strictly fresh. Thanks to an unprecedented effort on his part he was now in a position to convert from state 2 to state 1. Taking everything into account, should he? Oddly enough it was his difficulty with this question, not with the one just now about her state of mind when telephoning, that finally convinced him of what he had been suspecting for the last twelve hours and longer: he knew less about her than about the Hon. Mrs JRP Fane, knew her no better than any other female he might have happened to talk to for a few minutes, bar a hazy impression of what parts of her looked like with no clothes on, not that they had struck him as differing in any important way from the corresponding parts of other females. He must look at Joanna more closely.

Making up his mind not to bother to change the sheets after all used up so much of his energy that he flinched at the first job he had set himself for that morning, tidying up his biography stuff. At present this stuff consisted chiefly of hundreds of pieces of paper, some little more informative than bookmarks, some faxes or sheaves of typescript, some barely intelligible reminders and notes to himself, some in notebooks, some loose. They were parked on most horizontal surfaces in the room, including areas of the floor, and fully occupied his work-table and its immediate neighbourhood. He removed from the keyboard of his typewriter a xerox of a contemporary review of *The Escaped Prisoner* and found a new home for it on an unregarded section of windowsill. The way was now clear, if that was truly the word, for him to go on roughing out his remarks on this novel, but instead of doing that he went and took from the row on the mantelpiece the St James's Library copy of *The Battle Cruiser*, fifth novel of the Fane six. This one had been more successful, in terms of sales, than those that had come before and after it, though according to people like Brian Harris that was only because some first buyers had been misled by the title into taking it for a tale of adventure or even a work of naval history. Gordon had picked it out because he had read the text through only once and had studied little except the opening and closing pages. To reread *The Battle Cruiser* at this stage would be his nearest available approach to coming with a fresh eye to the works of JRP Fane.

Having removed from its seat half a dozen recorder tapes, Gordon settled down in his best and almost only chair to get as far into his task as he reasonably could by the time Joanna was due. He had made himself some fresh coffee and turned to a fresh page in his loose-leaf notebook.

The hero of the novel, presumably in some sense the battle-cruiser of its title, was the head of some agricultural and possibly agrarian concern in the north of England. His status and activities in this regard were less fully realized than his position as head of a family still centred in that area, not that anything very substantial was made out of that either. No matter: Gordon had come across fictions that survived a similar thinness at the centre. What made *The Battle Cruiser* hard to read was far more an ineptitude at the edges, understanding by these such outer manifestations of sensibility as dialogue and passages of narrative and description, down to phrases and individual words. The principle of selection here seemed partly one of perversity, preference for the unexpected when the obvious would have served perfectly well or even, perhaps, stronger in the context. How could the overall effect be described? As artificial, as influenced by a desire to be striking at the risk of being obscure, here and there as plain silly. Now he came to think of it, he had noticed this tendency at work in *The Escaped Prisoner*, but there it had seemed to matter much less. Was it possible to say anything sensible about why this might be? One could point out, at least, that *Prisoner* was a first novel and argue that as such it was likely to be better, because its author would have had a far greater freedom to choose his material than was possible for him in later works, where he had to depend on what he had not dealt with earlier. Or so he might feel, as Gordon remembered his father going on to say.

One advantage of having an excellent memory was that it put little strain on the powers of recall. Another – less comfortable, thought Gordon – lay in its power to remind persons who dealt in ideas that comparatively few of their ideas were original. But in the present case he wished he could have forgotten that it had been his father who had put forward this one in his hearing. The reason why he wished this was obscure to him, but it had something to do with wondering whether to allude to this fact in what he finally wrote, and if so how. He tried to puzzle this out for a bit, but then found himself overtaken by pondering the significance, if any, of Jimmie's often-advertised concern with the spoken language. Was that insistence of his on saying curriculum vie-tee related to the occurrence of the word *adscititious* twice in five pages of *The Battle Cruiser*? Why, incidentally, was there no hyphen between the two main words there? A discussion of this point, including comments by Jimmie, would at any rate help to bulk out what was coming to appear a thinnish book on the author and his works.

Gordon had still not reached any conclusion on this when his bell rang to announce Joanna's arrival at the flat. His feeling of pleased anticipation, raised at the sound and its significance, dropped back and further when he observed that she was blinking her eyes more often than usual and showing other signs that something was wrong. While he helped her off with her coat he was considering which of three or so possibilities was the most likely. In no particular order they were: something was wrong and she was jolly well letting it show, nothing much was wrong but she was pretending something was, and something was wrong and with the best will in the world she was simply unable to hide the fact, or a combination of any two of the three or all three. He also thought more dimly that some men, presumably including himself, were liable to get this sort of trouble with any and every sort of woman, while others, unlike himself, never got it with a solitary one. He tried to pack neutrality into his tone when he asked, 'Is something wrong?'

'Yes,' she said.

He might have been more surprised, he fancied, if a miracle out of science fiction had altered her bodily form, but only thus. He said aloud, 'What is it?'

'I don't know, I'm not sure, I can't think, I simply . . .'

'O soul, be changed into little water-drops and fall into the ocean, ne'er be found,' he said, again silently, and articulated, 'Come and sit down and tell me about it.'

Fortunately, and from a detached view mysteriously, there was a polished wooden bench of classic genre in the small space outside his flat. The two of them sat on it side by side and he put his arm round her shoulders. 'Now what's the trouble, what's the matter?'

Here she astonished him just a little by not at once bursting into tears by way of reply, and rather more by feeling for his hand and squeezing it. After a moment she said in a normal voice, 'It's this week-end he wants us to go on.'

'By *us* you –'

'I mean him and me. The week-end at the end of this week.'

'Well, that doesn't sound terribly –'

'He's up to something. I always know with Jimmie.'

'What sort of thing would he be up to?'

'I say, do you mind if we go through? It's a bit on the bleak side out here.'

'Sorry,' he said, remembering too late that it was a forbidden word. Joanna had not noticed, as perhaps was to be expected in the circumstances, but even so it was then that he decided that something was indeed wrong, whether or not she could define it.

'Christ,' she said when she saw his untidied biography stuff. 'Is this all to do with Jimmie?'

'In one way or another.'

'I had no idea there was such a lot to be said about him.'

'I'll clear a place for us to sit down.'

'Do you want a hand?'

'It'll be quicker if I do it.'

By the time they were settled on either side of the inoperative fireplace, Joanna's demeanour was more relaxed and normal than on her arrival. Among other things she was wearing a padded jacket and a thick scarf in the colours of what could have been a rugby club.

'Are you warm enough?' he asked.

'Another couple of degrees and I'll be in a muck sweat. How do you do it?'

'I don't do anything, it's just always like it in this weather and never mind and why don't you take your scarf off and you were going to answer my question about what Jimmie might be up to.'

'Don't you take that pissily complacent tone with me, my lad. You're part of the same deal whether you like it or not.'

'What the devil are you talking about?'

'Calm down, darling. You remember I told you about this week-end?'

'Well?'

'Well, you're coming on it too.'

'Oh, what nonsense, how can I be? Whatever Jimmie's got in mind he won't want me hanging round the place and getting in the way.'

'Sorry, darling, I should have explained.'

'I wish somebody would.'

Joanna's explanation, elicited piecemeal, made it clear that the week-end in question was not the sort one went off on like a coach trip but something one went to, like a theatrical performance or a fancy-dress dance only lasting that much longer. This particular week-end would take place at a house called Hungerstream situated somewhere in the south midlands, the country seat of the Duke of Dunwich.

'I don't think I've heard of him,' said Gordon.

'You wouldn't. I mean just he's quite rich but not very well known for a duke.'

But well enough known to Jimmie Fane, who had been trying to wangle an invitation to Hungerstream for simply ages, as Joanna put it. Now that the coveted summons had at last been extracted, it proved to include Gordon.

'Something fishy about that part, if you ask me.'

'I agree it does sound like Jimmie at his fishiest, but it also sounds like the duke at his most ducal. He is the most colossal wand-waver – you won't have come across people like that, darling. Jimmie said you happened to be mentioned in conversation at Gray's and His Grace said just let's have him along too. I can hear him saying it. Anyway, don't you want to come? Whatever happens'll be biographer's bully-beef.'

'You bet I want to come, but I don't want to turn up and find I'm not actually expected, as part of some merry jape of Jimmie's.'

'Again I agree that would be just like him as a rule, but absolutely not with a duke in the offing. He'll be as good as gold in that way while he's there. Incidentally if you're expecting an engraved invitation card addressed in secretary hand to Gordon Fcott-Thompfon Efquire, forget it. His wish is your command, if you follow my meaning.'

'M'm. Is there any more?'

'Only a little bit. Nothing really. How's my old friend Louise whatever-she's-called, that pretty girl chum of yours?'

'Fine as far as I know. I haven't had anything to do with her since you and I got properly started.' Gordon spoke quite artlessly.

'Did you have a terrific row, the two of you?'

'Nothing like that. Looking back I don't think we were ever all that close. No, one of us just didn't ring the other one up, I've forgotten which way round it was, and we sort of took it from there. Why?'

'I see. You know darling, when you and I got properly started, as you call it, I said to myself you were the best thing that had happened to me for ages. There is just one more tiny bit about the week-end. The done thing is, if possible to save it being awkward with the numbers and everything, you'll be bringing your wife with you or of course some other female. Why don't you ask Louise if she'd like to come? Just give her a ring and say you're going to Hungerstream for the week-end and would she like to come.'

'She's dead against all that aristocracy and grand houses stuff.'

'Want to bet? Just ask her. Right now, if you know where to get hold of her.'

'But I just told you I'd finished with her,' Gordon protested, without much force because he was still a little elated at being thought even as much as a passably good thing in Joanna's life.

'What was actually said?'

'I don't think anything was *said*, in so many words. It was all —'

'Tell her — bugger it, it won't matter what you tell her within reason if she decides she likes the idea.'

He succeeded in penetrating quite soon the layers of local-governmental bullshit that surrounded Louise in her borough counselling unit. Their conversation was decisive and not prolonged. Joanna looked over from the book she had picked up from the pile on the floor, like its fellows a volume of lacklustre memoirs in which there nevertheless figured a younger Jimmie Fane.

'So she's coming.'

'Hell-bent on it.' Gordon sounded puzzled. 'You know, I can't quite see what's in it for her.'

'Can't you? All sorts of people would give their ears to see Hungerstream from inside with its duke in it. She can drink it all in and have a bloody good time and then give the whole thing a right ballocking, perhaps even get her name in the papers in the end plus a spot of cash.'

'You don't sound as if you like her much.'

'What are you talking about, I've hardly met the girl,' said Joanna.

'Anyway, what's in it for you if she does come? That's another thing I don't quite see.'

'Well, it wasn't my idea in the first place, if you remember, and it could be rather fun to see Willie in action. Willie's the duke, by the way.'

'In action? Surely you don't mean —'

'Shaping up to wave more than his magic wand. He's quite a serious man, young Willie Dunwich.'

'What? I don't understand. What's the duchess going to say?'

'Not very much. She overdosed herself last year, perhaps you saw.'

'I don't know that I want anything to do with this,' said Gordon.

'Please come, darling.'

She looked at him with a forlorn smile and carefully replaced the book she had been looking at. As so often before in conversations with Joanna, he felt he had to take up an earlier matter.

'You haven't talked about Jimmie being up to something.'

'Oh, that.'

'*That?* You weren't taking it so calmly when you arrived, were you, not by any manner of means.'

'Oh, well I didn't know then that you'd be coming to Hungerstream.'

'I don't see what that can have to do with Jimmie perhaps being up to something.'

'Whatever it is, it won't be as bad with you there.'

'What, you mean having his biographer's eye on him will sort of tone him down? Possibly, but I must say this whole –'

'Yes, that's what I mean.' Joanna nodded her head emphatically.

'M'm. There's another point I'm not clear about. Rather a delicate one.'

'Come on, I think I can probably stand it.'

'Well, presumably as my wife or other female, Louise'd be sleeping in the same room as me.'

'I was going to tell you, we went to lunch there once and the guest bedrooms have dressing-rooms opening off them with beds in so you could barricade yourself in there if you felt like it. Or of course Louise could.'

'Or not, as the case may be.'

'What? How do you mean, darling?'

'Where do you want me to start? She and I used to be quite good together, well, on and off. She was very come-hitherish to me just now over the –'

At this stage, rather late in the day, Joanna did burst into tears. He sat on, stayed where he was, kept quite still, as if tears had a well-known way of clearing up on their own if left completely to themselves. The noises she was making and what he could see of her face were too unattractive, he considered, for there to be much that was voluntary, let alone deliberate, about her behaviour. It was not all that much less voluntary for him, after half a minute or so, to go over to where she was and, kneeling inelegantly on the floor beside her chair, embrace her, wet face and moist bits of hair and all. She cried harder and clung to him, but he had been ready for that. He said nothing.

Eventually she spoke. 'Have you got a handkerchief?' she asked, wiping her cheeks on the rugger club scarf.

'I'll fetch you one,' he said, and did.

'I screwed it up,' she went on in due time. 'I got carried away when you said you'd finished with her. I wasn't going to say anything to you about her being invited as well, I was just going to go back and say you didn't know where she was or something, but then like a fool I went and blurted out the whole story. I thought it would be all right. For a moment then I thought, I thought you felt the same about me as I felt about you. It was like being back at school.' Here she blew her nose.

Joanna's tears and words had severely shaken Gordon. He had never been the sort of man that women cried over, except possibly to express their boredom and exasperation with him. To hear one of them seeming to confess to strong emotions in his favour was an unfamiliar experience, but he now asked Joanna to explain herself a little, not in the hope of further gratifying his ego but because he thought she might want to, and in any case could not at the moment think of anything else to say. 'How do you mean?' he asked.

'I suppose I must have, well, if you don't mind me calling it fallen for you as soon as I set eyes on you, anyway I noticed you and I don't usually notice men your age.'

'It must have been my moustache you noticed.'

'Your what?'

'That moustache I used to have.'

'I must have managed to see through it. I don't mean that, I don't mean it like that, I wasn't trying to be funny when I said that. I suppose there's nothing much wrong with trying to be funny but it's a way of not taking something serious seriously and just ducking out. I'm sorry darling, I realize this whole thing was just meant to be a load of super fun and here goes silly old Jo-bags spoiling it all by taking it seriously.'

She said nothing more for a moment, her glance lowered, dabbing inexpertly at her nose with the doubled-up handkerchief, looking swollen round the eyes and the top half of her face in general and yet at the same time pitifully worn, a preview of her in five or ten years' time. Then she gave a long sigh, as if resigning something or the hope of something. A kneecap of Gordon's was hurting but not so badly that he had to move.

'I'll get hold of Louise again later on and tell her there was a mix-up about the week-end and she won't be able to come after all.'

'That wouldn't do any good.'

'Me turning up in person will turn the scale, you mark my words. Shall I have to put on a black tie at Screamborough or whatever it's called?'

'Hungerstream. Only if all your tartan ones and ultramarine ones are worn out. I'll give you a complete run-down on all that crap.'

'Right, come on, love.'

'Where are we off to?'

'Well, I rather thought bed.'

'Ooh, super, but isn't it a little early in the day for that?'

'No.'

Until the two of them were actually in the bed and for a few seconds afterwards, Gordon had imagined he had made his suggestion out of the feeling, not so much that a woman who had as good as told a fellow she loved him deserved to be taken to some such place at once, as that in the circumstances

Joanna and he had to embrace more fully and intimately than was attainable anywhere else. Even so he very soon discovered that he had a strong personal interest in what more usually takes a couple to bed together.

Then for a short time her face appeared to have lost all marks of age, to be completely untouched, unused, free of the worn look he had noticed on it earlier. But it was not long before those marks came stealing back, so that he noticed more clearly than ever before the lines across her forehead and the faint pinkish stains there, the creases at the outer corners of her eyes and even the incipient loosening and falling away of the flesh of her cheeks where they met her chin. He kissed her gently.

'You meant that, didn't you?' she said.

'Yes. Are you sleepy?'

'I am rather. I didn't get much —'

'Have a little nap now, just for a few minutes. I won't go away.'

She made a noise like someone sampling a more than usually delicious chocolate and turned on her side.

19

Gordon thought it would be better not to ring Louise at work a second time, a policy decision he regretted when she proved unreachable for the rest of the day and at any rate the earlier part of the night. She was reachable the following morning, however, though not at all friendly to the notion of meeting him to discuss arrangements for the Hungerstream week-end, as he perhaps not very brilliantly expressed himself.

'Tell me now,' she kept saying over the telephone, 'and I'll meet you anywhere you say.'

'I'd rather pick you up when you come out of the town hall.'

'I don't see why you can't tell me now.'

As eventually agreed, he reached the designated town hall shortly before six o'clock the following evening. Not for the first time in his experience, the tattered Edwardian grandeur of the building combined with the shifting presence of so many purposeful black people seemed to suggest contemporary life in a former African colony. It was very likely just his imagination, but he felt that those few who noticed him at all regarded him with some patronizing amusement as a quaint survival, an archaically clad white man just carrying on as if nothing had happened. He had hardly been there a minute before two young girls with plastic cards on their lapels and very shiny hair came up to him. They asked him if he knew where he was and then at once told him.

'I'm waiting for somebody,' he assured them civilly.

'Anyone in particular?'

'Oh yes. By the way this isn't a business call.'

'What is it, then?'

'I suppose you could call it social. Or personal, yes, that's more like it – personal.'

'Could you be more specific?'

By this stage Gordon would in different conditions have made some protest, sufficient at any rate to get himself either left to his own devices or perhaps made the object of a form of citizen's arrest. He would have had some idea of how to handle the situation had those who had accosted him been white and male. As it was, he turned through a right angle away from the main door, seemed to look to and fro among the swarming throng, waved at vacancy, shouted unintelligibly and took off, dodging once or twice as he ran like a wing three-quarter making for the line. After tripping slightly over an upward step he took shelter in the far side of a great shiny marble pillar with brown veins in it. While he was checking that there was no pursuit he heard a familiar voice speak behind him.

'Gordon. It is you, is it?'

'Louise, hi.'

They kissed minimally, as though against time.

'What were you doing peering round that pillar?'

He explained a little. 'I don't know what they thought I was doing here.'

'They probably thought you might have been off your rocker.'

'It was a bit like that. Why, do I look as if I'm off my rocker?'

'Well, trying to be completely objective, perhaps there is a touch of that, yes.'

'I can only assume that for reasons best known to yourself you're trying to be funny.'

'I'm not, honestly, I'm doing my best to help. It's only slight, as I said. Your eyes and all round them, that's okay. It's your mouth really, that and your top lip.'

'M'm. Somebody who was supposed to be a daughter of

Jimmie's, anyway, never mind. I had my moustache then, so it can't be anything to do with that.'

'What's happening to this country?'

The questioner was not Louise but a stout well-dressed woman in middle age who had come up to them as they stood momentarily halted in the street. She spoke with a noticeable German or eastern European accent.

Gordon, who had been taught at an early age that it was rude to ignore people, went on standing there and said something about not having any idea. Louise glanced at him in apparent uncertainty, the sort of uncertainty a hypothetical madman might well have encountered.

'They think if they say enough times the place is going to the dogs it will never go there. America they should consider. America has gone already. And what are you doing to stop the same thing from happening here?'

'I'm afraid I can't help you, I'm sorry.' Gordon started to follow Louise, who was walking on.

'Look out for yourself, young man!' The woman moved her head jerkily so that her blackrimmed spectacles caught the light. 'Be very careful or she, she there will cut your penis off!'

Like everybody else within a dozen yards or so, Louise had heard the last few words. When Gordon caught her up she dilated her eyes theatrically and said, or cackled, 'Don't be afraid, young man, it's safe with me. For the moment!'

'There's somebody who's well and truly mad, poor old thing,' said Gordon, and looked cautiously over his shoulder.

'Well, they do say it takes one to know one.'

'Look, give it a rest, for God's sake.'

'Sorry, I forgot you don't like being teased. You haven't got any mad people in your family, have you?'

'Not as far as I know.'

'I bet there's not one as far back as bloody Macbeth. That's your trouble, you know, Scotty. A touch of homicidal mania somewhere in your ancestry is just what a solid sod like you could do with. That cannibal chap who lived in a cave on the sea-shore about eight hundred years ago, for instance. Liven you up no end, my lad.'

For the next few minutes conversation languished, not through any failure of invention but because the two of them were perforce concentrating on crossing the road, reaching the point of descent to the Underground station, descending once there without being trampled to death by fellow passengers and eventually making their way aboard a train. Here any intercourse was limited by their having to sit separately, on opposite sides of the gangway and, after this was corrected, by a sufficiently powerful counter-attraction. This took the form of a youngish man, certainly some years junior to the lady with the spectacles, entering their coach at one end and departing at the other with his head leaning back and an ordinary pencil balanced under his nose. Before his progress had quite faded from the mind he reappeared and passed in the other direction. What perturbed Gordon was less this performance in itself than the lukewarm interest in it shown by those who gave it any attention at all. He promised himself he would keep a vigilant look-out for further cases of epidemic lunacy, but abandoned this project when a pony-tailed josser vacated the seat next to his and Louise slipped into it.

'Well, so what's on the agenda?' she asked Gordon forthwith. 'You were very mysterious over the telephone.'

'I didn't want to discuss this over the telephone. You see –'

'What? Discuss what? Why not?'

'I don't really know why not, I just thought I ought to tell you this face to face.'

'Tell me what?'

At this point and for some seconds afterwards the passing of a train going in the opposite direction effectively prevented communication. When relative quiet was restored Louise again asked him what he had brought her here to tell her.

'It's about this week-end at Hungerstream,' he replied.

'What about it? Christ.'

Trying not to show it, he took a deep breath. 'I'm afraid it's been cancelled.'

'*What?* When did you hear about this?'

'Oh, last night.'

At this she jumped to her feet, in annoyance he first assumed, but then concluded they were approaching their destination. No more was said while they waited, rather a long time he thought, for the train to arrive. In this interval, he noticed without appearing to that she took a series of furtive glances at him as if assessing his, well, something like reliability, not of course his actual sanity – it was clear now that that had been a joke of sorts. Then the train did arrive and they got out, walked along the platform, climbed stairs, were in a cold and also in other ways disagreeable street and shortly thereafter in a pub of the same general description. There was nowhere to sit down and an amazing level of noise from a variety of sources. Nevertheless they secured drinks and a place where they could at any rate stand and semi-bawl intelligibly at each other.

'You told me in that train the week-end's off.'

'I'm afraid so. It seems –'

'And when did you say whoever it was told you that?'

'Last night. The –'

'And who was it who told you?'

'I don't know, at least I'm not sure. Somebody who said he was speaking for the Duke of Dunwich.'

'As it might have been the duke's secretary.'

'Quite likely.'

'Yes. It's funny that when I spoke to that very person not much more than an hour ago she didn't say anything about the week-end being off or ever having been off and confirmed that I was expected. Yes, I rang from work, just to be on the safe side. Yes, Gordon, I got hold of the number quite easily considering. Right, now it's your turn to come up with something.'

Needless to say, Gordon's mind had been moving fast for some time and at record-breaking speed almost from the beginning of what Louise had last said. Unfortunately he had been unable to think fast enough.

'How extraordinary,' he said.

'Yeah, sure, and now try harder.'

'I was going to spin you a great yarn about Mrs Fane, that's Jimmie's wife.'

'So it is. I take it you've been having your way with her, or however you put it in your quaint oldie-worldie style of expression.'

'Yes. That is to say, yes. However you put it in your own style of expression.'

'You may not have realized it, but by agreeing to divulge that, you've made it possible for you and me to talk to each other. For a little while longer at least. And the Honourable Joanna was going to feature prominently in the tale you've now decided not to hand me.'

'I was going to tell you that on second thoughts you'd better keep out of her way because, because she's actually so terribly jealous and hysterical underneath that it would be better all round, like safer and everything, if you kept out of her way.'

Louise put her glass down carefully and stared at Gordon. 'And you reckoned that that would be enough to stop me coming.'

'It was all I could think of.'

'How long was it before it dawned on you it wouldn't do?'

'Ten seconds. Five.'

'What made you decide to tell me about it just the same?'

'I don't know,' he said. 'Can't we forget it now?'

159

'All right, after I've said I'm relieved you saw straight away it was no good, because if you'd tried it on seriously I really would have had to think you were mad. As well as fully prepared to insult my intelligence.'

'M'm. It looks as though I'd better let you have the truth.'

'I'll be the judge of —'

'But not here.'

Louise's flat was quite close by, close enough for the two not to have much time to converse on the way there should they have been minded to. In the event they exchanged hardly a word, being fully occupied in hurrying through a sudden downpour of rain. The flat was in a basement approached by a flight of remarkably steep steps where hanging on tight to the side rail was prudent. Scraps of saturated newspaper and cardboard lay underfoot. Inside it was dark, signifying the non-residence or supernatural assumption of the flat-mate. The breakfast dishes and pans were still in the kitchen sink and the whole place had a look of neglect, or more of being occupied for use only. The parchment-type shade round the main living-room light was crumpled on one side and bore an ancient scorch-mark.

'Would you like a drink?' asked Louise. 'I'm afraid there's only beer.'

'Beer would be fine, I'll get it myself.'

'Usual place.'

Eventually Gordon was saying, 'I don't suppose you'll believe this any more than the stuff about Joanna being terribly jealous, but it is true.'

'Really. Try me.'

'All right. I'm going on this trip myself because I have to — no, that's not quite right. Nobody's compelling me to go except myself. If I'm going to get this book written, which I must say is beginning to look doubtful, I've got to make it as good as I can, that's a practical thing as well as a matter of professional honour, and to pass up a chance of seeing old JRP Fane in his natural surroundings, or what he thinks or seems to think ought to be his natural surroundings, well obviously that's not on. With any luck –'

Louise interrupted him. 'I take it you have got a point you'll be coming to some time this evening?'

'I was just going to say, I've made up my mind to go, but I don't expect to enjoy myself at all. Quite the contrary. This Hungerstream joint may be Jimmie's habitat but it's certainly not mine. They'll all be watching me, waiting for me to make a fool of myself which I'm bound to do, probably more than once, and I don't want you around the place to . . . witness my humiliation. You know me and I'll know what you'll be thinking and even though I'm sure you won't say or do anything unsympathetic you'll make everything worse, so please don't come. I know you want to and I know I'm being selfish a well as wimpish just asking. Sorry, love.'

'Is that the lot?' Her tone of voice and her expression gave nothing away.

'Essentially. There's a bit about not wanting to have you despising me for kissing the arses of the ruling classes, but I'll spare you the rest.'

'But you can put up with being despised for being what you call wimpish.'

'Better than the other and I reckon it'll help you to believe what I've been saying.'

'Oh, I believe that all right.'

Gordon exhaled noisily. 'Well, that's something.'

'As far as it goes, that is, which isn't all the way. To begin with you're obviously not telling me the whole story. Mrs Jimmie Fane comes into it somewhere.'

'I was a fool to let you know about her and me.'

'Oh, I guessed about that ages ago but it was still good that you came out with it yourself.'

'You said to begin with I wasn't telling you the whole truth.'

'Did I? I must have done if you say so. All right, to be going on with whatever I say and however you may feel about it I'll be coming to bloody Hungerstream with you. You just haven't considered how supportive I can be.'

20

'Have you had much experience of puttock-sleighs?' asked the Duke of Dunwich.

That at any rate was how the question sounded to Gordon. The last word or pair of words was new in his experience and he was never to see it or them written down. It was also the case that the duke spoke indistinctly, touching only lightly on or near most consonants. Whether he did so because he was upper-class or because he was drunk or for some other, hidden reason, it seemed safe to Gordon to answer in the negative. Experience had already shown that if asked to repeat something the duke responded with slightly reduced clarity and lowered volume, though with eye-catching exaggeration of lip and tongue movements. No help towards answering his latest question was to be had from others round the table nor from the context, given his five-minute silence immediately before asking it. Whereabouts between aardvarks and zymotics its field of reference lay, if anywhere, must be left to emerge of itself.

Some of this sped through Gordon's mind in the second before he spoke. 'No, I have to confess I haven't,' he said.

'You'll soon get the hang of it.'

'I'm sure I shall.'

The scene was the lunch-table, or perhaps luncheon-table, in one of the smaller dining-rooms at Hungerstream. Gordon had worked out the one-of-the-smaller detail from the apparent size of the place – in the same league as Windsor Castle at a distance and still a bloody great building when seen close to. No doubt parts of it dated from one of the more prosperous periods of the Dark Ages, but in general it must have been given its present form only the other day, probably less than two hundred years earlier. Where the company was now sitting and the room where it had sat for its pre-prandial drinks had been just about warm enough, though the lofty hall and the far from narrow corridors had been cold enough for anybody's taste. But despite this, and despite their host's taciturn style, whereby no one got to be introduced and food turned out to be available rather than duly served, Gordon was in goodish heart. He had remembered not to shake any hands, the drink had flowed and his head was still on his shoulders almost two hours after he had crossed this seigneurial threshold.

As arranged, the group of four had been picked up that morning by a chauffeur-driven car that looked like a Rolls-Royce but was not. Nor was it strictly chauffeur-driven, the one who chauffed it being a tall hatless blonde wearing a matt black coverall that stopped only at wrist and throat. Gordon wondered a little at this and so, he could see, did Louise, but nothing was said, not even when the blonde snatched aboard the Fanes' substantial suitcases as if they contained only ping-pong balls. She spoke hardly at all, reminding Gordon by her demeanour as well as her dress of some global villain's hench-woman in a film of the 1960s.

An ordinary-looking chap in a suit had shown the four visi-tors into a spacious high-ceilinged room that might well have been a library, to go by the number and non-recent appearance of the books it contained. It also contained somebody sitting in a large scuffed leather armchair by the garage-sized roughstone fireplace, where unstripped logs smouldered and spat and hissed. The occupant of the chair was largely hidden from Gordon and the others by a spread newspaper, though the tweed trouser-legs and thick varicoloured socks rather hinted at maleness. No sound came from behind the newspaper.

Without hesitation Jimmie led the group over to one of several tall windows, from which they gazed out on apparently limitless lawn with a few full-grown cedars distinguishable between them and the horizon. This phase was soon ended when the person with the newspaper, evidently having read enough or decided to postpone the rest, quickly refolded it, shook it together, folded it again, hurled it accurately on to a sofa and rose to a standing posture. He was now revealed as indeed a man, though it was still not instantly clear whether he was actually a duke of something or a criminal psychopath energetically disguised as one. Rubbing his hands together and wincing, he sauntered across to the four by the window.

'Ah,' he said. 'So here you are at last. Glad you could come, all of you.'

By some prodigy of phonic aptitude he had managed to get his message across without apparently bringing his jaws together at any point. Seen at closer quarters, his possibly psychopathic look came down largely to his not having much in the way of eyebrows or eyelashes and a kind of blistering effect over the cheekbones. According to Jimmie as they motored down, this present duke had not had that title for very long, his father having shot himself to death climbing over a stile a couple of years back and his elder brother perishing from drink even more recently. One wife had run away with her driving-instructor, her successor died by her own hand, as was known, although whether she had intended to die was unknown and likely to remain so.

'Let's get the sightseeing over,' said the duke, who was perhaps three or four years younger than Gordon. Without looking where he was pointing he gestured to his left. 'Memling, Gheerardt David, Jan Mathys, Brueghel, Rubens, Allan Ramsay this end. *Hamlet*, *Paradise Lost*, *The Rambler*, *Lyrical Ballads*, *In Memoriam* the other. The orangery is supposed to have been worth looking at until my grandfather restored it. Right, now what are we all going to have?'

So saying, he led them down the room to a table with an inlaid top on which there stood a large silver tray on which in turn there were numerous bottles. Among them Gordon noticed three kinds of blended Scotch whisky and a Speyside and an Islay malt. Also on view was a part-emptied bottle of Trotanoy Pomerol 1979.

'I vote we all help ourselves to a drop of whatever we fancy,' said the duke, half filling a cut-glass tumbler with a VSOP cognac. 'I don't know about you,' he went on, 'but I find it saves an awful lot of fuss.'

'Isn't it a wee bit early yet?' said Joanna with a glance at Gordon.

'Good Lord no.' The duke shoved back a tweed cuff to reveal a wrist much hairier than his brows and a squarish watch showing figures but no dial. 'It's nearly twelve-twenty,' he said in a tone of mild remonstrance. Then his eye was caught a second time. 'Know how much I paid for this? Go on, have a guess.'

Nobody offered one, not even when urged anew.

'Two quid! Two quid! That's how much I paid for it. Keeps time to the second with no nonsense about winding for a year or more till the battery runs out and then you just chuck it away and buy yourself another. Uh-ooee-ahersh-ee-uh-ehee-ee-ung,' he added, but since he was yawning as he spoke what he had meant to say, if anything, was uncertain. More intelligibly he went on to say to Louise, 'Ah, I think you must be Norah.'

'Actually —'

'Let me top that up for you, Norah. Are you sure? I think we can leave these nice people to look after themselves while you and I go and look out of the window. There's a fair bit to be seen from there if you use your eyes.' And with his glass in his hand and the other with its associated arm round her waist, the Duke of Dunwich guided Louise back up the room to where the quartet had halted just before.

'Christ,' muttered Joanna.

'Oh please *shut up* darling, and try not to be so *bloody*

suburban.' Jimmie was crisp without sounding cross. 'Surely you can see that there's a man who isn't as other men are who's also been under a lot of strain recently what with one thing and another.'

'I shouldn't think that was his first drink of the morning, would you?' said Gordon.

Now Jimmie lowered his own voice. 'As I say, he's had a great deal on his mind and it's no wonder he finds an occasional stiffie helpful. It runs in the family.'

'So I've been told,' said Joanna. 'But what's all this strain he's been under? A great deal on his what?'

Jimmie did not answer these questions. He shifted the duke's folded newspaper and the three of them sat companionably down on the sofa with their drinks, just close enough to the fire for them to feel a small benefit of warmth. Near them stood a glass case on legs, in which Gordon had noticed an open copy of *Samson Agonistes*, the authour Ioh: Milton.

Unwilling to let the subject drop altogether, Gordon asked Jimmie, 'From your knowledge, is it a settled condition or does it fluctuate?'

'He means is young Tomnoddy pissed all the time or just some of it,' explained Joanna.

After giving one of his more tolerant laughs, Jimmie said, 'Quite honestly I don't know. I've only met him half a dozen times, you realize. But I've heard aristocrats talk like that who couldn't have been pissed at all. Chaps like old Lord Something-or-other, never touched a drop of anything stronger than tomato-juice and mumbled his head off whenever you happened to run into him.'

'I suppose a fellow like that reckons it's the other fellow's job to make out what he's said.' Gordon spoke in a neutral tone.

Joanna nodded vigorously but said nothing.

'I'm sorry if I sounded a little bit haughty a moment ago,'

167

said Jimmie, 'but it struck me as bad form to say disrespectful things about one's host behind his back, as it were.'

He had timed this reference cleverly or luckily to coincide with a burst of laughter from the duke at something he had no doubt said himself, but Gordon had felt less than easy about such matters since the three had moved nearer. 'I hope no one's been paying any attention to us chatting.'

'I know, you must find that feeling hard to shake off, but I can assure you that in my experience of them, my dear Gordon, aristocrats don't take any notice of whatever other people may happen to say while they're in hearing.'

'Not even when they're supposed to be having a conversation with them,' said Joanna.

At this point another couple arrived, having driven over from somewhere in the not-so-distant neighbourhood. Although no audible sirs or ladies or honourables clung about them or their names, both had the sort of accent that might have been calculated to go down badly in large parts of, say, Boston. In other respects, like dress and arrangement of hair on head and face, the new arrivals were ruffianly almost to a fault. The man in particular was rigged out with stained clothes and short-service bristle. Neither he nor his female companion seemed to be called Norah, though it was some time before Gordon was able to establish this for certain.

He got Louise to himself for a moment while they and the rest of them were trailing along to eat and said to her, in part, 'Did you hear who Norah really was?'

'Never. Her name came up quite a few times more, too. I got mine across in the end by Louise-ing away like buggery, you know, Louise, my old father used to say to me, Louise, he'd say, Louise girl, your mother and I had a rare old job naming you, Louise, anyway, Louise, I hope you like the name Louise, Louise. After about twenty minutes the message started to reach even that poor senile twelve-year-old brain and thereafter he hardly slipped back into calling me Norah at all.'

Gordon had halted in the passage at the place where a large picture of an ancestral Dunwich sneered down at them from the wall. The man was in all likelihood not a duke of that locality but marquis, earl or even viscount of it, for as Jimmie had pointed out, the Dunwiches had been made up to dukedom no more than a couple of centuries earlier. No informative plate was attached to the frame of the picture; as Jimmie would doubtless have explained, anybody who mattered would have known all about a thing like that already.

'Did he make a pass at you?' asked Gordon. 'The duke, that is.'

'You must mean how did he do it.'

'All right, how did he do it?'

'I'll tell you later. We'd better get back to the others before they all go off somewhere by helicopter.'

'I doubt if there's much danger of that kind of thing here, but I see what you're getting at.'

After lunch Gordon said to Louise, 'It's later now.'

'What? What are you talking about? Later than what?'

'Later than when you said you'd tell me later how His Grace made a pass at you. Of course, if you'd rather not discuss the –'

'No no, because it'll only take a moment. He said rather charmingly he was sure an attractive girl like me must have all manner of boy-friends, how he'd worked out I hadn't got a husband I'll never know, anyway I said no, not really, more to get his reaction than anything, and he just said, in that case what about him and that was it.'

'M'm. I take your point about it only taking a moment, if you really mean he –'

'No, that was *it*, but I did notice that it was one of the times he slipped back into calling me Norah, which I thought showed just how sincere he was being.'

'I think I get that too,' said Gordon.

'I know he looks extraordinary, but actually he's quite attractive in spite of that sort of burnt look he's got.'

'Oh, he is, is he?'

'Or even because of it. I realize I can't expect you to go along with me there.'

'Good.'

'Give me a kiss, then.'

Gordon's first response to this invitation was to back away from its donor, who lay stretched out on the bed but fully clothed. It was their bed standing in their bedroom, the first-floor room at Hungerstream that had been allotted for their use. Also allotted them, as Joanna had said, was a communicating room or dressing-room. As Gordon had himself checked within the first moments of arrival, this contained a thoroughly made-up bed and a usable reading-lamp. Now, without pause, before Louise could spring at him or anything, he started talking at top speed.

'Believe me it's not that I wouldn't like to, it's just that I know as well as you do how one thing leads to another and I won't bore you with my reasons which I'm not at all clear about myself but I don't want there to be any question of hanky-panky between you and me on this trip, in fact if I could have done I'd have made it a condition of your coming that you accepted that but I wasn't in a position to, so now I'll leave you to it and if it's of any interest to you I haven't got a date with Mrs Fane in the summerhouse.'

He said the last part as he left the bedroom, but before he had reached the middle of his speech Louise had turned on her side away from him. Feeling in no respect whatever like a man who has just done the right thing against odds he hurried downstairs and went into the library. Jimmie was in here, sitting in a high-backed chair with an ancient-looking volume open on his lap. He looked over his glasses at Gordon.

'A couple of mates,' he said, 'though I was two, and Buggins a hundred and four. It's no better when you read it in the original printing, is it? What's Louise up to? Having a zizz? Same like Joanna. It's never any different when these women get into the country, snoring their heads off from morning till night. Do you have a nap in the afternoon yourself?'

Gordon shook his head. 'I feel so terrible when I wake up.'

'Why, so do I, and so does any man, but I'm not going to let a thing like that stand in my way. That's when I'm in London. Nothing to keep awake for there. Different in the country, you know. I always think so anyway. Feel like going for a walk?'

'Frankly no.'

Here Jimmie in turn shook his head, but more slowly and consideringly than Gordon had shaken his. 'If you don't mind my saying so, and I really hope you don't, that remark merely goes to show how irremediably, and I doubt if that's a word you come across or use every day, you thought I was going to say middle-class you are, but you're wrong. Something much more like hidebound, unimaginative. Always remember that one impulse from a vernal wood can teach you more of man, of moral evil and of good, than all the sages can. Sorry about that but it's fresh in my mind. Very well, I admit I like walking. The one thing I miss in London, not that it's a small thing, is walking in the sense of going for walks. No point in it there. Every point in not. But in the country, well, you're not *in* the country if you don't walk.' Mumbling something about barren leaves, Jimmie shut his book with a snap and returned it to its place on a shelf behind a glass door, then turned to Gordon. 'Coming?'

Gordon was just opening his mouth to give another and firmer refusal when he caught a sound as of a heavy body falling somewhere upstairs, faint at this distance but no doubt substantial on the spot, not perhaps an unmistakable advertisement of the duke's presence near at hand but not mistakable enough for Gordon, who forthwith told Jimmie to lead on.

In less than a minute the two were leaving the house, overcoated, gloved, even scarfed, though the afternoon, for all its pale, bright look, was not really cold. Jimmie took them across to a white gate in an evergreen hedge.

'The shortest way out of the dominion of man,' he explained. 'Of one man in particular, let it be said. I'm afraid poor Willie Dunwich isn't what he was.'

For his age, Jimmie's hearing was good: probably he too had heard that overhead crash and been similarly reminded. 'Could it be the drink?' suggested Gordon.

'Do you think so?'

'Do I *think* so? I've never seen a –'

'It's not a matter of mere common or garden drunkenness, Willie's famous for never having drawn a sober breath in living memory, but he's always known how to control that. I mean I rather fear it's been getting to him in what I understand is now called the long term. I remember poor Gervase, Willie's late brother, you know, I remember Gervase developing that same, that same, I don't really know what to call it, a look, an air, anyhow imparting a sense of having ceased to bother about what sort of impression . . .'

'Not so long ago you were telling me that was a great aristo-cratic thing, not giving a toss about the impression you made.'

'Not giving a, oh yes, not caring a damn et cetera. No, I mean the impression made not on others but on oneself. I greatly fear Willie's stopped minding what he thinks of Willie. That's, that's a dreadful thought. Ah well, now I feel perhaps we've had enough of that particular topic.'

'Just one more thing while it's fresh in my mind. What's a puttock-sleigh?'

'A what?' asked Jimmie irritably.

'I heard it as a puttock-sleigh and what's he called, Willie Dunwich asked me if I knew much about it or them in the plural. Does the word mean anything to you?'

'Say it slowly.'

Gordon said it slowly. 'That's the best I can do,' he also said.

'Are you sure that's what he said?'

'No,' said Gordon. 'Of course I'm not sure that's what he said. People aren't, you don't, people can't expect to be sure of what he said any time, can they? Now let's drop it. I'm sorry I ever brought it up.'

'No, it's fascinating. Perhaps if I'd heard him say it myself I'd understand. One thing, I'm sure he wanted you to take his meaning. That is, he wasn't trying to put you at a disadvantage.'

'Even so he made quite a decent job of it. But no, he didn't strike me as a teasing sort of chap,' said Gordon, not going on to say aloud that surely most teasing sorts of chap used up a bit of curiosity on whichever sort of chap they happened to be teasing at any one time. What he did say aloud was, 'In fact altogether he wasn't what I expected.'

Jimmie halted dramatically on the verge of the small road they were about to cross. 'My dear Gordon, you can't be serious.'

'In some ways he was, of course, but I never got the feeling he was sitting there waiting for me to betray myself by eating peas off my knife, which was what I rather thought he might be banking on. I was completely off beam there.'

'You mean you were afraid he might be like Bobbie, you remember snobby-Bobbie, the old monster who put you through it over luncheon at Gray's that time.'

'I expect I was.'

'Mind you, a touch of what one might call *behavioural caution* is something of a prerequisite when a poor commoner like you or I comes into contact with persons of ducal or even baronial rank. I say, do you mind if we pause here briefly? We've come quite a long way in a short time and the view from here is quite remarkable.'

The view before them was certainly unusual in that, to the eye of a town-dweller at least, it contained nothing of the twentieth century, no power lines, no metal fences, no machinery, no advertisement. Gordon could see that what was before them was in general virtuous and might well remind Jimmie of how things had been in his youth, or appeal to him now as what they must, on consideration, have been rather like then. Such things, like all those to do with the passage of time, were to be respected. Nevertheless the scene made no more than a puny appeal to Gordon personally. It was green, brown here and there but mostly green, motionless, silent, unpopulated and asking for the addition of a passage in curli-cued italics about man's quest through the ages. And quite likely Jimmie was feeling and thinking nothing in particular, just getting his breath back.

For the moment, at any rate, he seemed to have nothing to say. With an abrupt inhalation like someone coming to after a doze, he set off again along the line of the ridge where they had stood. Soon their way took them through a patch of thin woodland, squashy underfoot here and there with the un-cleared remains of last year's leaves. The bare boughs kept off little of the sunshine and it was possible to imagine the coming of spring. Jimmie looked straight ahead or at the ground he was about to traverse. After they had gone some yards he said, still looking to his front, 'Do people read old Alfred Tennyson these days or has he never really emerged from the Victorian fug?'

'I don't think they read him unless they have to, which isn't often,' said Gordon. 'We're constantly being told he's taken his rightful place among the great English poets and anyway he wasn't all that keen on what we think of as Victorianism, but I doubt if he's got anything much to say to the 1990s. After all, he's been dead over a century now.'

'My God, so he has. Just so. Tell me, Gordon, do you read him yourself, read Tennyson yourself?'

'To be honest, no, not in the sense you mean, not unless I'm after something factual. He . . .'

'Do go on, dear boy.'

'I was going to say, I can never quite lay my hand on a sufficient reason for sitting down and reading him without an ulterior motive, so to speak.'

Now Jimmie did look at Gordon, gave him more than a glance. 'Not even *In Memoriam?*'

'I must confess I've never read more than a couple of pages, kind of thing.'

'I thought at least that was recognized as his masterpiece.'

'I'm sorry, Jimmie, I've heard that said, but really I wouldn't know.'

'You mustn't think I'm trying to drive you into some sort of corner,' said Jimmie, not at all reinforcing the literal sense of his words by again abruptly halting and wheeling round to face Gordon. But then he said gently enough, 'It's my favourite poem and has been ever since I first read it sixty-four years ago,' and he sounded almost apologetic when he added, 'I thought as my biographer you should know that.'

'I'll get hold of a copy as soon as I'm back in London.'

This time they had stopped in a small open space, too small to be considered a clearing, but big enough for somebody to have put together and lighted a fire in it as various blackened and now sodden remnants showed. Jimmie put his gloved hands on his hips and stared about him.

'It's a pity in a way there's nowhere to sit down,' he said, 'though we'd have to be getting back soon. But I was hoping you wouldn't object if we stopped here a couple of minutes before we move on.'

'Fine with me.' Gordon tried not to sound as wary as he felt.

Now Jimmie brought his hands round and clasped them in front of him. With his solemn expression and head slightly bowed, he looked really quite like somebody about to enter on a graveside oration. He avoided Gordon's eye.

'No doubt you know that Tennyson's poem memorializes Arthur Hallam, the young man whom he met at Cambridge in the year 1829 and who soon became the closest friend of his life. In fact in view of what later happened to Tennyson, or rather failed to happen, it would not be going too far to say that in Hallam he met the love of his life, whether the feeling was significantly reciprocated or not.'

Gordon was starting to feel uneasy about where this seemed to be leading. Not, he considered, in the obvious direction. By now he had talked to several people who knew Jimmie, not all of them entirely sober at the time, and had read several books in which he figured, not always to his advantage, and there had been no talk of that side of life in either case. Nevertheless, some sizeable disclosure did seem to be in train.

'If that love manifested itself in anything more substantial than a manly clasp of the hand, I should be very much surprised,' Jimmie was continuing. 'A characteristic close friendship in the Victorian style. Which is not in the least my own favoured style. In fact I have to confess . . .'

The biographer waited. He hoped very much that no abrupt revision of his estimate of his subject's proclivities was about to be called for.

'I have to confess to you that close friendships of any sort are not in my line, never have been. I suppose that means that men don't appeal to me much, certainly not compared with women. And I suppose that makes it faintly surprising that I should feel such a personal attachment to *In Memoriam*. Now of those two fellows it's Hallam who interests me more for the moment. It was he who pointed out to Tennyson his real duty as an English poet. Hallam wrote somewhere that unless a poet writes predominantly to create beauty, the result will be false in art. As we see from *In Memoriam* itself among other works, Tennyson didn't follow that advice. But I did.'

Parts of this speech were less easy than others for Gordon to take in. The less easy parts suffered from the distraction provided by a man approaching them, for the moment unseen by Jimmie. The newcomer was wearing a heavy tweed overcoat and a tweed hat of similar but not the same pattern, a hat in a rustic genre seldom worn by rustics. Under it the pale face of its wearer was frowning, and he waved a forefinger at Gordon in admonition before pointing it at Jimmie, whose voice died away as he turned and saw him.

'I recognized you there,' said the man in tweeds as he came up. He had a rustic voice. 'I trust you'll pardon this intrusion, sir. Of names I reck little,' he went on, 'nor am I accustomed to pay heed to such things, but the face of a great actor,' and he gazed at Jimmie's, 'I never forget. I thank you for all the pleasure you've given me. And thank you too for your attention just now.'

Jimmie surprised Gordon in more than one way by replying melodiously, 'It's I who should thank you, my friend. I can only say I deeply appreciate your kindness.'

'May I shake your hand, sir?'

'Of course. You honour me.'

They shook hands and the stranger departed.

'It might be interesting to know who he thought I was,' said Jimmie to Gordon. 'But I felt in the circumstances I could hardly ask him. Pity. But then I should be feeling glad at having cast some light into his wretched little life. Well, after that *intrusion* I feel I can hardly go on with what I was saying, whatever it may have been.'

'Oh, I can tell you that. You'd just said that Tennyson didn't follow Hallam's advice about writing primarily to create beauty, but you did. Follow it.'

'It does sound awfully wet now, I know. But I did try to do that to the best of my ability from the age of twelve. By the time I reached twenty, about the time of the outbreak of war, I could see that my ability was deficient, if indeed there was anything there at all. But I went on trying for another thirty years. During some of those years I tried to write novels, in the hope that it was there that my true gift lay.' There was no self-mockery in Jimmie's tone. 'Same result, unfortunately. No gift, true or not. Saw it sooner, fortunately. On consideration, something I don't go in for much these days, I should say that the best of me, or the least bad part of me, or the least bad part of what there is of me, or was of me . . . is in verse form.'

Gordon felt he could not say that Jimmie Fane had sounded rather old and sad in the making of his last few remarks, but that he had looked no older than usual and not sad at all. Nor could he, Gordon, summon up enough of the vigour necessary to any denial of those propositions, indeed there was nothing much that he wanted to say at all, certainly not about the rustic buffoon, now nowhere to be seen. So he kept his trap shut.

'Well, it's time we made for home,' said Jimmie briskly as they started to do so. 'I hope I didn't embarrass you too much by, by *holding forth* as I did – very self-indulgent of me. I didn't mean to say all that. In fact it wouldn't be far out to tell you I didn't know I had it to say. Past thoughts, they're like a room in one's house one's got out of the way of ever going into without realizing.'

Gordon slouched along at his side, by now not daring to say a word.

'You ought to hear it if anybody ought, I suppose. That kind of thing would come as no surprise to Joanna, but then I suppose nothing would.' The small sighs and groans Jimmie uttered during and after this pronouncement came as an indication, satisfactory to Gordon, that no meeting of minds on the subject of Joanna was to follow. There was a droplet more to come, however. 'One can't help feeling,' said Jimmie, but then at last fell silent, looking from tree to tree in wonderment as if it had only just occurred to him that they could be of different sorts.

What one could or could not help feeling was a question that soon ceased to engage Gordon. He felt as sure as he could

178

be without raising the matter with him that Jimmie knew nothing, whatever he might have suspected, of his wife's current spell of hanky-panky. That at any rate was how he felt at favourable times like the present. At less favourable times, like waking up unaccompanied in his bed at five a.m., he would remind himself that not all egotists were unobservant, especially not when their own interests were involved. He had even fancied once or twice there might be something in the view that Jimmie's celebrated warning-off proclamation to him had actually been designed as an egging-on, as Joanna had thought, or said. But wiser counsels, or at any rate more comfortable ones, on the whole prevailed.

This week-end, now, had had its minefield-like aspects, what with Louise as well as Joanna about and Jimmie in attendance, not to speak of the anti-personnel nature of the nobby ambience, but so far things had held together. Coming down in the car, for instance, he had shared the back seat with a quiescent, almost silent Louise and had a close view of the back of Joanna's neck, quite nice actually, and an almost equally close view of Jimmie's more weatherbeaten-looking neck. Little had been exchanged or audibly said on the journey. What followed it had not been free of difficulties, but the women had been as good as gold, had behaved almost as if they wanted no trouble. Gordon was not somebody who often visualized telling his grandchildren something, but if he had been then an account of picking his way among the present lot might have figured. So again he felt at times. At other times, as it might have been catching sight of Joanna across a room, he felt clean out of his depth, stripped of rules and models that up to now had always been there, and the whole thing was to do with her. He could only be sure of not feeling like that when he was alone with her. Perhaps he was in love, or was going to be.

Soon the two men had reached the small road they had crossed earlier and, as before, halted beside it. 'You won't mind if I stand here a moment and look at this valley,' said

Jimmie in a voice that perhaps showed his true age. 'I don't imagine I shall often see it again.'

Furtively, Gordon glanced at Jimmie. The venerable wielder of the pen was clearly doing his utmost to earn such a description, or at any rate to look and sound the part, a tall unbowed figure of some rugged grandeur, or at least a figure of that general description as presented by an expensive Italian movie-screen. There was no trace in him now of the dignified acceptance of failure that Gordon had seen, or thought he had seen, just before they started back. And yet you could consider yourself worthy of all sorts of things from admiration to pity and still be worthy of them. Gordon felt matters were getting out of hand again.

'And high bridge and indignant nostril nothing to do but look noble,' said Jimmie without explanation. 'I think I've rested my legs enough now. You know, if I walk more than a few yards these days they start aching. Give up smoking, my doctor said. I told him I hadn't smoked for nearly forty years. Good for you, said the quack enthusiastically.'

They set off again. Presently they came in sight of the ever-green hedge where they had started. 'One further brief cessation of ambulation,' said Jimmie, 'and then we can high-tail it for anchovy toast and Genoa cake served off a silver salver and washed down with oolong. I know you think I'm a frightful old arse-creeper of the nobility, and so of course I am, but you have to remember I'm not really out of the top drawer.'

'Oh, I thought you were absolutely sort of kosher.'

'Oh I'm *kosher* all right as far as I go. Actually that's quite far, but in one way not quite far enough. I come out of, I should have said I come out of *a* top drawer but not of *the* top drawer, the topmost of all, the one with dukes and marquises in it. I suppose from down where you are it all looks much the same but I can assure you it doesn't at all from up here. Not that parts of it don't look even funnier from up here than they probably do to you down there. While we're on the topic I'll have you know it ties up with what I was saying about beauty back in that sort of druidical circle. These days there's only one kind of place you can hope to come across it, that's beauty, outside art, of course I don't mean the kind of art that gets produced these days. Anyhow, with luck beauty is still to be found in the country, those few parts of it that man hasn't *gobbled up* and *spat out* again, and those parts in my experience exist only on the property of some great landowner in whose family it's been for centuries, before things started to go to pot. I agree it's hard to think of poor Willie Dunwich as exercising any beneficent –'

'Right on cue,' said Gordon, nodding over at the house, which he happened to be facing.

Round one of the corners of the building there had just appeared the aforesaid Duke of Dunwich attired for the saddle, and two groom-like figures, the elder of whom led a largish chestnut horse accoutred for riding. All four were sharply visible in the bright air, and Jimmie and Gordon had an excellent view of what followed. For the moment nothing did, beyond some discussion among the three men and a vigorous, almost violent, tossing of the horse's head.

'I've been giving those puttock-sleighs some thought,' said Jimmie. 'Are you sure he didn't say buttock-slaves? Think before you answer.'

'No need to, I can't swear he didn't say almost anything roughly approximating to puttock-sleighs. Anyway, how much better off are we with buttock-slaves?'

'Quite a lot, perhaps. Couldn't a buttock-slave be an admittedly fanciful but still intelligible term for a passive partner in sodomy, whatever it's called nowadays. It was a pansy when I was at school. A catamite.'

'Now that does call for thought.'

'It's funny, at that early stage I was quite sure a catamite was a kind of puma or jaguar. Not one's first choice for a bed-fellow. I must have got it mixed up with . . .'

Jimmie's voice died away as his attention became fixed on the scene below. The duke had got one booted foot into the nearside stirrup, the side fully visible to the two observers, and being unable to swing the rest of him up by his own efforts, had had to hop a few yards beside his restless mount. Now, while the elder groom held the chestnut's head, the younger one shoved his master up into the saddle. Through some trick of over-compensation he at once all but fell out of it again, now on the off side. By then the horse was in motion, indeed had broken into a full gallop almost at once. So the two progressed for a hundred yards or more with the duke still to be made out exerting himself. Perhaps a vestige of control on his part, or more likely just a whim of the horse, brought about a change of direction not quite sudden enough to be useful to the rider, who was now in open view again as he continued to try to climb into the saddle. Nothing in their relative positions had changed when man and beast disappeared round the corner of the house. For a few seconds the chestnut reappeared, this time with no one on or near his back, and then was finally gone.

'Reassure me, Gordon: he couldn't have done all that just for our benefit, could he?'

'Not possibly. He couldn't have laid the whole performance on in the time.'

'No, of course he couldn't. How ridiculous of me. Do you think a puttock-sleigh could be a horse, or a ride on one?'

'Except that when I said I didn't know anything about whatever they are he said I'd soon get the idea. Not quite what he . . .'

'M'm. It looks as if we'll just have to give it up.'

'Perhaps he was trying to be funny.'

'Not Willie Dunwich.'

They went down the incline, through the small gateway, across a paved yard where there were bushes or parts of bushes in tubs, and into the house. Here Jimmie at once said he must just go and see that Joanna was all right and disappeared up a markedly utilitarian-looking staircase. Gordon decided to assume without fear of contradiction that Louise was absolutely all right, or alternatively could do no harm in her continuing absence. He had been a very good boy so far and was determined to remain so, but was well aware that the less he saw of her the better his chances of not succumbing to her allure. That still left him in an unfamiliar part of the house, but after walking half a kilometre or so, always moving in the direction of increasing affluence of decor, he succeeded in regaining the library without assistance from any questing butler or other menial. Utter silence surrounded him from first to last. He wondered what state his host was in after having presumably fallen from his horse, but felt that the absence of domestic commotion indicated something on the right side of death or serious injury. He allowed his gaze to move round the shelves and cupboards where lay many of the glories of our literature in their earliest published form, and wondered why his desire to look at some of them should have sunk to such a low ebb.

He was in the middle of thinking this when the door of the room opened and, after a pause sufficient for a cursory look round the interior, somebody came in. The newcomer was recognizable as the blonde woman who, an infinity of time ago, had driven him and others down here from London. Clad now in an outfit less uncompromising than the black ensemble she had at first worn, she gave him a brief ward-nurse's smile and said in a high unwelcoming voice,

'Will you be requiring tea, sir?'

'Thank you very much, that would be delightful.'

She went out again and stayed away for some time, but at the end of it there appeared a trolley bearing all sorts of tea-things and possible food, propelled by a younger and smaller servant. After what was not really a very long interval Gordon had beside him a couple of fingers of toast, a damp, dark slice of cake and a cup of tan-coloured tea without milk.

'Got everything you want?' said a voice recognizably, and the Duke of Dunwich came into the room and poured himself a similar cup. Far from bearing signs of a riding accident he was dressed in a smart tweed suit like a successful country auctioneer and walked to his chair in what was very nearly a straight line. An instant before he spoke, Gordon had bitten off a large piece of cake, which he bolted at his best speed but not quite before the duke had said, 'Good, good,' in a tone of heartfelt relief. 'Jimmie not with you,' he stated or possibly asked.

'No, he said he was just going to look in on Joanna.'

'Nice girl, that little Norah, I must say.'

'Yes, isn't she?'

'What? But I doubt, I don't suppose you need my opinion on that, hey?'

By now Gordon had another mouthful of cake in place, so he merely wagged his head pawkily.

'Joanna now. What do you make of her ... er ... old boy?' Luckily for Gordon the duke had more to say, though its relevance was not at once apparent. 'Just between ourselves, you know, old Jimmie's a bit of a bounder. Do I mean a bounder? I suppose not really. If a bounder's a fellow trying to better himself, not too particular about how he moves up the social scale, like, well, like lots of fellows. Now old Jimmie, he's a social climber in his way, everybody knows that, dying to be asked here, not to see me or even my things, but so as to be able to talk about when he was last at Hungerstream hobnobbing with old Willie Dunwich, the duke, you know. But he's not a *bounder* exactly, m'm? More of a shit. You're supposed to be writing this book about him, surely you've found that, haven't you?'

Gordon actually stammered when he answered, 'Well, no, er, not really, no.'

'In that case you'd better start having a closer look, I'd have thought. Oh, he's good *company*, that's half the reason why he's here from my point of view, but a shit all the same, not least in his treatment of poor little Joanna, whom I must say I'm rather fond of. A moment ago I asked you how you thought she was bearing up.'

'Not too badly.' Gordon was fully conscious of the inadequacies of this reply, but was deterred from saying more by a galaxy of motives, from not knowing how long this conversation would last, to not being as sure as he would like to have been that old Willie Dunwich would not, on hearing more, incontinently snatch up the cake-knife and set about using it on old Jimmie Fane. The duke's eyes seemed to reflect the light in an odd way.

'Oh, good,' said the latter with a touch of sarcasm, but had time to add urgently, 'You know what's happening this evening?' before Jimmie himself came into the room along with the ruffianly couple who had arrived shortly before lunch, looking somewhat less ruffianly now with a dress and a collar and tie here and there, but with cranial and facial hair still in place. The medium-intensity giggling of all three as they entered might have suggested that all three had seen that Joanna was all right. The next moment Gordon hurried out, doing his best to look like a man in sudden need of a pee, and ran upstairs.

Outside the Fanes' door he raised a knuckle but lowered it again. Assuming Joanna was talkable-to, what was he to say to her? Just then the door opened and showed her ready for parade in a new buttercup-and-brown outfit with a wide shiny belt. She stared at him.

'You look nice,' he said.

'What's the matter?'

He realized he had rushed up here in order to warn her, but all he could think of to warn her against or about was something due to happen that evening, if as much, so instead of anything cautionary he said, 'The duke fell off his horse but he's all right now.'

'And Jack and Jill went up the hill to fetch a pail of water.'

'What?'

'Have you ever wondered why I don't lead you a dance?' She spoke in a friendly tone.

'I don't think so.'

'Well I have. Wondered, I mean. I usually do with men. Lead them a dance, that is.'

Frowning with self-dissatisfaction, he said, 'If there's anything you want me to do, now or later, I'll do it.'

She opened her lips and closed them again. Then she said, 'For now, you'd better just bugger off before Jimmie comes up to make sure I haven't bumped my head on a William and Mary cornice. That'll do to be going on with.'

So Gordon buggered off, and eventually the whole party had gathered in the library and seven or eight people came for drinks, some of whom the duke seemed to know, by sight at any rate, and that went on for some time without detectable damage to anyone present. Eventually there came the moment whose analogues Gordon had always found strange, not that he had experienced many of them, the moment when drinks-guests were intended to leave and dinner-guests progressively arrived, the first lot dismissed by implication as too drunk to be allowed anything more, the second lot kept off until now as too keen on the booze to be allowed free and uninterrupted access to it for six hours or more. But eventually that moment too had come and gone, leaving Gordon's senses blunted to what seemed to him an appropriate degree.

'I didn't have time to ask you how things were going,' he said to Joanna.

'What things, or rather which things?'

'Jimmie things, Jimmie plots,' said Gordon daringly but, since Jimmie was talking to the duke and Louise on the other side of the room, perhaps not as daringly as all that.

'Those things have been quiet. I reckon I must have been wrong when I thought something was due to happen on this week-end. He's making a bomb all right, but it doesn't look as if it's set to go off yet awhile. How's Louise?'

'I think she's quite smitten with the duke. He with her too a bit, but then I expect girls quite often smite him in that sort of way.'

Joanna looked at him. 'Is that all you have to report from the Louise direction?'

'Well, I've managed to keep her hands off me, which hasn't taken much doing. I sometimes get the impression she's not really a very sexy girl.' His statement about his impression was true enough, though it was also true that at other times he got a different impression.

'Gordon.'

'Yes?'

'You find this sort of four-cornered deal we've got down here a touch on the bizarre side, don't you darling?'

'Yes. Since you ask me.'

'All right, but don't knock it. You're part of it yourself, remember, and quite a prominent part at that. You're the only one with your fingers in both pies, if you'll pardon the expression.'

It could not really have been at this exact point, just that Gordon ever afterwards remembered it so, that the door of the room opened and a number of assorted people came in, evidently the dinner-guests arrived in a body. Among them was a tallish, thinnish woman whom Gordon at first took to be about fifty but after a moment saw was some years older. Nevertheless she had kept herself in trim, what with a close-cut green woollen dress, hair expertly tinted to a sort of auburn and a peering, disgruntled expression that indicated to him her membership of some privileged social group. But most of this he took in later; what he caught an immediate glimpse of was Jimmie's face, well displayed in the light in that part of the room and showing for a moment pure and intense consternation. Old Jimmie might or might not have been good at hiding his true feelings in general, but then at least he registered sincere dismay.

Nobody else seemed to have seen what Gordon had seen, though it was clear enough that Joanna had seen something. 'For your information,' she said in a strained voice, even touching his hand for a moment, 'the lady who has just come in is Mrs Jimmie Fane number two.'

'Oh yes,' said Gordon dully. 'What, what of that?'

'Oh darling, it's Jimmie's bomb, I know it is,'

'How, I mean how is it, how do you know, what sort of bomb?'

In those few seconds the newly arrived lady and Jimmie had officially recognized each other, nodded, smiled. The lady looked much less surprised to see Jimmie than he to see her. The duke and others moved towards them.

'What sort of bomb?' Gordon repeated to Joanna.

'A Jimmie sort of bomb.' She had evidently recovered her composure. 'But I can be much more specific than that. We've got a couple of minutes yet because nobody's going to expect Mrs Jimmies two and four to make much of a fuss of each other. Now then, oh by the way have you ever met her, yes, the female over there?'

'No, I did run into her daughter just for a moment quite recently.'

'Bloody little Periwinkle. She doesn't half take after her mother, that girl. Actually it was Periwinkle turning up the way she did that first started me thinking about bombs and things. This is maddening of me, I know. Okay, the said bomb consists of Jimmie Fane leaving his fourth wife, me, and taking up again with his second wife, the person he and the Duke of Dunwich are at present in conversation with. Darling, please try not to look at me as if I've gone mad. Things like this happen every day.'

'I didn't know I was . . . Not that, not that that would be wildly inappropriate.'

'Darling, you're so predictable. That's not the kind of behaviour they go in for where you come from so nobody at all goes in for it, eh? Right. One, my father died last year and he didn't cut up as well as forecast, so Fane's standard of living is under threat, theoretically at least. Two, some time in the last however many years it is, Rowena, that's Mrs F number two to you, her by the fireplace, she used to be called Rosie but it's Rowena now, not only that but *Lady* Rowena on account of her dad's unexpectedly coming into an earldom. Just imagine all the places that would get him invited to! Or he thinks it would. And she's never been hard up for a few bob. Three, things like him always saying what a great girl old Rosie-Rowena used to be until he got the idea for his bomb and then shutting up about her overnight. Oh, give it a rest, Gordon, do – no one's watching us, you're quite safe. Yes, and four, this may still be all balls from start to finish but it isn't *self-evidently* all balls. Jimmie Fane's perfectly capable of – I must get myself another drink. Don't worry about me, darling, I'll be all right, I've seen it coming for long enough. The only thing I don't quite understand is what the fair Lady Rowena is doing here. Just stirring up trouble as usual, no doubt.'

Gordon had no chance of either improving or throwing doubt on this reading of motives in what followed. Quite soon he was introduced to Lady Rowena and experienced some minutes of her being charming to him in his capacity as Jimmie Fane's biographer, a role she plainly thought of as on a level rather below that of the great man's physiotherapist but well above his bootmaker, say. Something about her carefree tolerance made it seem unlikely that in her view Jimmie had any sort of claim to be a figure of eminence, let alone in a field conventionally regarded with respect among the educated. Putting this point to himself made Gordon feel like a good deal of a pompous dunce but, he reflected, better that than a philistine. At the time the set of her shoulders, it might have been, or the way she lifted her nose as she started to speak, made it not impossible or revolting to imagine her, when younger, the object of male interest. Well, all things considered, including the durability of Joanna's looks, it was clear that old Jimmie could pick fillies with staying-power, as people like the present duke's grandfather would no doubt have put it.

After a short while there presumably sounded some buzzer or kindred device inaudible to Gordon and all at once Lady Rowena withdrew her attention from him so totally that he felt like glancing down at himself to make sure he was still there. By the time he had recovered, she had moved away with Jimmie and the duke's eyes were on him or somewhere near him. His Grace seemed no drunker than before, but no less so either. He allowed himself to be taken aside.

'Charming woman that Lady Rhona or Rowena Thingummy,' said Gordon in the kind of fluctuating whinny he fancied was a serviceable rendering of the mode of speech generally affected by the company. 'Knew she was coming, did you?'

'Absolute charmer, isn't she? Absolute, er, you know, what do I mean? Charmer.'

Gordon took a fresh glass of gin and Dubonnet from the butler's tray. 'I asked you if you knew in advance she was coming.'

'Oh yes, yes,' said the duke. He appeared puzzled.

'I mean you did know Lady Rowena was coming over tonight for dinner.'

'Fellow she's been staying with, old Something-or-other, he asked if he might bring her along, and of course I said the more the merrier. What exactly –'

'Tell me, Willie, do you think she knew she'd run into Jimmie here?'

'Oh yes.' The duke showed no signs of puzzlement now.

'But that's little Rowena all over. One of these wenches who like giving things a shove every so often.'

'Somehow I doubt if Jimmie knew she was coming.'

'Really? I say, that makes me out to have been rather remiss. I certainly intended to drop a word in his ear. It must have slipped my mind. That's if you're right, of course. Oh dear, I find all sorts of things have slipped my mind these days, I tell you frankly.'

Before any instances could be given, a tall fair-haired woman approached whom Gordon found distinctly attractive. 'We've met before,' he said.

'Indeed we have, Mr Scott-Thompson, several times, the first having been when I picked you and your party up in the car this morning.' She turned to the duke. 'I think we could go in now, Willie.'

'All right, my dear, thank you, Polly. This is Polly,' he explained. 'She runs my life, I don't know what I'd do without her. She's been being hostess for me here ever since, er, ever since . . .'

'For quite a while,' said Polly. 'You go on, love, and we'll come along after.'

'So you sort of act as hostess for the duke at dinner-parties and things,' said Gordon without feeling in the least degree proud of doing so.

'You've got it. It's this way.'

'You aren't one of these characters, are you?' he found he had said.

'We're in here tonight,' said Polly. 'More of a chance to spread ourselves.'

There was, or they had, in one of the larger dining-rooms at Hungerstream. Gordon sat down among people who were completely unknown to him. Even protracted ocular search failed to reveal anyone he remembered having seen before except the duke, although the Fanes and Louise were presumably close by. His kneecaps were cold and bit by bit he

191

perceived that other parts of him, like his fingertips, were cold too. The soup, when it came, warmed him a little without to any degree impressing itself on his memory. Nobody took any notice of him except the old man opposite who was wearing a dinner-jacket and who said confidentially of it,

'Don't know why I put this thing on. Habit, I suppose. Makes a fellow feel a damn fool, I can tell you, being the only one. By the time somebody told me it was too late to change back. Don't want to bore you. How have you been getting on?'

'Oh, not too badly, thanks.'

'M'm. Didn't you do not too badly at Doncaster?'

'Where? I don't think I've ever been there in my life.'

'What are you saying? You must have been in Doncaster, my dear fellow. In fact I remember you did frightfully well there only last year, or perhaps it was the year before. Never been to Doncaster, eh? You'll be telling me you've never seen a horse next.'

'As a matter of fact I saw one just a . . .' Something happened to Gordon's vision for a moment that he thought might be the result of his head spinning. He said carefully, 'I'm sorry, but I think there must have been some mistake. Who, who do you think I am?'

Until this point the old chap's demeanour had been the very soul of cordiality and good humour. Now he frowned and his manner sharpened at once.

'Don't be ridiculous,' he snapped. 'I know who you are. I don't think, I know.'

'In that case, what's my name?'

'Look, if you want to pretend you've never met me that's entirely your affair. Reasons best known to yourself. I won't say another word to you, never fear.'

Without much hope, Gordon started to give his name and occupation, as to a policeman. Before he had said it all, however, the man in the dinner-jacket cut him off in effect by shutting his eyes, abruptly raising a hand and remaining frozen in this posture till he had achieved the outcome he wanted. On resuming normal bodily movement he never again glanced in Gordon's direction. Neither did anyone else, indeed from the start of their exchange the two had attracted no perceptible attention whatever, a testimony either to laudable tact or uncommon blockishness.

Gordon had not yet decided which alternative was the likelier, though on reflection inclining to the second, when he noticed that the wine-glass in front of him still or once more contained wine. He drank it down and set about marvelling at the irreversibility and speed with which the dinner-jacketed man had put him in the wrong from what one might have thought was a position of grave weakness. Such a stroke, in his world, was rarely so much as attempted except by women, but then his world was, so to speak, not this world. Either his marvelling went on a long time at one go or he kept going back for a further instalment of it, because he was still or once more engaged in it when he noticed that people were leaving the room. He got to his feet and joined them.

Some time later Gordon was happily urinating in the nice little lavatory that opened off the bathroom that in turn opened off the bedroom allotted to him and Louise. When he had finished in the lavatory he went back through the bathroom and bedroom, thinking how pleasant they were, and into the dressing-room, which he thought even more pleasant with its pleasantness concentrated in the made-up bed he had noted earlier. This was so inviting that he decided to lie down on it for a moment, or found that he had started to do so.

When he woke up it was to notice that the overhead light was very much on, that it was seriously dark outside and that he felt extraordinary, awful too but more extraordinary. When he woke up a second time the centre of attention was concentrated on the inside of his mouth. He was pouring water into and through his mouth when he heard somebody come into the main bedroom: Louise, as it proved.

'Never felt this way before.'

'Oh, come on, don't let me down. Have a shot.'

'No. It'd only make me feel worse. Did anyone notice I was drunk?'

'Oh yes. I couldn't speak for absolutely everybody, but they all seemed to except the duke. That old boy I saw you chatting to, he said all the other champion jockeys he'd met were tremendously abstemious. You must have given him a nasty shock.'

'What? He can't have been talking about me,' said Gordon indignantly.

'No, he was talking about you all right. He described you to an absolute T.'

'Oh, he did, did he? What did he say, can you remember?'

'Of course I can. He said you were rather large for a jockey, he thought, and you had a sort of nervous look. I couldn't have done better myself in a few words.'

'Nervous of what, did he say that?'

'I can't see why you want to know all this. Well, he said he couldn't tell if you were nervous about anything in particular, it was just that you seemed, you know, nervous.'

'Oh yeah. The man's a raving lunatic. Anybody with a tittle of wit would be nervous of him.'

'I don't think he'd have thought you were of anything if you still had your moustache.'

'Oh, I see.'

'You'd better get yourself to bed, chum. In milord's chamber, not in here with me. Your heart, let's call it that, your heart wouldn't be in anything coarse, would it? And come to think of it your heart wouldn't be in it either, that's heart in the more genteel sense, of course. You can't expect to make those sort of goo-goo eyes at a female without Auntie Louise noticing, even if the female is, I'll spare your blushes over what I think she is, but for purposes of identification she's the one married to the toffy-nosed scribbling twit with the snowy locks. On your way now.' And she turned her back.

21

'Tea, coffee or fruit-juice, sir?' asked Alec Walker in an unexpected voice. Then it immediately became clear that it was not the captain that had spoken but the ordinary-looking chap in a suit visible at the duke's front door and on later occasions the previous day, identifiable as a butler. Gordon said something back and the chap came out with something about India, China and-or Ceylon which evidently needed a reply, so Gordon mentioned India, a country about which an uncle had given him a large illustrated book one Christmas, and fell asleep again for what was probably no more than a few seconds. When he awoke the chap was in the middle of asking him a question about the Channel Islands, or at any rate Jersey and Guernsey, which he answered with a mutter indistinguishable even to himself. After that he once more fell asleep, for a bit longer this time, he suspected, because when he again awoke it was to find a cup of what he discovered was cooling milky tea on the bedside table. He found out it was lukewarm in the course of drinking it, found out too that it was unsweetened, greasy in texture and of mildly unpleasant flavour, but down it all went to the last drop. He reflected that he would have welcomed the chance of opting for lemon instead of milk, but then perhaps he had slept through that part.

By cautious degrees he established that Louise was not immediately about. It was not that he had any great objection to her presence, just that as he felt at the moment the thought of talking to her, indeed to anybody at all, was insupportable. Still moving slowly, if not with positive caution, he shaved, dressed and otherwise prepared himself to move away from here before the advent of an assiduous chambermaid or other domestic. Without any thought of breakfast he went downstairs unobserved and along and into the library where he had first encountered the Duke of Dunwich, not because he wanted a book and very much not because he was hoping to encounter the duke again, but merely because he could not have faced venturing into those extensive parts of the house where he had not been. To visit a part he had at least seen before gave him a feeling, however illusory, of being in touch with events, even perhaps of having some influence over them.

He had barely arrived in the library when the audible threat of another arrival there drove him to scoop off the shelves a book, any old book, some book or other, and carry it with him at top speed to a handy chair, one no doubt of some antiquity. There entered the chap in the suit Gordon had come across in the context of early-morning tea.

'Excuse me, sir,' he said politely, 'but have you seen His Grace anywhere?'

Gordon was rescued from having to reply at once by a quite unexpected compulsion to retch. By the time he had yielded to it without further offence but quite loudly, something that evidently caused the suited chap no concern of any kind, he was sufficiently master of himself to be able to say, distinctly enough, 'I'm sorry. I'm afraid not.'

The man nodded but did not speak. Instead, he went on a brief tour of the room, perhaps to assure himself that his master was not concealed anywhere in it, finally returning to a nearby point. 'If you should happen to see His Lordship, sir, would you be good enough to tell him that Nigger will be saddled up and ready for him at eleven o'clock.'

'I most certainly will,' said Gordon heartily, in the confident assumption that Nigger was some kind of horse and not, say, a stable-boy. 'As soon as I see him.'

'Thank you, sir.' The butler nodded again, with more amplitude than before, and left.

After an interval only long enough for Gordon to heave a lengthy sigh, retch another couple of times, still without issue, and open his book, the duke came in. This arrival disconcerted him less than it otherwise might because he knew exactly what to say to him for at any rate the first few seconds of their meeting.

'Good morning. That butler chap asked me to –'

'Good morning to you, and thank you but I saw Jenkins in the, in the, and he told me.'

'About –'

'I told him to stand Nigger down. I don't really feel like an outing today. Now what's the book you've found for yourself?'

'*Culture and Anarchy*.'

'M'm. The fellow found himself a good subject there, what? Interesting subject, I mean.'

'He certainly –'

'Or subjects. No, I don't feel like an outing today, but I know what I do feel like. And hey, I've just had the most marvellous idea. Why don't you join me?'

'Join you in what exactly?'

'Just a little glass of fruit-juice. Say you will. Splendid.' The duke went over to what was doubtless a bell-rope, swathed as it was in some rich damask stuff, and pulled it – twice, Gordon saw. 'The two rings are for two glasses,' said the duke. 'You can save an awful lot of time with a simple code for things like that.' After a moment he said, 'Funny sort of name for a horse, isn't it, Nigger? I mean it's not as if he's black or even brown. I suppose you'd call him more of a red roan than anything else, you know.'

'Who christened him?'

'Now there's a funny thing if you like. It can't be more than a couple of years ago, so it's got to be yours truly, and bugger me if I can think what I had in mind. I mean I must have had something in mind, it stands to reason. But please, don't let me keep you from your book.'

'No really, I only picked it up because there was no one to talk to.'

Not for the first time, Gordon wished he had something to call the Duke of Dunwich. Duke – too American. Dunwich – too familiar, too egalitarian. Willie – too familiar and very likely too egalitarian as well. Your Lordship – too humble and too much like a policeman in a police-court, if they still had police-courts. Your Grace – much too humble and like a servant. For a short period Gordon thought of writing a newspaper piece on this anachronistic class barrier in modern Britain. Then his attention became concentrated on his right knee, part of which was aching slightly and continued to do so until he moved that leg an inch or so. Then the suited man appeared with a bottle of champagne and two glasses on a silver tray. The champagne bore a label to the effect that it was a Veuve Clicquot-Pontsardin 1943, which struck Gordon as satisfactorily long ago and far away.

'I find a glass of this stuff very comforting at about this hour,' said the duke. 'Talking of which, what precisely is the hour? M'm, a bit early, it must be said. That's if this damn watch isn't slow, which wouldn't surprise me in the least considering I only paid two quid for it. You can't expect much for two quid these days. Well, anyway. Your very good health, my dear fellow.' And, with a smile of what looked like pure friendliness, he lifted his glass and drank a good deal of its contents.

'Yours too,' said Gordon.

'Thank you.' The duke lowered his glass again and tried not very successfully to smack his lips. 'M'm, most comforting. I feel better already, you know. Tell me, do you ever suffer from alcoholic remorse? I don't mean alcoholic's remorse, I mean alcoholic remorse. Feelings of remorse for recent actions imperfectly recalled but suspected of having been unworthy in some way and certainly performed under the influence of drink. Do you know what I'm talking about?'

'Oh yes, absolutely.' Gordon tried to sound encouraging.

'The thing is, I think I may have made a bit of a grab at young Norah last night. Now I see no harm in that sort of thing in general, in fact quite the reverse, a girl likes to feel she's been noticed. It's just as much of a compliment if the fellow's some way from being love's young dream and may even have started on his second glass of sherry. M'm. No, as I say, I think that sort of thing's perfectly innocent in itself. It's when it goes, what's that useful tag, *over the top* that one starts feeling a little awkward the next morning. No use apologizing, of course. Bad habit altogether, apologizing.'

'What did you actually, I mean . . .'

'I'm afraid I can't tell you that. I don't mean I won't, I mean I can't. If I could remember anything more than the haziest possible outline I promise I'd seriously consider telling you. Has Norah said anything to you?'

'What? No, no, not a word. Why don't you just forget all about it? She's knocked about a fair bit in her time.'

'Who has?'

'Well . . . Norah has.'

'You know, it's a funny thing,' said the duke, topping up Gordon's glass and refilling his own, 'but I could have sworn you called her something else once or twice. Pet name, perhaps. Anyway, never mind. Well, that's a relief. You didn't happen to notice anything from where you were, I suppose?'

'No, but then I'd had a fair bit to drink myself.'

'That's the idea.'

'You did seem to think you might have forgotten to tell Jimmie that one of his ex-wives, Lady Whatsit, Lady Rowena was coming over for dinner.'

The duke drained his glass with a sucking sound. 'This is an innocuous bally drink,' he muttered. 'Would you care for something a bit more grown-up?'

'No thanks, this is fine with me.'

When the duke came back from the drinks tray he was carrying a tumbler half full of a dark-brown liquid and was also frowning. But as he started to speak his expression cleared, to Gordon's relief.

'No no,' he said affably. 'I distinctly remember dropping a word in Jimmie's ear to the effect that the lady concerned would be putting in an appearance in these parts. He didn't like the prospect any more than I did myself, in fact rather less actually. But after all, what could I have said to her hosts? Don't bring her? Tell her to go out in the garden and eat worms while we feast our heads off? The trouble is, you know, my dear fellow, we're all trapped in a sort of conspiracy to pretend everybody's forgiven everybody else and nobody minds anything any more and we all know life's not like that but what can we do? Now my advice, for what it's worth, is either finish what you've got there or just forget about it and have a proper drink.'

'Could I trouble you for a small Scotch and water?'

'One standard-sized Scotch and water coming up.'

Later, more than at the time, but not only later, Gordon thought about the duke and some of the things he had said. Among much else it could have been argued that to talk of the reputation for eccentricity enjoyed by members of the English upper classes was not really to call things by their right names. Consistency of character, logical behaviour, reliability, sense of duty, however admirable and however resolutely to be pursued, were middle-class virtues and to some extent under the control of the will, became moral qualities and as such imposed restraints on freedom. Jimmie had said more than once that the upper class enjoyed the true freedom of not caring what anybody else thought about them. Like children, perhaps. If that had a bearing, there might be a connection here with the boyishness of such people noted by some outside observers, including Indians under the British Raj and later.

At this point in his ruminations Gordon became aware that the duke was standing a couple of yards away rotating his glass, which seemed to have slightly more in than before, and rocking a little from foot to foot. 'I say,' he said.

'I'm sorry?'

'I was just going to say, have you got everything you want there?'

'I think so, yes, thanks.'

'Not bursting for a pee, for instance? If you are, for God's sake get it over quick like a good chap. I don't want you to go dodging out of the room all of a sudden in the middle of a conversation like, like a, well.'

'No, I seem to be all right at the moment.'

'M'm.' For once in his life the duke seemed momentarily at a loss. 'The fact is, my dear fellow, there was a bit of a dust-up last night. Jimmie and Joanna, you know. I wasn't really involved myself, any more than anybody else was, I'm happy to say. Well, I call it a dust-up, nobody was actually throwing things but there was a definite atmosphere, no, that's not right either, more than an atmosphere. What it seemed to be about was her, Joanna, going on at Jimmie for being fed up with her in a big way, you understand, and Jimmie saying he wasn't. That's about it. Quite enough when you come down to it. Oh, there was something about Lady Rowena sticking her nose in, but that was separate as far as I could tell. It was a bit late on by then. Anyway, now is the time for all good men to come to the aid of the party, meaning I'd as soon not be left alone in here to cope with the pair of them. Then there's the matter of young Norah, as I was telling you. I'm not exactly pining to meet her unescorted either, as no doubt you can imagine.'

Gordon made reassuring noises, did so as persuasively as he could considering how impressed he was to find Willie Dunwich admitting to the possibility of embarrassment, even taking precautions to ward it off or at least to minimize it. That used up a few seconds, and then hardly at all behind cue the door opened to admit not the Fanes, not Louise, but the ruffianly couple first seen almost exactly twenty-four hours before. Something far from unimpressive had brought it about that they were entirely transfigured in dress and accessories and yet no whit less ruffianly than before. They were quickly followed by a couple of couples of additional scum mobilized as short-service guests, and by the suited butler and an underling or two. Before the camaraderie of their foregoing chat should have quite dissipated, Gordon said to the duke,

'While you and I are still in touch . . .'

'Yes, old chap?'

'. . . I wonder if you'd mind explaining what puttock-sleighs are.'

'What what? What? I'm terribly sorry, I don't seem to have quite . . .'

Gordon gave it up. Paddock-something perhaps, he thought. It occurred to him that the duke's inveterate slurring of consonants in his speech might have originated from an innate difficulty with several, such as L, R, S and Th. Something that dawned on Gordon later was the irreducible cost of this hypothesis, entailing as it did identical genetic speech defects in some thousands of persons of noble birth. He quickly gave that one up too when he had identified it.

For the moment there was plenty to occupy him, though perhaps not at any profound intellectual level. Even so he soon found he was at the centre of a small group of youngish people who asked him questions about himself and even seemed to be listening to his answers. He had given several of these before it struck him that, though asked in a perfectly friendly way, their questions seemed designed to elicit biographical facts that could have been of no particular interest to the company. Or so one might have thought, and yet what he said was listened to with mysterious attentiveness.

For instance, the female half of the ruffianly couple said to him, 'I expect you go back up to Scotland quite a bit to see your folks and old friends and so on.'

'I haven't been to Scotland for years. I doubt if I go there more than anybody else who doesn't live there.'

'Would you say you were English or British or Scottish or what?'

'It's something I never think about except at times like this,' said Gordon, who was already starting to tire of the subject of himself.

'Which do you think you are when you do think?'

'If it has to be one of them I suppose British. As I said I was born in London. But I don't quite see what –'

'You also said your father kept up his connections with Scotland,' said the ruffianly male.

'I read somewhere that over fifty per cent of those who call themselves British have at least one grandparent who wasn't English,' said somebody else.

Then Gordon said something. In the last minute he had come to one or two tentative conclusions about the way he was regarded by the ruffianly couple and others present. To them he was an object of curiosity rather than interest, as if he had been a spaceman or an Australian aboriginal. Seen in this light he was a mixture of the hackneyed and the incomprehensible, exotic, perverse, forbidding, part ridiculous, part marvellous. At the same time a more serious inquisitiveness was at work, a genuine desire to know something of a kind of person little seen or studied or called to mind, namely a commoner, one of the majority.

But at the moment this imbroglio took up less of Gordon's attention than wondering where on earth Jimmie and Joanna were and what they were doing. Perhaps they were preparing to leave without telling him, perhaps they had already left. Neither of these hypotheses appeared to him in the least likely, but between them they finally edged out of his mind all speculation about his questioners' motives, with a farewell hint that they should go and stuff themselves. But just then Joanna came into the room followed by Jimmie, and Gordon switched tracks again.

Humorously berating the rest of the company for frowsting indoors on a fine morning like this one, Jimmie explained that the two of them had been out for a health-giving walk. Certainly at that moment there seemed to be colour in his cheeks over and above what decades of assiduous boozing had put there. At his side, Joanna too had a fresh-air look. Nothing about them suggested that they were other than a decent, respectable, well-behaved, moderately posh, rather boring couple. It was hard to believe that husband was about to ditch wife or that wife was about to suffer ditching. But then again he found it hard to believe that, say, Joanna was a persistent fantasist. Harder.

All the same, he found himself inspecting Joanna quite carefully when he got her alone, or rather, to be strictly fair, she got him alone. Whichever way on it was, the mutual isolation process was achieved thoroughly enough to make him forget all about the people he had been talking to.

'Did you have a nice walk?'

'It was all right as far as it went.'

'Did anything emerge?'

'Well, that you could have knocked old Jimmie Fane down with a feather to find old Rowena swimming back into his ken after so long, and at the same time how unsurprising and humdrum it was, just the sort of thing that happens. Oh dear, he's usually better than that. He was so open and artless and friendly that any girl at all would have realized something, well, something rather horrid was on the way, let alone one who's been married to him for something like twenty years.'

'And who still doesn't really know what she thinks of him after all that time. You know, Joanna, before long you'll have to decide about Jimmie.'

Gordon had spoken lightly but he saw at once that he had said something she would very much have preferred not to have heard. She concentrated her gaze. 'I think that's all wrong, the way you're thinking, if it is the way you're thinking. I made up my mind about Jimmie a dozen times when I thought it still mattered, of course I did. It doesn't matter what anybody else decides about Jimmie, what counts is what he decides about other people.'

This seemed to Gordon almost unbearably neat as well as depressing but he let it go. Instead he again spoke rather out of turn. 'Has he made up his mind about you?'

'Yes, and for your information what he's made up his mind to do about me is leave me and go back to Rowena.'

'Oh. Would she have him?'

'I reckon that's what she came here for last night, to tell him the good news in person. And without putting anything in writing, of course.'

'Oh, come on, love, when he saw her come in he was flabbergasted and furious at the same time. I'll swear to that.'

'Swear away, darling. He must have thought as I did at first, that Lady Rowena had turned up to pursue her favourite sport of stirring up trouble.'

'You've got an answer for everything.'

'So I have.'

'So when's he off?'

'He hasn't said anything about when. In fact you might as well know he hasn't *said* anything as yet, not in so many words. But I know, for sure, surer than if I'd heard it from his own lips, and for Christ's sake don't tell me I'm being hysterical, there's a good boy.'

'Why not?'

'Do you really think I sound it or look it?' She certainly looked much as usual, except if anything healthier and more blue-eyed than ever, and sounded as usual too, except perhaps less nervous.

'No, I have to admit you don't, not to me, but then I don't know much about how people sound or look when they're being hysterical.'

'Now there's a couple of per cent chance I may be wrong, here and there at any rate, but put it this way, if I had that amount of reason to believe he was a spy and I was a security copper I'd arrest him even if my career depended on it.'

'M'm,' said Gordon. It was all he could think of to say.

'He was marvellous when we were out for that walk, funny and charming and kind, if it doesn't sound too much of a hoot. He hasn't been like that for years, at least not to me. He'd stopped worrying, you see, he'd made up his mind. I remember reading that thing about some chaps who're going to commit suicide being on top form for their last few days, because the struggle's over. They've decided.'

Gordon had been about to tell Joanna as if for her own good that now she was being melodramatic when, perhaps fortunately, a well-remembered fuzzy voice said, 'Oogh ah *awww* er *errghgh*,' this no doubt occasioned by a sudden access of pain at the base of the back, and then after a few moments' self-massage, 'It's no use you two thinking you can sneak off and have a nice little chat on your own, you're at a *party*, which means every couple of minutes you switch to something even less interesting than before if possible, no no you be off out of it you two little things I haven't time for you now, but, but, but *you* have a lovely fresh drink, dear Joanna, and you too, Gordon, my dear fellow, if you'll just excuse me a moment,' and the Duke of Dunwich moved by a slightly curvilinear path to where Louise had just then arrived in the library.

Impressed as he was by the other man's retention of his name against so many odds, Gordon got no nearer to him for the time being. But he had little leisure to consider that when a kind of spreading wave of vacancy ascended in his insides from somewhere like the pit of his stomach. He had had nothing to eat for over twelve hours, a condition in effect hidden from him earlier by the internal presence of the large amounts of water and other fluids he had swallowed since waking. Lack of food had been further masked by the alcohol he had ingested more recently and by occasional fits of nausea. These last seemed to have fallen off sharply in the past twenty minutes. Was he getting drunk again? Yes, but as against that he felt generally the better for it and was confident, too, that long before or at least before attaining last night's state he would have fallen asleep, perhaps from a standing posture. To appear normal he chatted to other guests of about his own age, as far as theirs could be determined. He found it a strain to make a whole remark without forgetting its second half, but evidently no one noticed or cared. With a total blank in his memory of the conversational ground covered he drifted along with the others when the time to eat came round.

Eating took place in buffet style, which meant among other things that when Gordon ultimately got his food there was nowhere to sit down. This suited him very well, in that it offered him a chance of alleviating his hunger before drowsiness overcame him. At the last moment he put down his almost-finished plate of risotto, found a chair in a nearby unpopulated room and was instantly asleep.

The next moment, or so it seemed, Jimmie was literally shaking him awake with enough violence in face and manner to be momentarily scaring.

'Wake up, I tell you, wake up! We're going!'

'What?'

'I say we're going, we're off! Get moving!'

'What?'

'Oh for Christ's sake stop saying *what* in that cretinous way. Can't you take in the simplest possible idea? We, you and I and the women, are leaving, immediately, by car. You clearly grew up in some appalling place where the menfolk take their collars off after Sunday *dinner* and have a proper *kip* but you're not there now! Get up!'

'Jimmie, if you could just give me a few seconds to pull

myself together, I was dead asleep, you made me jump out of my skin.'

At this appeal Jimmie calmed down somewhat but not all the way. Gordon's discomfort changed direction. Sitting up on the edge of his chair he felt simply terrible, meaning he felt nothing else much, not even sleepy, and could have got no nearer saying how he did feel.

'I have things to do in London,' said Jimmie. 'I dare say you could stay here overnight if you really wanted to.'

'What about Louise?'

'She seems to be coming with us, with Joanna and myself.'

Gordon got to his feet. 'If you'll hang on for five minutes while I put my things together I'll see you outside.'

Jimmie compressed his lips and shut his eyes briefly. He made a movement with his head as if dodging a blow. All traces of impatience had left his voice when he spoke next. 'Take as long as you like, dear boy. I'm afraid I might have sounded rather cross when I roused you, but Joanna had been going on at me to get us all on the move. You know how one minute they're lounging about as if they wouldn't dream of stirring until the middle of next week, if then, and the next they're standing by the front door looking at their watch and tapping their foot. I didn't mean —'

'Say no more, we've all been through that.'

Gordon said no more either, but hurried out of the room and upstairs. What he would have liked to say but could not say was that he had never seen Jimmie in such a state as when he had woken him up just now, much too extreme to have been the product of ordinary marital irritation. The real cause of the trouble would have to emerge of its own accord, if it ever did.

Only a short time after the limit he had set himself, Gordon with suitcase in hand reached the front of the house and went up to the car, the one that looked like a Rolls-Royce but was not, where it stood in the turnaround part of the drive. The sky was clouded but it was a milder afternoon than of late. Needless to say there was not another soul about, or so Gordon would have thought until he had disposed of his luggage and taken his former seat at the back of the pseudo-Rolls. Then he caught sight of Louise and the duke slowly approaching out of the middle distance, and shortly afterwards, from a different direction, Joanna, Jimmie and Polly, the châtelaine-chauffeuse, now restored to her black rigout and for the moment carrying various impedimenta. With a vague idea of seeming helpful and perhaps polite, Gordon got out of the car again.

'Sorry you've got to rush off,' said the duke. 'If it had been me I'd have left it till tomorrow morning and taken my time. For my own part I never rush anywhere. Bad habit altogether, rushing.' He had drawn Gordon a little aside. 'I hope you haven't been too bored.'

'Not at all, everything's been most enjoyable.' Gordon had been going to say what was actually truer, that he had found everything most interesting, but decided at the last minute it might sound a bit clinical and investigative put like that.

'Nice of you to say so. Just one word in your ear before you vanish. I don't know the ins and outs and I don't want to be told, but perhaps I can ask you to keep an eye on my poor little Joanna for me. I think I told you I'm rather fond of her, and there she is having to cope with that shit Jimmie. Well . . .'

Uncharacteristically, Gordon got as far as saying, 'Why did you ask him here if that's what you think of him? Good company you said – is that all?'

The duke picked at one of several food-stains on his waistcoat. 'Oh, he makes up the number, doesn't he? I don't say there's anything you can do bar keep an eye on poor little Joanna. Nice girl, that. Louise, now, she's another nice girl. Thank you for bringing her. Well . . .'

Again remembering in the nick of time not to shake hands, Gordon muttered some reciprocal words of thanks and moved towards the car. Before he reached it a shout from the duke made him stop and turn.

'That phrase you wanted me to explain. I knew what it must have been almost as soon as you asked me. Actually you hadn't got it quite right. It was –'

Willie Dunwich's mouth went on opening and (nearly) shutting, but whatever he might have been saying was lost in a mechanical roar as Polly, perhaps impatient to be off, started and revved up her engine. Gordon could think of nothing to do but smile, wave good-bye and climb aboard next to Louise.

22

It would not be accurate to say that Gordon was again startled into wakefulness by Jimmie, if only because of the several brief awakenings that preceded the final one on the approach to the Fanes' house. Nevertheless it was not until he was getting out of the car that Gordon attained something like full alertness.

'I'll be off then,' said Louise.

'Why don't you and Polly come in for a cup of tea?' asked Joanna.

'Jolly nice idea,' said Polly, 'but I think we'd better be getting along, if that's all right.'

'Sure.' Louise turned to Gordon. 'So long, old fellow. Thanks for taking me to that remarkable place. A fair treat it was.'

'Glad you enjoyed it.'

'See you soon.'

They embraced affectionately. The two girls drove away in the gathering dusk. Gordon stood next to Jimmie on the pavement and waited with him for the car to turn and come back past them, as it would have to do.

'So it's straight to Louise's digs,' said Gordon.

'Where Polly helps her pack.'

'And then drives her to wherever she's arranged to meet Willie.'

'Very likely the airport.'

'En route for Monte Carlo?'

'Quite possibly Monte, though this time of the year it's more likely to be Bermuda or the Caribbean.'

'Bit of luck for Louise whichever it is.'

'Or for Willie. No, let's say *and*.'

Both men waved diligently at the car as it went by, then started to look about them.

'Where's Joanna?' said Jimmie.

With a piece of luggage in hand he hurried into the house, followed by Gordon similarly burdened. For some time the latter moved uneasily round the upstairs sitting-room, not daring or at any rate liking to sit down. Then Jimmie came back in. He looked at Gordon with an expression hard to read, hostile but by no means altogether hostile.

'Your turn now,' he said. 'I've done what I can and it isn't any good at all. You go up and see what you can do. It's the first right on the second floor, that's if you don't happen to know that already.'

There were immediate signs that Jimmie found something less than satisfactory in this last speech, perhaps in its closing few words, but Gordon disregarded such considerations and went straight up to Joanna's room, of which he indeed knew the location, though without ever having crossed its threshold. He knocked at its shut door, waited a moment in vain, then went in. It was now quite dark outside and the curtains were undrawn, though the lights were on.

Joanna was sitting at her dressing-table on a padded stool but now turned round on it towards him. Apart from taking off her outdoor coat she had done nothing to her appearance since coming into the house. Her face had changed, though, as if some internal string that normally held things together had been cut or released.

Gordon came half way into the room. 'What's happened?' he asked.

'Oh, nothing much has actually happened,' she said in an only slightly flatter tone than usual. 'I merely saw something I should have seen before. Sit down on the bed and I'll tell you about it, it won't take long. Would you like a drink?'

'No thank you,' he said, sitting as directed.

'I'll make a cup of tea in a minute. Now, you may have

wondered how I managed to take it so calmly, comparatively calmly anyway, when I added up two and two about Jimmie's plans for himself. Actually he and I had a high word or two on the point last night, nothing much out of the ordinary but poor old Willie was quite shocked, it must be the sheltered life he leads. Where was I?'

'You were going to explain how you managed not to act up.'

'Oh yes. Well, you see, I thought if things came to the crunch, and there's always a part of you that thinks they never will, I thought that's all right, I've got someone else.'

He thought she must mean him but felt he must not assume so. 'Who?' he asked.

'Why, you, you bloody fool. I must have forgotten I'd made the same mistake just the other day when I thought you must have fallen for me the same as I'd fallen for you because you said you'd finished with Louise.'

'But I had and I still have and anyway she's got the duke now.'

'For a bit, at least. What I saw, I was going to tell you what I saw, what I saw was you and Louise saying cheerio for now just now.'

'But I've just told you —'

'Oh I don't mean anything like that, I know that's all over, but what'll never be over is how much younger you are than me. Do you know, some of the time, well all the time in a way I thought it didn't matter, we were the same age really, you and I, what had a few years got to do with anything these days, as if that came into it at all. I thought we'd go off and even get married and everybody would just accept it. I even thought, never bring this up will you, promise me you won't, but I even thought that one day, perhaps you saw in the paper about that woman, something like ten years older than me she was, she'd been trying all her life to have a baby and thanks to whatever it is they can do now she was going to.' A single tear caught the light as it fell to the green part of the pink-and-green rug that surrounded the padded stool she was sitting on. 'I'd known it could never happen but I didn't really realize it till I saw the two of you kissing good-bye just now. You're nearly as young as she is. Now will you please promise me you'll forget I said any of that.'

'Look, Joanna, first of all I was born in —'

'I don't want any of that. Or being told I'm barmy or exaggerating or imagining things or Jimmie won't be able to face all the upset and commotion if it ever comes to it and at least wait till he makes a move. I don't want to be told anything at all.'

As she spoke the last words they heard the front door emphatically shut and, in the quiet street, footsteps receding. Gordon turned his head.

'That's him.' Joanna got up, looked at herself in the glass and drew a comb through her hair, not greatly improving its appearance. 'Off to Gray's.'

'Will there be many people about on a Sunday evening?'

'You can be quite certain there'll be someone about, someone worth his while.'

'As a matter of interest, how will he get there? Surely not by bus?'

'Christ no, he'll pick up a taxi in the King's Road. Are you ready for that tea now, darling?'

'Later.'

She watched him while he went and drew the curtains together. The curtains themselves were much nicer and posher than the ones in his flat, but not quite as nice and not nearly as posh as the medieval-chasuble style of drape at Hungerstream, though these here did run on old-fashioned brass rings, each one chunky enough for the Minotaur's nose. When he was satisfied with the effect he started to take off his tie.

'What makes you think it'll work as well as it did that time at your place?' asked Joanna.

'This isn't meant to be the same as that. To start with, that was there and this is here.'

'So it is. Do you remember my saying to you I didn't feel right about having this sort of performance taking place in this house?'

'Yes, I do remember. But the situation's changed since then, hasn't it? I didn't feel right about it then either, by the way, not that I imagine my objection went as deep as yours.'

'Oh, I don't know. Is there anything else?'

'Nothing I can tell you about in words.'

She seemed to consider for a moment, then began unhooking her dress.

Gordon had not been much taken with his last remark, had indeed been somewhat relieved to find Joanna apparently prepared to tolerate it. At the same time he had tried to excuse himself to himself with the thought that he had had to say something to that effect and had at least been in earnest when he spoke. He had another thing he wanted to tell Joanna, much more serious and unsayable, to do with him and her. Too many bad people had used the words in question, too many people both bad and good had used them lightly, too many people had used them. Nor could he get round the point that to tell her what he wanted to tell her conferred obligations on him, obligations he had not attended to enough. When was he going to have attended to them so? And if there was a strong case here and now for not saying the unsayable, there was a stronger one for not letting it go unsaid. He would have liked to say it without thinking, but unfortunately it was too late for that. At least he had never said it before.

'I love you,' he said.

At his side, Joanna said nothing, not even a word of acknowledgement, nor did she move at all. She was either asleep or what was in effect the same thing, closed for maintenance. Never mind, having said it once he would of necessity find it easier to say a second, a third, an nth time. He was pleased all right and knew he always would be to have got it said, but felt already something of the full force of those obligations, which he resented not at all but was a little scared of. Then there was the question, most easily imagined being asked in his father's voice, of why the hell he had got himself so deeply involved in a social class whose code of behaviour, if any, was to say the least not the one he had been brought up in. The only comforting thing about that problem was that its still sizeable interest was now largely academic.

'What about that cup of tea?' asked Joanna.

'I'd rather have a drink.'

'So would I.'

'You stay there, I'll get them.'

23

Gordon had sufficiently mastered the posh code of behaviour, and had enough sense, to be aware that in such circles knowing something was not the same as avowing knowledge of it. So Jimmie must beyond doubt have had a working knowledge of how matters stood between his wife and his biographer, but for reasons of his own had chosen not to be seen to allow this to colour his behaviour. Meanwhile, in other words while this professed ignorance lasted, there was plenty for Gordon to get on with.

For example, whatever anybody might say or not say they believed, there was still some sort of book about the life and works of JRP Fane to be got into a publishable state. More immediately than that, the very next morning, Monday, was scheduled as an occasion when Gordon should report his progress in the matter.

Back in his flat now, he got up early, something that proved unexpectedly easy, and settled down to the task of recording in abbreviated form what Jimmie had told him during the Saturday afternoon just past. At the same time he had found, sensed, a kind of forlorn, dried-up romanticism in Jimmie's professed feeling for the Tennyson of *In Memoriam* and in Tennyson's own feelings for the so prematurely dead and end-lessly mourned Arthur Hallam. But now Gordon found it impossible to recapture that softer aspect and was driven up against the coarseness of fact. But he noted down as much as he remembered and hoped that something would return to him in the interval that must elapse before he should commit him-self to a final version.

Since Gordon had last come to his office, Brian Harris had had his hair cut and had shaved a mere couple of days earlier. Though still of course tieless he was wearing the sort of shirt whose neck could without implausibility be encircled by a tie. For a couple of weeks now he had seemed to be not so much smartening himself up as pursuing a more house-trained image. Already he would have passed the head waiter's inspection at any but the least innovative London restaurants. Perhaps, knowingly or unknowingly, he was helping to start a trend.

After some preliminaries he said to Gordon, 'I read that stuff you sent last week,' as if it was a mark of unusual favour for him to have done so.

'What did you think of it?'

'We'll come to that in a minute if that's all right. In your covering letter you said something about perhaps wanting more time for delivery. Is that still the position?'

'If not more so. Fresh material keeps turning up.'

'That's good, I'm glad to hear it, but on the understanding we publish in the autumn of next year, then we'll need to have your final manuscript by the end of this coming October. That'll be our real deadline.'

Without having had much in the way of direct dealings with publishers, Gordon knew enough about their behaviour to understand that in their world a real deadline was no more a real deadline than a manuscript was expected to be handwritten and that, after months of futile attempts to produce a cover design and of damaging the text by subjecting it to the expert attention of copy-editors, a proof rich in imported error would emerge accompanied by an unapologetic note requiring its return corrected by first light the following morning. But he also knew enough to say no more than that he thought he understood the position.

Brian appeared to be satisfied. He wanted to know, or at any rate asked, 'You're still enthusiastic about the project, yeah?'

'More than ever.'

'Great. There's just one point I want to take up with you. You remember when we talked before we agreed there were obviously going to be two sorts of stuff in your book, what you might call literary, about the old boy's works, and, you know, personal, what he got up to. I told you then there was bound to be more readership interest in him and all those wives et cetera. Right. I also said, what was quite obvious, that we really seriously need to sell an excerpt or two to one or other of the heavy papers to go probably in its Saturday edition, one excerpt minimum, more if possible. We frankly expect not to do all that well from sales with this one so we've just got to recoup on serial rights. That's where you come in, my old Gordon, yeah I know you come in everywhere in this but it's up to you to show me a couple of meaty excerptible chunks pretty soon, and when I say meaty you know what I mean but I'll spell it out for you just to be on the safe side. I mean personal, which is to say sexual, to do with Jimmie and his wives and other females, more outspoken as some of them still call it than, er, what you've shown me so far. If you've no objection I'll take a hand in placing the excerpts, I've got one or two useful contacts there.'

'So you think there's a chance?'

'Oh *yeah*. Don't forget the old boy's the sort to not only reveal it in private but to make the right kind of affronted noises in public. Newspapers like that type of thing. And there are some shit-hot libel lawyers around. Now I hope you reckon you can help out.'

'What do you mean when you say pretty soon, being when you want me to deliver these chunks of bawdy?'

'Who said anything about bawdy? The moral tone will be elevated throughout, will it not? We'd like them by the end of the month, okay?'

'Okay,' said Gordon. 'I'll enjoy it. Blowing the gaff on that toffy-nosed old twit. Or perhaps son of a bitch would be more suitable.'

'Mind your language, doctor. I knew you were having a second thought or so about him but I never thought you'd swung this far.' Brian paused and looked Gordon over before continuing. 'How does he get on with his wife, his present wife that is? By the way how do you get on with her? Quite pretty still, isn't she?'

If Gordon had not been thinking at that very moment of how nice Joanna looked with no clothes on he would very likely not have jerked slightly in his chair at Brian's last question, let his mouth fall open and stepped up his rate of blinking. Anyway, he could not face the tedium of denying the implication. 'A shot in the dark, I hope,' he said.

'One that landed, too. Don't worry, I won't tell anyone. In your position you're bound to get a bit of that. I saw something in a diary in one of the rags.'

'What? Where?'

'Don't *worry*, just some prat had seen you and her out at lunch somewhere. I'll send you a xerox. It was nothing at all.'

If, again, Gordon had not been charged up with adrenalin just then he would almost certainly not have retorted, 'Well, that sort of stuff's obviously fresh in your mind these days, isn't it, Brian?'

Brian Harris showed a superiority of something or other by not betraying the success of any shot, whether aimed or at a venture. Scorning to ask what that was supposed to mean, etc., he contented himself with looking the picture of low-priority incomprehension.

'Well, you've cleaned up your act, haven't you? With it you may still be for all I know, but you don't half work away at being a long way away from it. What tipped me off first was your conversational style. For a publisher, you used to go on as if you couldn't read a book title without moving your lips.'

'Pithy too, eh? Then what? Sorry, I mean what did you notice after that?'

'General get-up. Clothes, accent. But the chief thing was all those sentences with verbs in you kept reeling off. Only one thing could get you rejigging yourself on that scale – what you used to call a slut.'

Brian was silent for a space, almost imperceptibly nodding his head several times. Then he said, 'My lady friend's ever so grand, I don't mind telling you. She says piss awff. What about that? Clever bit of deduction on your part, though. I didn't have you figured for somebody who notices that kind of thing.'

'It was a lucky guess, and I'm just back from a week-end at Hungerstream, which you'll doubtless know at least by repute, so the subject was sort of fresh in my mind.'

'Hungerstream, Christ. Well, as I used to say, it takes one to know one. Hey, I'll tell you something, my old Gordon – until I started going round with this bloody aristo and mixing with her mates I'd have said that snobbery, the genuine old-fashioned article, you know, Ascot and Henley and I'm more important and just *better* than you because my dad's a marquis and yours is only a viscount, I'd have said that was all over, thing of the past. But is it *buggery* a thing of the past.'

'Here to stay as never before.'

'Are you free for lunch?'

24

After lunch, which lasted for some time, Gordon went back to his flat, intending to do some preparatory work on his couple of excerptible chunks for Brian, and indeed put in fully three minutes on that before falling asleep in his chair. Evidently he still had some catching-up to do. When he awoke he telephoned the Fane number for the second time since returning but, as had already happened more than once that day, got only the utterly remote voice of Joanna on the answering-machine. He did no better on a couple of subsequent goes but did manage to get hold of Madge Walker and invite himself round there that evening.

No. 14 Pearson Gardens, with its photographs of archaic battleships and 1950s style of decoration, was so much as before that Gordon might never have left it, but Madge herself was not quite as untouched by time, even though only a short stretch of it had elapsed since his last visit. She was again dressed as if taking part in some historical reconstruction, but had lost some of her former look of robustness. By the reckoning he had years ago heard from his mother, Madge had suffered one of those sinkings from one level to a lower one that old people underwent from time to time.

'Bless you for remembering our ridiculous hours,' she said. 'The captain's safely tucked up. He was asleep when I last had a look at him. Tell me, Gordon, did you notice any sort of funny smell when you came in?'

'No,' he said truthfully, though it was also true that his nose had not been on the alert for one.

'That's a relief, it's such a nuisance with the gas-men

trampling all over the place trying to find a leak. I'm sorry I started putting you through the third degree when you'd hardly sat down, but they do say, don't they, that one's more likely to notice anything like that when one's coming fresh to it. Are you sure you weren't aware of anything?'

'Absolutely certain,' said Gordon, and added at once, as if turning to a new head, 'How's the captain been?'

'Oh, perfectly marvellous as always. Well, in fact he hasn't been too well this last week or two, nothing serious, just some temporary thing, hardly worth calling in the doctor. But he is so marvellously cheerful and brave the whole time. I've never known him utter a cross word and he never complains, I wish I could be like that. I sometimes think with Alec it's all that naval training he had, but then I think that was no more than just a help to him. It's character that counts, the way one was born. Do you think there's anything in that?'

'Yes, very much so.'

'Dear Gordon, it is nice to see you. Now is there anything I can get you? Would you like a drink?'

'As a matter of fact I would. Just a small one.'

'You always say that.'

'Ah, but this time I can see to it that my wishes are respected.' And he brought out the unopened half-bottle of whisky he had had ready.

Madge looked at it in an affronted way. 'Gordon dear, I can't have you –'

But he had his story ready too. 'This is a new brand that's just come on to the market, I thought we might see what we think of it.'

Mollified by this couple of lies, she went to fetch water and glasses. 'You don't like ice, do you?'

A jug was being audibly filled out in the kitchen when the telephone rang and Gordon found he could answer it without rising from his chair.

'Hallo.'

'Is Mrs Walker there?' asked a youngish female voice with a London accent.

'Hold on a minute.'

Long before a minute had elapsed, in fact after only a few seconds, Mrs Walker was indeed there, her face troubled, her attention all on the handset. 'Yes,' she said into it. 'Speaking. Thank you.' She said more, not closely attended to by Gordon, who went in search of the makings of drinks and otherwise tried to efface himself but saw no reason why he should not pick up what he could. This amounted to the recognition that the caller had told Madge that something had gone well so far and Madge had told the caller that that was most satisfactory and she would telephone in the morning. Alec was not alluded to, still less mentioned, but Gordon knew that he came into it somewhere.

'I'm terribly sorry,' said Madge as she put the telephone back. 'What a nuisance that woman is. Oh, well done, my dear.'

'You did mean these glasses, didn't you?' Gordon broke the seal on the whisky. 'Say when.'

'M'm, I think this is really quite good,' she said after a sip, to his hidden disagreement and herself not seeming to voice any deeply held belief. 'Auld Antipathy,' she read off the label. 'That's a strange name if you like. Now you tell me what you've been doing.'

'Well, about the only thing is I'm just back from staying at Hungerstream.'

'Ooh, how thrilling. That's Gervase Dunwich, isn't it?'

'It was, but he, er, I gather he died suddenly not very long ago and it's his brother Willie now.'

'Really. Tell me all about it.'

Gordon told Madge a great deal about it, though he left out several things, including what Jimmie had said on their walk. He went into some detail about the unexpected manifestation of Lady Rowena and some of what had ensued.

225

'Oh, she's called that now, is she?' said Madge. 'She was plain Rosie when I first heard of her. How fascinating. It would be just like her to have arranged to turn up in that sort of way in the hope of putting the cat among the pigeons, just like her.'

'What do you think of the idea that Jimmie's, how shall I put it, Jimmie's planning to stage a come-back in her life, to last until further notice? Would that be just like him, or at all like him?'

Madge looked grave, but she answered readily enough. 'Well, Gordon dear, you understand this comes from somebody who's been on the outside all these years and who doesn't know any of the ins and outs. Would it be just like Jimmie, no it wouldn't, he hates causing upsets and he hates causing other people pain if he can avoid it. Would it be like him, well still not very. But if you sort of come down the scale to would he be *capable* of it, there I have to say that he bloody well *would*, you know. He mightn't like doing it, it might really cause him real pain, but he'd do it. He's one of the nicest and sweetest men I've ever met, but he'd do it. That's to say the Jimmie I used to know would have and I don't think people change much about that kind of thing, do you?'

'M'm. Madge, do you mind if I ask you something?'

'Gordon dear, you can ask me anything you like, but as the barmaid said, whether I'll tell you or not, dearie, well that's a horse of a different colour.'

'It isn't that sort of thing. What you told me about that awful evening when you realized, that's to say you found out later you'd been ditched in favour of somebody called Betty Brown . . .'

'Oh yes, I told you that whole story, didn't I, I remember.'

'Is she still, I mean do you know where I could get hold of her?'

'I don't suppose you feel very much like asking Jimmie, and anyway she walked out on him a long way back, but I'm afraid

I've no idea where she is, I can't help you, I'm sorry, but as far as I know she's still alive, yes.'

'I've got to get hold of her if I can to ask her about Jimmie.'

'Of course, for your book. How's that going, are you nearly finished?'

'I'm hard at work on one bit of it which I hope I'll finish soon.'

'Ooh, super. What's the bit you're hard at work on about?'

'Well, it's sort of Jimmie's marital career.'

'His sex-life, you mean. Better and better. Can I see it when it's ready?'

'Well . . .'

'My dear, there's no need to hesitate if it's because you're afraid for my delicate sensibilities, where Jimmie's concerned I haven't any of those left, they went out of the window God knows how many years ago. No, it would do him good to have some of the nasty truth about him out in the open. That's a figure of speech of course, nothing would do Jimmie Fane good, short of being flogged round the fleet, and you can trust him to avoid anything like that. No, you show it to me if you feel like and if you don't then publish it anyway and jolly good luck to you.'

Soon afterwards Gordon took his leave, not wanting to wear out his welcome, noting too the glances Madge had started to send in the direction of the bedroom in which Alec presumably lay. When Gordon got back to his flat, he settled down at the telephone and, after some thought, rang the Fane number, which answered at once with the voice of Joanna in the flesh.

'It's me,' he told her.

'Hallo. I thought perhaps you'd gone away somewhere.'

'What? Far from it. In fact I was going to suggest —'

'Actually it might not be such a bad idea if you did go away somewhere for a spell. No, it's all right, darling, it's just that as things are at the moment you might do worse than keep your distance.'

'Is Jimmie about at the moment?'

'Just this minute taken himself off to Gray's. I know he was there last night as well, but there must still be plenty of chaps he hasn't yet had a chance to impress with having stayed the night at Hungerstream, Willie Dunwich's place, you know.'

'Why don't you just come round here straight away?'

'Because, one, I'm expecting some people, and two, Jimmie's bound to ring up about something and I want to be here for that. As to three, well . . .'

'Yes, what is three?'

'It's really *all right*, darling. I'll come round tomorrow and explain. What do you say to that?'

Gordon saw it was all he was likely to get. When he had finished talking to Joanna he went and made a cup of tea, which he carried back to the telephone. There, taking a small card from his pocket, he punched a number unfamiliar to him. A man answered.

'Mr Cooper?' asked Gordon.

'Norman Cooper speaking,' said the youngish north-country voice.

'You won't know me, Mr Cooper, but my name's Scott-Thompson.'

'If it's Gordon Scott-Thompson, then indeed I do know you from what Mrs Walker's had to say about you.'

The two of them spent a few moments on that. Then Gordon said, 'I told Mrs Walker I wanted somebody to help look after a friend of my mother's.'

'Oh yeah.'

'But what I really wanted to know was how Mr Walker or Captain Walker is.'

'I'm afraid I can't discuss my clients' state of health or anything else about them.'

'I'll come and talk to you in person if you say the word.'

'I'm sorry, I can't discuss such matters with you under any circumstances. Now if you'll kindly –'

'Forget it, then. Forget that, anyway. If I ask you another question, will you please treat it as confidential, I mean that I asked you?'

'All right. Let's have your question.'

'Remember I'm asking this as a friend of them both. I hope Mrs Walker's given you that sort of impression of me, that I'm on their side.'

'Well, yes, I suppose I could say that. Get a move on now.'

'Right. How well off are they, the Walkers? I know they're not very, but as far as you know are they managing all right, or aren't they?'

The dead silence at the other end lasted so long that Gordon's nerve was severely tested, but he managed not to speak. In the end Norman Cooper's voice said, 'Hallo?'

'I'm still here.'

'I'd like you to understand I'd have hung up on you long ago, Mr Thompson, if it were not for the way Mrs Walker talks about you, all right? Anyhow, to cut the cackle, the answer to your second question is that they're not, they're not managing all right, or they soon won't be. She's got a little bit of capital which she's spending as slowly as she can but obviously it won't last for ever. Not that that's a requirement in this case, I do see. As regards your first question, I'll answer it after all, as far as to say that Captain Walker's condition has taken a small turn for the worse which it's hoped won't prove irreversible. Though the effect on the bank balance already is. I'd like you to regard all this information as confidential, in the same way as –'

'Just to interrupt you there, Mr Cooper,' said Gordon, 'could you give me an estimate of what kind of sum of money is going to be needed and a rough idea of –'

'Twenty-two hundred by the end of this year at the latest. Madge and I worked it out between us.'

'Thank you. Noted.'

'Can you do anything?'

'I'll have to see.'

'I'm afraid I can't do anything myself.'

25

After a toilsome morning in the course of which he finished off the first of the two excerptible chunks about Jimmie, Gordon had a cheese-and-pickle sandwich and a glass of Callow's best bitter at the pub across the park. He had told Joanna that he already had a lunch engagement, but his true reason for choosing not to eat with her was more basic, namely that his expectation of the main event of the afternoon was already uncommonly vivid and would probably have risen to uncomfortable heights during any sort of shared meal taken before the off, if indeed he managed to get anything solid inside him at all. It was bad enough on his own in the pub.

Fairly soon after Joanna arrived, Gordon assaulted her as apologetically as he could. It occurred to him meanwhile that he could have done this before, not after, a meal taken together, but that was only in theory. The pre-lunch option had a savour of possible bad form about it. The thought soon passed from his mind. Afterwards he waited as long as he could, or felt he could, before saying,

'You told me yesterday you'd explain when you saw me.'

'I'm sure I did, darling. Explain what exactly?'

'Well, sort of, here we are, going to bed together and all that, and yet we're not, well . . .'

'Living together, you mean?'

'Yes.'

'Let me turn round so I can see you. Now. I spent all day yesterday at the St James's Library.'

'Quite the little bookworm.'

'Oh do shut up darling or I'll never get to the point. They

231

found a tiny room for me with no one in it and no telephone and I just sat there and thought. Chiefly about just that. In the end I had the answer but I don't know what took me so long because when it came it was perfectly straightforward. You see, there are only three places where we could live together: one, here, this place, two, there, my place, and three, some- where else. Okay? There's no room for me here with even a fraction of my stuff. My place has got Jimmie in it at the moment and then there's only somewhere else, which would get us into all the papers. No darling, you just go on keeping quiet, you'll get your chance when I finish. Now there's one objection that applies to all three. Which is in each case that I commit myself, I say to everybody, look, I've got this chap – you know what I mean. Putting Jimmie in the clear, you see.'

She paused for long enough for him to get as far as, 'I'm not sure I do quite,' before she broke in again.

'There's one thing I may have got a bit wrong. I'm as sure as I ever was that he intends to be off with Lady Rowena but, do you remember when I talked to you on Sunday after he and I had had our walk, do you remember I said what Jimmie decided would happen was what was going to happen?'

'Vaguely.'

'Anyway I might not have been quite right about that. Dar- ling, what I mean is he's all for going but I sort of left out of account the, well, the possibility that she might not want him to come on the whole. In other words she's not as keen as he is. Perhaps.'

'Does that mean you –'

'Darling I do think you might make a bit more of an effort to follow what I'm telling you. If I move in with you before he moves in with her it puts him in the right and you must see I can't have that.'

'In whose opinion? Puts him in the right according to who?'

'One way of putting it would be the chaps at Gray's.'

'Oh don't be ridiculous, Joanna.'

'Of course I don't just mean it literally, you owl, but I bloody well mean it literally too. It's Jimmie's whole life, that place, or at least he wishes it were.'

'But you don't see it like that, for God's sake.'

'Darling, listen. I didn't make the rules and I don't say I like them, but they are the rules, and one of them says a woman who leaves her husband to go off with another man is let's call it seriously at fault.'

'What about a bloke, what about somebody like Jimmie who leaves his wife to go off with another female, where does that leave him?'

'The actual leaving is entirely his affair. It's a man's world, you see. Naturally if he's improving his financial and-or social standing by going off like that then there may be talk of bad form, but half the chaps have married money themselves, so any muttering noises soon die down.'

'Good God,' said Gordon. 'Where does that leave the deserted wife, morally I mean? Is she free now to do as she likes?'

'You're learning, but if she goes off with another man too soon afterwards, that puts the chaps firmly on the errant husband's side for smartly leaving a woman who's now come out in her true colours.'

'I get it. Just confirm, would you, that we're talking about the 1990s.'

'The 1890s were probably a bit more liberal, a bit more free and easy. The rest of the world was more settled then.'

'M'm.'

'Let's get up, I'm hungry. I didn't really get any lunch.'

'I'm afraid there's not a hell of a lot here.'

'I noticed an Indian restaurant in the next block. I could just about manage a tandoori chicken.'

'In that case we needn't hurry.'

There was of course nobody else eating in the very clean eatery where they went and where a strange jangling noise, not unrelated to music, was to be heard. As always at such times, Gordon wondered how the business survived and then, having no solution to advance, let his attention lapse. He ordered a whisky and soda for himself and a glass of the house white wine for Joanna. The waiter, who was wearing a very clean white shirt, asked him if he wanted ice and he declined.

Joanna watched this. 'Why don't you want ice in your whisky? I thought you preferred it with.'

'If I did, I still wouldn't ask for it here.'

'Why not?'

'You don't know what sort of water it's been made from.'

'What do you mean, what sort of water? Water's just water, isn't it?'

'Very likely. I just wouldn't fancy it, not here. I don't mean anything more than that.'

'Whatever you mean exactly, it appals me that somebody of your age and education should be so . . .'

'Common?'

'No such luck darling. So boringly middle-class.'

'Boring or not,' said Gordon emphatically, 'I'm saved from wondering about what the chaps at Gray's are going to think.'

'Darling, please don't let's quarrel. You may have something on the last point, though I still think you're ridiculously suburban about the ice.'

They clasped hands across the very clean white tablecloth but unclasped them again when the drinks arrived. In Gordon's whisky a large piece of ice was after all floating, but before he could do anything or even betray any emotion Joanna had fished it out with her fingers and dumped it in the water-jug the waiter had brought.

'I wondered whether you might like it neat for a change,' she said.

Gordon sipped appreciatively. 'How long shall we give Jimmie?'

'What about till the end of the month. If he hasn't gone by then or firmly named a day, we have a chat about what we do next. As soon as he does go I go off with you.'

'Straight away? Won't that be a bit soon? Show you in your true colours?'

'I'm not a member of Gray's myself and to do him justice Jimmie'd be quite pleased for me.'

'Maybe. Anyway, if you were right it would put the chaps more on his side.'

'Exactly.'

'Come on now, Joanna. Now, you're not a member of the club both literally and not literally. All that stuff about the rules and being seriously at fault was just a cut-glass way of saying you don't fancy leaving Jimmie when he still hasn't actually, correct? I don't mind, in fact I rather approve if anything, and I still agree to your time-table. But I'm right, aren't I?'

'Suppose so. Sorry darling.'

'You're forgiven. In token of which I intend to take some of your money off you.'

'How much?'

'Two thousand two hundred pounds. It's for Madge Walker, or rather for her house-bound and incontinent husband, to see to him being taken care of. I remember you think she exaggerates but the figure I quoted isn't her estimate and is solid, I guarantee. It's a lot of money for you to give somebody you've never met and I know you're not all that well off.'

'Let's just say that plus or minus two-two-double-o isn't going to make an appreciable difference to me at the moment.'

'Good. Thank you. Of course the money should come from Jimmie by rights, because he's the one that owes it if anybody does and is also the only person Madge would willingly accept it from, that's if she'll accept it from anybody, which is a sizeable if. But I haven't been able to think of any way of getting a sum of money like that to Madge via Jimmie, with say Jimmie's signature on a cheque. I can't, love, but perhaps you can.'

'And you also can't think of anyone but me who's got their hands on that kind of money and who you feel you can ask.'

'That's right.'

Joanna seemed to consider for a little while, but Gordon could never determine whether she was really thinking about real possible ways and means and such or whether she was just good-naturedly putting in some time seeming to be. Finally she said, 'Why should I take your word for it that this is on the level?'

'No good reason, except why should I go through all this rigmarole? No that won't stand up either, so no good reason at all. But my father said once he'd rather be cheated than not trust somebody he thought he could trust.'

Joanna opened her bag and took out her cheque-book and a pen just as the waiter arrived with his order-pad.

26

It was a couple of mornings later. Gordon got up early and crouched over his typewriter as if it bestowed a magic protection upon one like him, confronting in the next hours three trials of ascending severity. He also used the instrument for typing and got off a few lines of guff about the limits that should or could be set on the legitimacy of interest in the personal lives of creative artists.

When the time came, or when he could put it off no longer, he went out into a bright but mild morning and embarked on a bus journey that brought him to Pearson Gardens. A few strides would take him the rest of the way but his watch told him it was not yet five minutes to ten o'clock, so he waited on the corner until just before the hour, when a youngish man with a dark beard and heavy glasses came into view. He looked so unlike Norman Cooper's voice that Gordon nearly let him go unaccosted, realizing that was silly when it was almost too late.

'I can only stay a moment,' said bearded Cooper after identities had been established and mild astonishment and pleasure expressed.

'I've brought the money you told me Madge Walker needed.'

'Oh bloody marvellous. But this isn't your cheque, is it?'

'No, Jimmie Fane's wife's. His present wife's.'

'I can't see Madge caring much for that one.'

'Tell her it's not for her, it's for him, Alec.'

'No, you tell her. Come up there with me now and tell her.'

'You don't need me along.'

'Indeed I do, lad. Now we've got to go straight away or I'll be late.'

When Madge let them into the flat there was no sign of Alec. Gordon mentioned this after a pair of warm embraces and the expression of further mild astonishment and pleasure. It seemed that, as usual at this juncture, Alec was in the bathroom. When Cooper had gone off in that direction, Gordon handed Madge the cheque and started to explain. Before he had finished she tried to get him to take it back, a threat he countered at first by backing away, but rather than have her chase him round the room soon stood his ground and allowed her to stuff the offensive slip of paper into his top jacket pocket.

'And don't you let me hear from you any reasonable nonsense about its being for the captain and not for me because that's not the point.'

'No, the point is that it's charity, isn't it, you silly old woman?'

'Don't you dare call me a silly old woman.'

'Why not, you are one if you think you're so grand you're above charity, private charity that is, state charity's all right, eh? And take note of this. Who's the one person you might have accepted charity from, who you consider rather owes it to you?'

'I suppose you want me to say Jimmie.'

'Wouldn't that be fair? But, leaving out the fact that his money is her money anyway, he's so mean and dishonest that there's no possibility let alone a fighting chance of him sending you a cheque for that amount or any other amount, that's what we decided, we being Mrs F and me, and we were right, weren't we?'

'Talking of the amount, you must have got together with Coop behind my back.'

'It was the only place he and I could do it, and you should be grateful to him.'

Madge blinked a few times. 'I don't know what to say.'

'How about thank you? To Coop and Mrs F through me? Yes? And think of the fun you'll have writing to Jimmie and explaining about the money and saying exactly why everybody voted to leave him out of the enterprise completely.'

'He wouldn't condescend to take notice of anything like that.'

'Oh yes he would. Anything to do with him is of absorbing interest to him. It sounds to me as though you've got out of touch over the years.'

'It would be like water off a duck's back.'

'That's where you're wrong. He'll read and mark and inwardly digest every word of it. You said he didn't like causing pain, well here you go reminding him that once upon a time he caused somebody some.'

With an air of preoccupation, Madge took the cheque out of Gordon's pocket.

'Coop'll have the captain in the bath soon,' she said. 'He usually comes out and has a cup of coffee then. Would you like one?'

'Yes please. I didn't mean it when I called you a silly old woman.'

'It was very hurtful. I understand your reason for saying it but it was still very hurtful.'

'Sorry, Madge.'

'It's all right, dear Gordon.'

When Cooper reappeared it was with the news that the admiral seemed slightly better that morning than the day before and was now safely in his flagship. At the end of ten minutes or so he would get out of the bath, dry and dress himself and be installed on his chair in the sitting-room. Before that stage had been reached Gordon was off.

Soon he had embarked on another bus journey that took him at an angle to his previous path. This bus was rather full, but he noticed on an inner seat up front the back of a man's head that, with its abundant snowy locks, reminded him of Jimmie. It would be fun of a kind to quote, in chunk and-or main text, from whatever Madge wrote to him.

Gordon had not been to his present destination before and got out of his seat too early. As he stood waiting near the door of the vehicle he noticed a vacant outer seat beside him and slipped into it. Not till then was he fully reassured that the man nearby was no more than a reminder of Jimmie Fane, not the man's self. Only in medieval Galicia, perhaps, or the Seychelles before Christ might it have been possible to handle such a situation, not here and now.

The house, when Gordon eventually approached it, was not right as any kind of permanent abode. It was large but recent-looking, not actually guilty of coach-lamps or comparable enormities yet with a mean air of success about it, acceptable to the higher orders of society only as rented accommodation. In answer to his ring a manservant let him in and took him into a long but low-ceilinged room in which two people sat, a middle-aged man Gordon had never seen before and the presumably more than middle-aged woman he had run into at Hungerstream, Lady Rowena as they called her.

'How nice of you to come,' she said warmly. She wore a long white garment with gold trimming and, today at any rate, had a pair of rather mad eyes, but the way she lifted her nose on speaking was still in place. She now brought forward the middle-aged man and introduced him as Derek Hoyt, but Gordon had no time to notice more about him than an expensive American accent and a beard much more thoroughly organized than Norman Cooper's before she said with some emphasis, 'Mr Hoyt has come over from Philadelphia specially to counsel me.'

'Has he really? Have you really?'

'You can guess what about,' said Lady Rowena with further emphasis.

'Well . . .'

'I'm afraid we're rather in the middle of things, I hope you don't mind.'

'Of course not.'

'And you wanted to discuss . . .'

Surely, thought Gordon, she had not forgotten their telephone conversation of almost exactly twenty-four hours ago, when she had seemed to show complete understanding of his purposes and ready acceptance of his proposal of a chat concerning JRP Fane past and present. Trying to speak lightly, Gordon now said, 'Your second husband in times gone by.'

'Oh, *Jimmie*,' she said as if she had not thought of Jimmie for a twelvemonth or more. 'Why not? But Mr Hoyt and I have our conversation to finish.'

'I can always go away and come back later.'

Derek Hoyt now spoke for himself. 'Nothing I may say is confidential in the slightest degree. I'm not ashamed of the work I do and whatever benefit may accrue from it is available to all. Unless this gentleman has some reason of his own for leaving, I am resolute that he be able to be present through the balance of our exchange.'

'Oh, in that case I'm perfectly willing to stay.'

So it came about that Lady Rowena and Derek Hoyt resumed their former seats and Gordon found one from which he could see both of them without having to move his head. There he waited in a state of some expectation for the balance of their exchange.

Hoyt opened with the words, 'We were mentioning five hundred in the first place.'

'As a minimum, not a grand estimate. That would take us nearer eight hundred.'

'If you say so. Then can we fix eight?'

'There'll be more available by October 5th, say four hundred.'

'Is that stable, Lady Rowena, remember, nothing in writing, as you said.'

'Again it's a minimum. As such, totally stable.'

After some more of the same kind of thing, it was borne in upon Gordon that what Derek Hoyt was counselling Lady Rowena about was not her recent bereavement nor her alcoholism nor her terminal cancer, but her money, and not counselling her about it in the sense of helping her to feel better about having it, either. She confirmed this herself when the financial guru had departed, seemingly en route for an aeroplane back to Philadelphia.

'I go a tiny bit woolly about heaps of things these days but never about money. In fact I think I can say I may even have got slightly better about that over the years.'

'How are you about things like your life with Jimmie?'

'Relatively woolly, I'm afraid, relatively woolly. Everything seems to tend to sort of go into one big blur.'

'Are you going to set up with him again?'

'Now that's exactly the sort of question that makes me go really quite woolly. If Jimmie says I'm going to then it's quite possible that I am. What does he say about it?'

'I haven't asked him.'

'I know he's a fearful old liar but you're more likely to get the truth of a thing like that out of him than out of me. You seem quite a nice young man. I'm afraid I couldn't make out what you were doing at a place like Hungerstream, no never mind, anyway I'll remind you that to *go* woolly about something isn't the same as to actually *be* woolly about it. I rather like to keep people guessing, do you see. You know that marvellous expression, to catch somebody on the wrong foot? I rather enjoy that, I'm afraid.'

Just then the front doorbell rang and Lady Rowena cowered theatrically back among the cushions on her chair. 'Oh dear,' she said. 'So many people coming to see one. Well, I'm afraid you won't get anything out of me about Jimmie or me-and-Jimmie.'

'Why did you ask me to come round?'

'Perhaps to see what would happen if Jimmie found you here.'

'What!'

'I know he wanted to come round some day like today. So it might really be him.'

It was not Jimmie or anyone like him but Mr and Mrs something unrecognizable to Gordon by name, recognizable enough in the flesh, however, as the daughter Periwinkle and her husband perhaps Oliver encountered once and briefly and some time ago. Neither treated him with overt hostility, but he decided against giving any of the hidden sort a chance to work its way to the surface and was off within a minute, forgetting what excuse he had made as soon as he had made it. Once more, with rain in the air but still not actually falling, he stood and waited for a bus, thinking to himself as he did so that despite hefty evidence to the contrary he had not in fact wasted the last thirty-six hours or however long it had been.

His latest journey took him to a building that he found much more unwelcome in appearance than either of its predecessors, detectable by its very appearance as a place confining people whom the rest of society rightly or wrongly had no wish to be bothered with. It was the sort of place where visitors went on arrival to a central desk where information and directions were dispensed. Gordon went to it.

Without anything that could be called a delay he was taken to a room on an upper floor where nobody would go except to see somebody. Again he had no need to hang about before somebody was shown in.

If Gordon had not known differently he might well have supposed this person to have been a man, an old man rather short in stature wearing a loose shirt outside unpressed blue trousers, the hair white and closely trimmed, a handsome old man despite deep furrows round nose and mouth and at the corners of the eyes.

243

After an exchange of amicable smiles, Gordon said, 'Mrs Easton?'

'I beg your pardon?' The voice was masculine and senatorial.

'I am addressing Mrs Easton, Betty Easton?'

'That's my name, certainly. And you are . . . ?'

He gave his name and started to explain why he had come, but had not got very far when it struck him that the other was not listening. He smiled again, perhaps over-cordially this time, and said, 'Didn't they tell you anything about me or what I was after?'

'Forgive me, but didn't who?'

'Well, the people here, the . . . whoever it was told you I'd come to see you.'

'I'm sure everybody behaved impeccably. They're all very nice and helpful and conscientious, I think I can safely say that. They're all very nice.'

'Oh, I'm sure they are. Let me just tell you very briefly why I've come to see you. I'm collecting material, that's to say I'm writing an article about —'

'Excuse me, Mr . . . I'm afraid I didn't catch your name, I'm sorry.'

'Scott-Thompson, Gordon Scott-Thompson. I'm working on a —'

'What can I do for you, Mr . . . ?'

'I'd be most grateful for anything you can tell me about somebody called Jimmie Fane. I understand you —'

'I beg your pardon?'

'Jimmie . . . Fane. JRP Fane. He wrote books.'

'What, what sort of books?'

'Oh . . . novels, er, stories. Poems. Poetry. Lots of different sorts of book.'

'Who do you say wrote these books?'

'Jimmie Fane. You remember Jimmie.'

'I'm afraid I can't remember reading any books by . . . that author.'

'But you were . . .' Gordon drew back at the last moment from saying that Mrs Easton had at one time been married to the Jimmie Fane he had introduced into the conversation. Instead of that he thanked her for talking to him, apologized for taking up her time and in due course left.

'Just checking out,' he said to the chinless but friendly girl at the central desk. 'Mrs Easton.'

'Oh yes, how did you find her?'

He shook his head wordlessly.

'M'm, I've always said there's a case for telling people in your position not to bother to come, but you see we have this rule against doing anything to discourage outside visits.'

'Of course, I understand.'

When Gordon had left the building he walked a hundred yards or so to the nearest pub and went in. He was already starting to feel better at not being in Mrs Easton's company, but the improvement went into reverse for a time when, without meaning to, he thought about the fact that she had been the female that the youthful Jimmie had married. It also occurred to him to imagine the two of them engaged in – well, nothing much more than holding hands, actually, but it was quite enough to send his imagination reversing at full speed. He ordered two large Scotches in quick succession and started feeling better again, more because there he was drinking them than from anything they were doing for him in themselves. He went home by taxi, feeling that his chat with the first Mrs Fane narrowly justified the expense.

27

Soon the two excerptible chunks were ready. In a half-hearted attempt to make them seem like two parts of a whole, Gordon had put something about Jimmie's wives and girl-friends into the chunk that was mainly about his works, and something about his works into the chunk that was mainly not. The latter piece had cost him some trouble and he had had to take it through several drafts. Much of their respective contents had oscillated between portraying their subject as a greedy lord-loving egomaniac, redeemed only by flashes of lust, and making him seem no worse than any other creative artist, with exacting standards of comfort and support, perhaps, but with no history of alcoholism, theft, venereal disease or other literary characteristic. Satisfying Brian Harris without alienating Jimmie himself was a tricky requirement. Or so it seemed to Gordon. He wished he could send his final version straight to Brian, but he thought that both honour and policy required the imprimatur of the central figure.

Accordingly, when the chunks existed in fair copy Gordon took them along to Jimmie's choice of venue, the members' lounge at Gray's club. It was a few minutes before noon on a fine spring morning with quite noticeable sunshine slanting in from St James's Street.

'Come along, my dear boy, come along,' said Jimmie, his effusiveness perhaps evidencing knowledge that it was not strictly all right for a non-member of the club like Gordon to be where he was at such a time. 'I expect you know these chaps, don't you?' There were three or four of these chaps, boasting two or three baronial names between them, soon distancing themselves in one way or another from host and guest. 'Have a glass of champagne,' continued Jimmie, 'I've worked it out that you actually make money if you drink it like this before luncheon.' He was wearing a pale-grey suit that was new to Gordon, perhaps new absolutely, through which he managed to radiate an appearance of health and relative youth and affluence. 'Now do correct me if I'm wrong but I rather fancy you've *put together* or even actually *written* something you say you want me to cast my eye over, or am I simply talking through my *hat*?'

By this early stage Gordon was more than half reconciled to having put together or actually written a couple of paragraphs unhelpful to a laudatory general view of Jimmie and his activities. 'Would you like to take this stuff away with you and study it,' he said, 'or would you prefer to have a look at it now? It's in two lots, one critical, one personal.'

With a touch of magisterial impatience amid all the bonhomie the old artist-man thrust out his hand. 'Pass me the critical stuff, I'll give it my best attention at leisure. The personal stuff or whatever you call it I'll go through with you straight away.'

'Right.'

Jimmie took about half a minute to get through the first page of personal stuff. 'Have I really got to read all this?'

'Not if you don't feel like it. Concentrate on pages four and five.'

Jimmie concentrated, but not very hard. 'Yes . . . yes . . . did I really do that? I expect I did . . . yes . . . oh *no*, how thoughtless of me . . . yes . . . well of course.' He put the papers in order and handed them back.

'Aren't you going to just glance at the end?'

'Oh, very well.' Some ten seconds later Jimmie said, 'There. You know, dear boy, I don't really care what you or anybody else says about me and what I've got up to in my time, never have. Well, that's not quite true, I suppose I care what people like Willie Dunwich say about me but anyone less exalted is free to say whatever he chooses. Or think it. I've lived in the world, I can't really object to being judged by the world.'

'What did you get up to during the war?'

'Oh bless my soul.' Jimmie threw back his fine head and laughed abundantly. 'I fancy I know where that came from. For your enlightenment, dear Gordon, I joined the civil service on 28th August 1939 and before I could turn *round* I was neck-deep in scrap-metal collection. It was inordinately boring but one stood only a very small chance of being shot or blown up. M'm. Do you kindly reflect that there are some whose curiosity it's a duty as well as a pleasure to leave unsatisfied.'

'How does Willie Dunwich think you spent the war?'

'I'm sure he's been told but he wouldn't have noticed.'

'Why not?'

'My period in the civil service was over before he started going to school.'

'What about the war itself? He must have noticed being told about that.'

'Too large an event to miss altogether. Anything on a smaller scale would have to have happened to one of his ancestors or immediate family.' Jimmie looked over Gordon's shoulder at somebody who had just come into the room.

It was in fact two persons, the Bobbie and Tommie met with on these premises before. They came over and Bobbie, nodding at the typescript, said in his melodious voice, 'Paper in the club.'

Gordon would not have remembered thinking about the matter much in the interval, but now it was clear to him that Bobbie's demeanour was conditionally hostile, ready to retreat into humour if confronted. 'How do you mean?' he said.

'He means one isn't supposed to work in the club,' said Jimmie, 'sign papers or conduct business or anything like that.'

'Actually a very good rule when it was instituted,' said Tommie. 'A long time ago now of course.'

Bobbie nodded with a touch of impatience. He looked word-lessly at Gordon in a way designed to draw attention to the presence now and in this quarter of a non-member of the club, again with a smile in reserve.

Gordon liked and approved of the way Jimmie saw this and reacted, elaborately apologizing with a display of shame and distress that put Bobbie firmly in his place. In the middle of the whirl of counter-apology that emerged he found room for the observation that all cultures had their rituals.

'Sometimes I'm not quite sure where I stand with Bobbie,' said Jimmie as they left the room.

'Sorry?'

'I can never make up my mind whether he feels a rankling personal hatred for me or just dislikes me enough to enjoy teasing me.'

'I should imagine he dislikes quite a few people enough for that.'

'I've thought of asking Tommie but I can't summon up enough interest in the answer. What about another drink? — in the bar this time, you're allowed there.'

'Well, yes, please, just a small one.' As often over the past weeks, Gordon accepted a small drink much less for itself than because of what Jimmie or another might let fall at such a time. Jimmie probably understood this, but what of it?

In the bar, where the barman was the only sentient being on view, Jimmie even so said, 'Gordon, dear boy, I really brought you in here to say thank you.'

'Why, what on earth for?'

'Just . . . undertaking and constructing this work of yours on the subject of JRP Fane, man and artist. You may be sur-prised and even pleased to hear that whenever I've mentioned it round the place, in confidence of course, the response has been not merely encouraging but specifically encouraging. No fewer than, well, several men shall we say not unconnected with publishing and bookselling have assured me that when this work appears it will *trigger off* a large revival of interest in what I've written. And in myself too, the one reacting upon the other. It doesn't matter that some of my actions have been, how to put it, offensive to conventional morality, in fact it's a great advantage, which is another reason for accepting your warts-and-all treatment as seen in that ... disquisition you showed me. These days the public *like* to think of an artist as a, as a *shit*, known to behave in ways that they themselves would shrink from. Did it harm either the reputation or the sales of that Danish fellow or whatever he was when the public learnt how monstrously he'd behaved? Far from it, far from it. I myself don't aspire to his level, but the principle's the same. I don't think I need go on. But I did just want to say,' and here he shifted position a little so that Gordon could see his face in profile, '. . . thank you.'

'Think nothing of it, Jimmie.'

'Will you have another of those?'

'I'd like to, but I'm afraid I really have to be getting along.'

'I'll telephone you if I may to let you know of anything I might like to see changed in that ... treatise you gave me to look at.'

The place Gordon was bound for now was near the distant end of Piccadilly. It was an Italian restaurant that was unusual in having Brian Harris in it. Round the corner from Gray's Gordon boarded a bus and was presently joining Brian at the table where he now sat.

Even in the brief interval since they had last met, the publisher had moved some further distance back towards a style of appearance his predecessors might have tolerated. Given some negligence in the execution he might have been freshly shaved, and his neck was encompassed by an actual tie, shaggy, irregular in cross-section but definitely a tie. Even his voice was less harsh. He used it now to bid Gordon welcome.

Gordon finished arriving, accepted a small Campari-soda and apologized for being a few minutes late.

'I hope you used them to get a bit of drink down you,' said Brian.

'I suppose you could say –'

'Because I'm afraid I've been rather knocking them back here. This is my second.'

'Not like you.'

'It's working in publishing that does it, you know, Gordon, makes you hit the old firkin. People talk about the ruthlessness of property tycoons and what are they, asset-strippers, but they're angels of mercy compared to the bastards who run publishing these days. I mean really run it, not the sort of tweedy twit who used to offer you a glass of pale sherry when you went to see him among his panelling, so legend said anyway. Still, don't let's go into that now. Look, do you mind if we order, I've got a meeting this afternoon and there's some stuff I want to look up first. Right, now you tell me what you've been up to. How's Jimmie Fane getting on?'

'If you mean JRP Fane in italics followed by a colon and some piece of crap like lyrist and libertine, in other words my critical biography of that literary figure, then it's getting on as well as can be expected. If you're asking after old Jimmie, then that's not so easy.'

Gordon considered his distinction between book and subject rather neatly phrased, and was mildly irritated to find that Brian seemed to have missed it, had started to deal with the waiter instead, was giving instructions as to the serving of his avocado pear.

'These days if you're not careful they take it out of the skin and slice it up and spread it out on the plate in a sort of fan instead of letting you dig it out for yourself,' he explained to Gordon. 'No doubt it's how they dish it up at American ski resorts. Now what are you grinning at?'

'I was thinking, that's exactly the sort of thing Jimmie would say, especially the bit about America.'

'Oh Christ, it must be the influence of that classy babe of

mine. She's still the centre of my existence, by the way. Which reminds me, how's the lovely Mrs Fane?'

'Lovelier than ever, which speaks well for her considering what a shit Jimmie's being to her, or contemplating being to her. A new vile scheme of his.'

'Tell me about it.'

'Sure, but just – you did get those faxes of mine, those two sort of extracts?'

'Yes, they're okay, I'll tell you later. I want to hear about Jimmie's new vile scheme first.'

This lasted them through the meal, which was washed down with plenty of wine. Brian listened attentively, but was also interested in keeping Gordon's glass filled. Was he trying to get him drunk? Why should he? No no, merely helping him to catch up with the party. Anyway, by the time Gordon had covered his visit to Betty Easton and coffee and grappa had arrived he had become quite eloquent. He had also reached a decision.

With a show of grimness, Brian said, 'That was something, to go through that. But it's just how things turn out, I suppose. No one to blame.'

'No, but it does seem a bit unfair.'

'So do lots of things. Fair and unfair doesn't enter into it.'

Gordon cut short this banal interchange by saying, 'At least I hope that's taken you away from your publishing worries. Worse troubles at sea.'

Brian scowled and sipped grappa. 'It's not just a matter of a bit of aggravation here and there, you know. I happen to think publishing's a very important job.'

'Oh, absolutely,' said Gordon without any great sense of urgency.

'You don't know what's been going on, do you, otherwise you wouldn't be so fucking smug. All these financial deals going on, who cares a toss who owns this or who's paid a hundred million quid for that, I agree. The trouble comes when the bloody philistines who've bought you up start looking at the books, and I don't mean the books of exciting new poetry or the books of vibrant innovative prose, I mean the *books*, the sodding account-books. One fine day one of the bastards happens to glance at the page that shows the annual profits on turnover of the various enterprises the company owns, and the fellow starts making a few comparisons. He's one of the smart ones who can count on his toes as well as his fingers, and after some time he notices what intellectuals call a disparity. Soft-drinks chain, profit last year, twenty-six per cent, breakfast cereals, thirty-six per cent, telecoms, forty-six per cent, Brontosaurus Books, six per cent. Say that again slowly – *six per cent*. Now any actual publisher who nets six per cent in an average year knows he's doing very nicely, thank you, but this sod isn't a publisher, he's only a businessman with a head for figures, which means he can spot the fact that Brontosaurus Books is much less profitable than even the lousiest oil-well. Perhaps he can't cure the disparity but he sure as hell can reduce it, and if he can he obviously must. That means –'

Here Gordon interrupted, but not for long. 'If this is a way of working up to telling me –'

'You'll get your turn in a minute,' said Brian, and drained his glass of grappa. 'So businessman consults a friend of his who can read, and friend explains there are things called bestsellers which are more profitable than other things that get published. The best-sellers may not be as, well, since nobody's listening you and I can call it between ourselves *good* as some of the other things, but that's a matter of opinion and only to do with culture. That means that books that are clearly never going to be best-sellers –'

'Like *JRP Fane: lyrist and libertine*, by Gordon Scott-Thompson, will have to move over to make room for something that'll show a handsome profit, or a profit at any rate.'

Brian said without expression, 'You took the words right out of my mouth.'

'Actually you took them out of mine. I decided before you started your lecture that I wanted nothing more to do with any book on Jimmie. There are limits to how much of a shit one can face writing about.'

'Of course,' said Brian inattentively, looking over Gordon's shoulder for the waiter. A little later he added, 'I should have seen this coming, well in a way I did, but you know how you get.'

'I can imagine.'

Quite soon the two had agreed that the contract between them should be rescinded as from that moment, that Gordon should be free to sell wherever he pleased the fruits of his labours and that he should not be called upon to refund the advance he had so far been paid in consideration of his honest endeavours under the said contract.

Of course, as Brian had said over Gordon's shoulder of course there was nowhere to put on record the fact that the money-men at the publishing house had done nothing more than decide to get out of the Fane commitment if they and it could, and their and its ability to do so had come about because of what Gordon had decided to do or not to do, a decision taken quite independently. If anyone should ever care to ask, Brian Harris had been deputed to tell him that the thing was off and off it was at once and the record said so. Well, what did it really matter?

One final point was that the two excerptible chunks faxed to Brian were in his judgement and that of his contacts uneven in commercial quality, so much so that the chunk about Jimmie and his wives and girl-friends would need a good deal of beefing up before being offered to a quality newspaper, while the chunk about the works of Fane was probably too tame and intellectual to be worth offering at all. Brian added that the fact that no book was now contemplated would very likely take a thousand quid or so off what such a newspaper would pay.

'It's rather a pity that the bastard concerned didn't put off looking at the books a bit longer,' he said on parting. 'Another couple of weeks and we'd have got ourselves in too deep to pull out. Thanks for being so helpful over this. My expert handling of the situation'll probably give me more time to look for another job. Not necessarily within the world of books.'

'So you're leaving this lot soon?'

'It's not up to me, my old Gordon.'

Another bus-ride took the ex-biographer to one of the places he had originally visited in search of Fane material. On arrival he decided to leave the matter of his change of status for a different occasion. A man's voice spoke to him out of the wall when he pushed the bell at 14 Pearson Gardens: Norman Cooper's.

Upstairs in the Walkers' flat, Gordon thought Madge was looking no worse than he remembered, though in a way hard to define more closely she did look smaller. But again it was obviously not a time to go in for any peering or wondering about things like that.

'I was so sorry to hear your news,' he said.

'Thank you for coming, Gordon dear.'

'I suppose it was all rather sudden, wasn't it?'

'When it came it was. I piped him down as usual, everything was as usual then and during the night, and then when I went in to him this morning he just hadn't woken up.'

'There's no need to go through it all again, Madge,' said Cooper.

'I want to hear,' said Gordon.

'Of course he does, Coop dear. After all, there's not an awful lot to go through. The doctor was very sweet when he got here. I hadn't really taken to him in the past but the captain always swore by him, said he was tough as well as kind, that was the sort of combination he always looked up to, the captain. And he was marvellous this morning, the doctor was, he said . . . that Alec wouldn't have known a thing about it, couldn't have done, which really put my mind at rest, honestly.'

'You sit down with Gordon now, Madge,' said Cooper, 'and I'll get us some tea.'

While tea was being made, Gordon heard how Madge was glad the captain had gone so suddenly and painlessly, glad too for his sake that his life was over. In the past he had kept up with old shipmates, gone out to lunch with them, done a bit of sailing, attended reunions and reviews, but those days had been brought to an end years before. Since his illness he had never talked about his feelings or even referred to them except when he had had to, but Madge had known him well, not that it had been difficult to guess a certain amount, such as what went through his mind first thing in the morning. No, she said, they had not had many visitors after the first year or so.

'Well, perhaps people get lazy,' said Gordon. 'And don't like journeys.'

'Oh yes, of course, but sometimes I think it's a kind of embarrassment that keeps them away. They think they ought to come more often than they do, perhaps, and it makes them uncomfortable to keep apologizing for leaving it so long since the last time and promising it won't be so long till the next time. Once they've realized that they may start finding it too far to come at all. And they're not getting any younger themselves.'

'I suppose you haven't had time to think what you're going to do yet.'

'Oh, I've had plenty of time before this morning. I'll start by getting my grand-niece over for a week or two. Well, actually she's Alec's grand-niece but we've always got on quite well, she and I. I rang her up and she'll be coming along tomorrow.'

Cooper arrived with the tea in time to hear this last bit. 'Not till then?' he asked.

'No, she's got to get a child off to school.'

'That leaves tonight,' said Cooper. 'I can't do tonight.'

'Don't worry about me, either of you,' said Madge. 'I'll be fine on my own.'

Cooper continued to address himself to Gordon. 'In fact I really ought to be off about six.'

'If I leave in a few minutes I can easily be back here by six,' said Gordon.

'There's really and truly no need,' said Madge.

'I'll hang on for you,' said Cooper.

28

Now that Gordon no longer had any obligation to write any sort of book about JRP Fane, artist and man, he found his estimate of the old boy had changed in both aspects. Jimmie himself seemed slightly less of a towering shit than when last encountered in Gray's. This relative leniency towards him might have issued from a sense of having disappointed some of his expectations, however richly they might have deserved to be. The sense of gleeful anticipation with which Gordon had looked forward to passing on his news was largely abated. On the other hand, with all pressure towards impartiality removed, the novels instantly struck him as the most abject piss, well beyond any excuse of a comprehensive change of taste, simple passage of thirty years or more, etc. The interesting ambiguities he thought he had seen in *The Escaped Prisoner*, for instance, were now revealed as no more than a boring attempt at mystification that failed totally to obscure the lack of conflict at the centre and a conclusion so thoroughly foregone as to make all but the first few pages predictable in every detail above the smallest. No doubt his opinion of the Fane writings would ascend again in the future, but not far, he thought, not as far as it had fallen, just far enough with luck to recall to him what he had found in them that had made them seem worth writing about in the first place.

Gordon sat at his work-table, though he was not doing any work. It was twenty minutes past four the following afternoon and Joanna had been due at four o'clock. Unlike some women he had known, she had an observable sense of time, perhaps having grasped that one person waiting for another is effectively debarred from doing anything else but wait. So it was with Gordon now. He sat on for a short while waiting in vain for Joanna to arrive, then went to the window as if looking into the street would cause her to appear in it. Much to his surprise she was indeed to be seen at that moment, approaching the front door of the building, though not in her usual brisk, head-down mode, almost at an amble. When she reached the door she failed to stop by it or even glance at it, continuing on her way instead at the same strolling pace. A couple of dozen yards down the pavement she came to a halt and stood without turning. Although the sun shone the air was not warm.

These antics, which were in no way characteristic of Joanna, disconcerted Gordon. He had almost reached the point of opening the window and calling down to her when she seemed to come to herself, swung round and walked actively back and pressed the doorbell. Not wanting to be seen as over-expectant he took his time about going to let her in, but it was not very long before she was there in his flat. She proved to be wearing a shirt of some deep red colour and a shortish leather skirt which showed off her legs. He was dimly conscious of having seen her in these clothes before, though he could not have said on what occasion. For all that, he also sensed he was better off not remembering. She unemphatically avoided their customary inaugural kiss and was not so ready as usual to look him in the eye.

'What's wrong?' he asked, already knowing a large part of the answer.

'Nothing's wrong exactly but something's changed. Jimmie isn't going.'

'Oh.'

'He told me the whole story last night and I mean the whole of it. How he'd worked it all out and come to the conclusion that he'd be so much better off back with Rosie that it was going to be worth all the upset and boredom and everything of making the switch and never mind what the papers said.'

'I can't see Jimmie bothering much anyway about –'

'Rosie held out against the idea for a bit but she finally caved in and after she told him so at Hungerstream he felt fine.' At this point she gave Gordon a quick smile of defensive apology, almost as if asking him not to judge the old boy too harshly. 'But then quite soon, he couldn't have said exactly why but he found himself asking her for a sort of stay of execution, putting off the moment when he finally took the plunge. I think that was him changing his mind but not liking to admit it to himself straight away. Well, he's admitted it to himself now and to Rosie and also to little me. So . . .'

'What's to stop him changing it back again?'

'Pride. Or conceit if you think that's a better name for it, which it probably is. Plus the fact that Rosie wouldn't let him near her in a hundred years for a second bite at the cherry. Actually it would be a third bite, wouldn't it?'

'What do you think made him change his mind about taking the plunge?'

'Rediscovering what Rosie was like. There are limits to what a chap'll put up with for let's call it money. Of course, I'm biased.'

Gordon got to his feet from where he had again been sitting at his work-table. He felt as if his future had been dismayingly and irrevocably settled. Without much sense of what the words meant he said, 'Where does this leave you and me?'

'Darling, if Jimmie and I are going to make a fresh start together we'll have to do it completely, without any attachments either of us might have had.'

'I thought what you and I had was more than just an attachment like any other.'

'Of course it *was*.'

'But then you . . . it dawns on you . . . you just decide he's more important to you than I am and always has been, but that's only because of what he's decided he's going to do.'

'You do realize you're trembling.'

'No, I mean yes, why shouldn't I be, naturally someone in my position would be or might be, surely you can see that.'

She stayed where she was, sitting on the edge of a chair it was hard to imagine anybody ever having relaxed in. The tension she had shown until only a few moments earlier had transferred itself to him or had disappeared. Still without moving from where she was she spoke in a gentle almost a wheedling tone. 'Darling, let me tell you where we've got to and what's going to happen, can I?'

'All right.'

'I still think Jimmie is a rotten man and I know more about him than you can hope to. At the same time, not but, just at the same time, I do know him after all these years, and his attractive side which I also know about makes up for his rottenness, not by much and not all the time but on the whole it does. And I'm married to him and not to you. You're a better sort of man than he's ever been or ever will be, but when it comes to picking husbands that sort of thing doesn't seem to matter as much as, as much as it probably should. Do you see what I mean?'

'I should have asked you to marry me,' said Gordon.

'If you ever had I'd have turned you down. Not because of you but because of me. I'm too old. In a few years I'll be sixty and not attractive any more and don't interrupt me. I've worked it out that with you there I could face any amount of public fuss and not-public as well as public jeering and serious talks from old friends and I expect you could manage too if you had to, but me waking up every morning and wondering whether it was going to be today I first saw you thinking I'd started to look my age, just the thought of it scared me so much I had to make sure it would never happen. Right, that's it. You can say something now if you want to.'

He said nothing at first, but then he said, 'I suppose you've talked to Jimmie?'

'Yes, I told him about you so to speak officially and he was decent enough to pretend parts of it were news to him. I didn't tell him anything private.'

'Of course not. But you did tell him what you were going to do about me now.'

'Yes.'

'Would it be all right if I came to see him in the morning?'

'What about?'

'Just stuff to do with my book on him.'

'Will it be affected by what I've been –'

'No, all that stays exactly as it was, well, twenty-four hours ago.'

'Good. Come about ten and I'll see he's there. I'll go now, after I've said two things. One is, please don't ever try to remind me of how it was before in any way at all, which sounds harsh but isn't if you think about it. The other thing is, you and me, that's over, finished and done with, but I'll always love you. No, darling, not a word, seriously.'

When Joanna had gone, Gordon sat on where he was for a few minutes, after which he went into his bedroom and found quite soon what he had not felt confident of finding at all, a quarter-full little bottle of sleeping pills left over from early the previous year, when he had painfully ricked his back playing squash. The bottle was in his pocket when he went out and across to the pub. Here he drank two glasses of Scotch whisky in quick succession and bought a half-bottle of the same to take away. Back in his flat he switched on the television set and settled himself down in front of it. At first he watched snooker, then some national news followed by weather, then some regional news, then more snooker. After that he watched a programme about Liverpool followed by one about food and drink. While he was watching the latter he thought how lucky he was to have something to do, something to occupy his time, and wondered what previous chaps suddenly deprived of their girl-friends, not just girl-friends, very serious girl-friends any-way, had done for the rest of their waking hours. While he was watching some strangely attired people sitting at desks and guessing things, if that was what they were doing, he remembered that his doctor had warned him that it was dangerous to drink alcohol while he was taking the sleeping pills. Washing down a couple of the pills with diluted whisky he thought he would probably be all right, and anyway for the moment it seemed to him slightly more important to get off to sleep that night than to be there in the morning. In the end he swallowed the last of the pills with the last of the whisky while the TV was showing professional golf.

29

The next morning Gordon woke up to find his bed had grown enormous during the night. This was much less tiresome or frightening than it might otherwise have been because he discovered on investigation that he too had grown enormous, and in exactly the same proportion. When he looked further he established that this was also true of everything else, including what he could see out of the window. He went on assuring himself repeatedly that this new belief of his made literally no sense, but in vain. Then when he had made himself a cup of tea he noticed that the world and its contents were back to normal, so firmly so that he had quite forgotten what it had felt like to suppose any different. As against this he now had a sort of headache right at the top of his nose, between the eyes.

In the same general way as his mistaken view of visible reality, Gordon's nose stopped hurting behind his back, as it were, when his attention was elsewhere. This took place during his bus journey into the Fane neighbourhood. The front door of the house stood ajar and very soon he was in the upstairs sitting-room face to face with his former biographee, for the moment presumably unaware that he had recently become former. Jimmie was wearing the pale-grey suit Gordon had seen him in when they last met at Gray's, but he showed little trace of the well-being that had been noticeable in him on that occasion. Without showing actual hostility his expression was not welcoming or cheerful. He stood on the fringed hearthrug with his back to the grate, where an electric fire glowed.

'Joanna told me she had a talk with you yesterday and the

two of you agreed to put an end to your liaison,' he said, pronouncing the last word in the French rather than the English fashion, causing momentary difficulty but no real misunderstanding.

'Yes.'

'Is there anything you want to say to me on that subject?'

'No.'

'Then I'll say something. Or rather remind you of something I said to you a little while ago. I cautioned you briefly against having an affair with my wife not because such a thing would inconvenience me, which it duly proved not to do, but on the grounds I seem to remember that no good result could be expected to result from such an entanglement. An entanglement between two people of such different backgrounds, such *disparate* upbringings and, er, and origins. Do you remember my saying that?'

'Yes, I do, but I can't see what . . .'

'What about it? What advertence? Very little. None at all directly. But it's not often an old man is given the chance of triumphing over a younger one, especially in such a, what you probably call *sensitive area* as this, and I meant and mean no more than to avail myself of that chance. I've no thought of turning it to my advantage.'

'Avail away and welcome. I can't think where that chance would have come from if you hadn't made yourself available to Joanna after all by deciding to turn down your Lady Rowena or Rosie option. Which downturning, having recently seen her, I may say I fully support.'

Gordon was conscious of having put his point with something less than unimprovable clarity and force. Jimmie shared this general view, or affected to. He nodded busily with half-shut eyes and said, 'Just so, just so, I willingly concede that and more. Now I think we might profitably leave this, er, sensitive area and pursue the object of this visit, the notorious *book* I presume you still intend to complete and publish.'

'You presume wrong,' said Gordon quickly, to give Jimmie as little warning as possible. 'I've dropped the whole idea.'

'Ah. Have you told your present publisher of your decision?'

'Yes. He, the firm, won't mind, in fact they made the suggestion before I'd got as far as – '

'Oh, it was the publishers's proposal, I see, that the venture was shelved.'

'In a sense, but I'd already made up my mind before he'd put forward the – '

'Of course you had, dear boy, of course you had. Now for goodness' sake let's sit down and see what we can salvage from the wreck.'

Jimmie's tone had perceptibly lightened since the subject had changed, and although Gordon's news, whatever it might have been in detail, could not exactly have pleased him, his manner remained buoyant. It was almost vivaciously that he sat himself down in a honey-coloured chair of some foreign provenance, clasped his hands together and arranged them over his knee and gave an encouraging nod.

Gordon would have rather liked to stay on his feet, but he knew well enough that the era of preferring to stand when invited to sit had passed with the discontinuance of the JRP Fane novels, if not earlier. So he too sat and said coldly, 'I'm afraid there's no question of my being able to salvage anything.'

'Why, does your publisher, or former publisher, retain some sort of ownership of the work you've done up to this point, or imagine he does?'

'No, it was specifically agreed that I should be free to sell any of the stuff I've got by me to anybody I like.'

'In that case our next step is clear. I told you some of my friends in publishing responded favourably to the notion of a book on the present theme. Well . . .'

'Jimmie, you don't seem to have taken in what I've said. As far as I'm concerned the project is over. I've written no book and never will write one about you and the work I've done up

266

to this point to all intents and purposes has ceased to exist. I intend to sit on it indefinitely. Any new writer or researcher would have to start from scratch. Now do you see?'

'Of course I do.' Jimmie might or might not have seen, but it was doubtful if he had accepted. 'May I ask what has prompted this change of heart? I expect you think people never talk like that, but be assured that some of them do.'

'Oh, is that so? In a nutshell, which is about the right size of container, what's done the prompting is deciding once and for all that you're such a . . . massive and multifarious shit that I disdain to be associated with you in such ways as having my name with yours on a title-page. And the operative part of *that* was funnily enough our last conversation, yours and mine, in Gray's club. You actually thanked me for portraying you as a, as a reprobate among other things and by doing so advancing your esteem among the public. You're not a reluctant shit and certainly not an unconscious shit, you're a self-congratulatory shit.'

'As I remember the matter, you didn't go quite that far, dear boy, in that extract or whatever it was you showed me.'

'I'd probably have put it in later, when I got a proof of it if not before.'

'How sorry I am that that piece will presumably never see the light of day. It would have profited us both. And just to anticipate you, I'm afraid I rather took against that other thing, the critical one, when I considered it closely. I'm afraid I couldn't have let it appear.'

'No good for the paper anyway,' said Gordon. 'Too thin-blooded.'

'That too, indeed. It occurs to me, did it play any part in the reaching of your momentous decision?'

'I read it over last night. I found it over-indulgent to your weaknesses as a writer is a short way of describing what I felt.'

'You know, old fellow, all things considered it may be just as well that this work of yours about me and my works will not now appear. I doubt if it would have furthered my reputation.'

'I understood your bookish pals thought it would trigger off a JRP Fane revival. And just a minute ago you –'

'Did I really say that? I'm afraid I was rather exaggerating in the hope of cheering you on. May I just suggest quickly that what you delicately called my weaknesses as a writer one might be inclined to see instead as evidence of your unsuitability for your task, an unsuitability nothing to do with the powers of your mind in the ordinary sense.'

'But everything to do with the irreducible gap between our respective social groupings.'

'Yes, Gordon,' said Jimmie with great emphasis. 'Yes. Exactly so.'

'When did you decide that that was a fatal weakness?'

'Oh, right at the start, as soon as I heard you speak. I thought it would be amusing to proceed even so. And it has, in my view and I hope in yours.'

'That too, Jimmie.'

'It would distress me somewhat to think that you've suffered financially through me, though I fear there's not very much I could –'

'I've no complaints, none at all.'

After a moment, Jimmie said, 'I'm sorry, I am getting deaf, would you mind terribly saying that again?'

Gordon started to do as he was asked, then stopped and stared. 'You old bugger,' he said without either hostility or affection. 'You wanted to be sure about whether I say *c'mplaints* or *kommplaints* and whether I say *none* or *nonn*. I suppose if I got them wrong you'd have had to decide between me being culpably Yorkshire-Lancashire or criminally tainted with spelling-pronunciation. You old *bugger*.'

'I haven't the faintest idea what you're talking about.'

'Oh yes you have. You looked at me in just the same appraising sort of way as the time you asked me if I pronounced the T in *often* or whatever it was. You were seeing if I fitted into your pattern of horrible nouveau people. Come on, Jimmie, admit it.'

'Oh very well, perhaps the thought did cross my mind. I confess I am a little bit naughty like that once in a way, but we all have things like that about us, don't we? Childish things? M'm? And now perhaps you'll join me in a farewell glass of champagne.'

'Oh God. In one way there's nothing I'd like better but in another I just can't. Too dull and literal-minded and self-righteous.' Gordon would have liked to find a way of putting into words his feeling that he stood for a whole dismal army of buck-toothed scholarship boys with pens and pencils clipped to the V-necks of their grey sweaters who had to be supported to the end against the bucks and rakes, but he could not think how, so after a couple of seconds he said Sorry and left.

He happened to be quitting the house just as Joanna Fane was returning to it. He had not yet pulled shut the front door of the place behind him when she came stepping down from her taxi, so he hesitated a second time and left it. He stood irresolutely back while she paid the driver and went into the building, acknowledging him with the kind of mixture of intimacy and impersonality to be expected between mistress and family servant. Just before she disappeared from his sight she raised her hand to him in an awkward salute. Well, that time, just for a few seconds, he had caught one of them at a perceptible disadvantage.

Gordon looked at his watch and calculated. If he now walked without hurrying to the nearest point of the river where he could board a water-bus, he could then be delivered by one within further walking distance of the newspaper office that held Desmond O'Leary.

That literary journalist was indeed behind his desk when Gordon appeared. He remained in a seated posture only momentarily before bounding to his feet in apparent alarm, seizing the telephone and gabbling into it, 'Security? A strange

269

man I don't much care for the look of has just come bursting in. I'll try and hold him in play till you get to me. Quick as you can.' Then he said to Gordon, 'Who are you and what are you doing here? There's no money to hand except what's in my wallet and a couple of quid in the petty-cash tin. If you'll just leave quietly we'll forget the whole thing.'

Gordon said and did nothing. Experience had taught him that O'Leary's cameos finished faster if it was left to him to keep them going and, sure enough, there soon came a change in the man's expression. Signs of puzzlement appeared there.

'Wait a minute,' he said, lifting a forefinger. 'I could have sworn I'd seen you before somewhere, when you . . . No, it's gone. No! I thought so, you remind me of a fellow, what the deuce was his name, used to hang round here looking for a book to review, many years ago it must be now. Perhaps he was a relative of yours. I've not set eyes on him for, oh, it can't be less than . . .'

'Come off it, Des, I was in here last week three times including Saturday and from now on I'll be coming in . . .'

Gordon's voice too died away. Staring triumphantly at him over his half-glasses, tearing the paper off an oblong cigar by feel alone, O'Leary said in a thrilling voice, 'Has something happened? Something you feel I should know about?'

The cigar was not much burnt down by the time Gordon had told him all it was necessary for him to know. Its recital made it sound tame, the account of a failure of nerve, a prim unwillingness to overcome personal scruples. It seemed that O'Leary found nothing very surprising or reprehensible in any of this. He might have been restrained by scruples of his own, or just as likely he was not listening very hard. Wherever it might have come from, some sort of mildness of manner had kept O'Leary where he was instead of long since having been thrown out of his office window on to one mudflat or another. He said now, 'Without wishing to presume, perhaps we may look forward to your being able to put together something on

JRP Fane for our forthcoming series, the one provisionally entitled *Where Are They Now?*'

'I don't want anything more to do with that old scrounger.'

'We'll discuss the matter further when you've had the chance to distance yourself from the thought of him and from the necessity of seeing him.'

'A century won't be too long for that.'

'Don't you be too sure.' O'Leary's manner became more direct. 'I caught myself being quite tolerant about that old fart EM Forster not so long ago, only in my thoughts, admittedly. I bet you haven't thrown anything away, have you?'

'Not yet.'

'Not on your life. There'll be more in what you've written than you remember. Well now, I won't say I told you so but nobody can prevent me from thinking it. I'm also relieved to see you alive and well and presumably back. I am right in thinking you mean to give us the benefit of your full support in the days that lie ahead?'

'You're saying we can go back to our original arrangement.'

'Yes, which is very decent of me. My old heart must have been touched by the spectacle of the return of the prodigal journalist to where he belongs.'

'You told me once it was important for everybody to know where their limitations are. Oh shit, and as you know I don't say that lightly.'

'What's the matter?'

'I can't drive out of my mind the thought of that old sod Fane picking me up for getting my sequence of tenses wrong.'

'What would he have said?'

'I have to confess, dear boy, that in the context I feel you must mean limitations *were* rather than *are*, surely. I'm afraid that's not very good, Des, I'm sorry.'

'The words were all right but I agree it wasn't much of an imitation. Not your forte, what? Have a word with Harry while you're here.'

271

30

A habit from his early life Gordon had retained was that of devoting a couple of moments to looking at each item in his morning mail with a view to guessing its sender, should this not be irrelevant or instantly obvious. Nearly always, of course, it was one or the other, if not both at once, with possible interest confined to noting if a correspondent had added to the existing corpus of misspellings or other distortions of Gordon and-or Scott and-or Thompson. A previously unrecorded version turned up rarely now.

Then, one fine morning in the early summer of that year, he found on his doormat a postal packet that broke new ground. All his names were correctly rendered, even though in a larger face of typescript than he had thought existed outside dyslexic institutions or the like. The entire object weighed a few dozen grammes, was several millimetres thick and resisted bending. When he had glutted his curiosity without result he rent the envelope asunder.

Inside it was a card with a thick dark-red edge that was obviously more expensive than any mere gold. Some very black embossed printing on it quite soon yielded the information that somebody called Clarence William Dunwich, viijth duke and xviijth earl of Dunwich, whom Gordon was pretty sure he could identify, was inviting him to be present to celebrate his engagement to be married to someone who revealed herself almost at once as old Louise, his, Gordon's, erstwhile girl-friend. Well, well. At first blush, something of a surprise, on little further consideration, not so much of one. The envelope also contained a letter on perhaps simulated calf's-skin including part of a train time-table and with an actual two-way ticket clipped to it. The whole thing seemed a world away from the relaxed manner of Gordon's last invitation from that source, but this, after all, was a bit special. Somewhere it was said that he was expected to be wearing a lounge suit rather than the full armour with casque his fancy first suggested to him. Before he or anyone else could think better of it he telephoned the RSVP number, which consisted of a great many digits, and accepted the invitation.

Once or twice over the intervening couple of weeks he wondered why he was bothering to attend this upper-class junket now that he had no biographical or literary reason to do so, and told himself by way of reply that so disencumbered he would be freer than before to indulge his curiosity, or in simpler terms there was no knowing what he might pick up there, even if it was no more than a piece of first-hand knowledge of what actually went on at such do's. He might even be able to turn such knowledge to his own financial benefit, and mentioned the possibility to Brian Harris on looking in at the latter's office.

'You're going down there anyway, are you?' he asked.

'I thought it might be fun.'

'Fun, Christ. Some people have funny ideas of fun. Or did you develop a taste for that kind of life when you were working on the works of the great Jimmie? As regards your original question, why don't you try your own paper? I'm not your agent, you know, despite what I may have tried and failed to do for you in the past.'

'I did try them, but they said a bloke from their gossip page was set to cover the thing.'

'And if I were your agent I'd be reorganizing my list of clients in a way that unfortunately had no room for your name on it. I don't much like saying this, my old Gordon, but recent events have signally failed to bring you to the forefront of sophisticated attention. I particularly dislike saying that the experts here may not have got it so wrong when they made no-no noises to your Fane book. The close-down of that project raised about as much of a stir as a warning of the cancellation of a dentists' quarterly get-together in South Shields. Sorry, but there we are.'

Gordon had no thought of delivering a riposte when he said, 'Staying in publishing, are you, Brian, or not?'

'Oh, a shrewd thrust, I declare. I finish at this place at the end of the year. No practical alternatives on the horizon as yet.' Brian checked himself and his demeanour quietened. 'I'm sorry,' he said, 'I'm in rather a bad mood today.'

An actual apology from that source was rare and, as for the mention of any mood, bad or good, Gordon had supposed Brian Harris entirely and blessedly free of all such disincentives to action and purposeful thought, and said he was sorry to hear it, though not very, he silently added.

'Every day that passes I feel more like getting out of this racket altogether. Not so long ago I thought of myself as a, I thought I was really a, you know, I don't know what you'd call it, sort of new modern publisher, like one with a whole set of new ideas like thinking publishing was the wrong word for what I was supposed to be doing. Now I think I'm cut out to be just an old-fashioned publisher who brings out books like they did in Graham Greene's time. Or would like to. Does that make any sense to you?'

'Not really, no.'

'Be a museum curator or something. How's Mrs Fane?'

'Fine, I hope.'

'I see. Well. My upper-class lady is still in place, you'll be relieved to hear. It's the only thing that keeps me insane. Yours won't be attending this rave-up, I suppose?'

'I shouldn't think so.'

Nor did she. Nevertheless Gordon found it hard to expunge her image from the events and the locale of that engagement party when the day came along. The first part was all right, consisting as it did of catching and then travelling by a train without the surcharge of encountering any obvious fellow guests. A couple of couples in the buffet-car queue peered and frowned and blinked a good deal in his direction, but they ruled themselves out by their docile bearing and muted voices. Above all, there they were in the buffet-car taking their turn to be served just like everybody else.

Things took a modest turn for the worse when he finally descended on to the single platform of the designated small country station. In its yard he came upon a group of a dozen or more persons of about his age or younger who all looked at him to see if they knew him, some of them swinging round to see him better, and then simultaneously resumed their former postures in some disappointment. Gordon was uncertain of what to do next, but at that moment a single-decker bus-like vehicle drove up and the party regrouped round its point of entry. He was still in some doubt when a tall blonde woman leapt athletically down from the driver's seat, and not just any old tall blonde woman either but one he had seen before in the present connection.

'Polly,' he said to her with some sense of personal vindication.

'That's right, sir, how are you, and will you be requiring tea?'

'Not yet. I think. My watch says twelve-twenty.'

'I meant before you set out on the return journey.'

He made a noise indicating uncertainty and Polly moved off.

Not for the first time in these parts Gordon felt as if he lacked access to some body of information or wisdom denied him for many a long year, perhaps since his birth and by reason of its circumstances. He boarded the bus and settled in a rear seat away from the other passengers, but a backward glance or two suggested to him that some curiosity about who or what he might have been still lingered. To be on the safe side he should have adopted Brian's sure-fire stranger-repellent device and got hold of a large newspaper in Greek or Cyrillic print. Then he wondered why he should want to keep at arm's length the very kind of people he had come all this way to make merry with. He must have forgotten, or until now had been less than fully aware, how much he disliked the English upper classes. As with other social groups of which he was not a member – blacks, queers, women, landlords – they tended on further acquaintance not only to disimprove but also to be seen as increasingly similar among themselves. So if you want to go on thinking that upper-class chaps are not so bad or not so much of a muchness when you get to know them, be sure not to get to know them. That last bit sounded like a piece of advice, one he could foresee himself taking on his departure from Hungerstream later today.

For the moment, in fact any moment, he would have to stand up to arriving at the place. The country road ran through a small village with cottages in or near it. Some of them no doubt held the contemporary descendants of a peasantry reaching back a century or more, others retired civil servants or council employees and their wives, neither kind of occupant enjoying any advantage over the other when it came to being invited to the great house a quarter of a mile or so further on. Even more than before this struck him, when it came into view, as ridiculously vast for just a couple of people to live in, though to feel as much brought him no sense even of attaining equal terms, let alone superiority. Well, he no longer needed to decide what he thought about any of it or of them.

They were there. When, a short while after the others, he descended off the bus into the middle of a large green sunlit space, the first person he saw was Louise in a shiny dove-grey outfit too advanced in conception for him to know what to call it.

'You need a drink' – those were her first words to him, and until she said them he was unaware of their profound truth. A young man with a silver tray propelled a glass in his direction.

Gordon took it. It held some kind of white wine punch, but gin was also present, and not faintly either.

'I worked out you were pretty sure to be part of this bus-load,' said Louise, 'and here you are.'

'Indeed. Whose idea was it to ask me?'

'Both of us's. Why?'

'I don't know really. Just, the other guests I've seen so far are all posh people by the look of them. And the sound of them.'

'All right, I suppose of the two of us it was William who thought of you first.'

'William? Oh yes, of course, William. How nice of him.'

William! This use of the full name was clearly a kind of running-up of the flag, Louise's own personal flag, certainly nothing to do with her fiancé, who within a couple of months would have the pair of them called Willie and something like Boofie everywhere they went if Gordon knew his duke and his upper classes. It was a middle-class wifely habit to give a husband's Christian name a supposed face-lift in ordinary conversation and transform Mike back into Michael, Tim into Timothy, Jim into James. A plebeian wife would never have bothered, though an occasional plebeian mother-in-law might.

'He thought there should be somebody from my side,' Louise was explaining.

'Very thoughtful. But surely he didn't remember what I was called.'

'He wouldn't have taken in a thing like that the first time or two round, but all he had to do was mention the young fellow who came down with me and Jimmie Fane and his missus.'

'They're not here, are they, by any chance?'

'No. One, they're staying with royalty somewhere. Two, they weren't asked.'

'Understood, the first part anyway. But why on earth weren't they asked?'

'William decided he didn't really care for Jimmie. Pushing sort of fellow, he said. You expect that, of course, but you want a touch of charm with it. The way William saw it, he'd paid him back by asking him that first time.'

'Paid him back for what?'

'Well, me, really. Willie told me there was an evening at Gray's when Jimmie was going on and on about, sorry, but he was saying he'd met the most gorgeous girl he'd seen in years, just right for an enterprising fellow like the eighth duke of Dunwich. So to cut a long story short you and I got asked down here and Jimmie had to be asked too at the same time, you see. In a way I've got Jimmie to thank for all this. It makes you wonder.'

'It does indeed.'

'I hope you feel up to meeting him, William I mean, because that's what you do now. In fact you should have done it by rights as soon as you arrived. Where has that man got to?'

Actually he had not got very far, spatially at any rate, in other respects further. He had a glass in his hand from which he refreshed himself twice in under a minute, soon afterwards refilling it from two nearby bottles of which one recognizably held champagne, the other nothing recognizable. Perhaps he was fortifying himself to deal with a semicircle of men of about his age and aspect. The conversation, if that was what they were having, had reached the stage where one of the group, not necessarily the same one each time, would make a loud word-like sound in an unnatural voice and the others would respond with remarkably uniform laughter. When this cycle started up for the fourth time since Gordon had wandered into hearing, he looked over at the duke, but he was drinking freely from his glass. At some point, however, he had presumably spotted Gordon, for after a moment he started to move towards him.

'So glad you could make it,' he said as he came up. 'Keeping pretty well, I imagine?'

No doubt Louise had learnt that, with her fiancé, seeming to recognize someone did not inevitably imply full recognition. 'You remember Gordon Scott-Thompson,' she told him now.

'Who? Of course, little one, of course. Lot of boring old shags to put up with on a day like today,' he went on without lowering his voice at all. 'Speaking of which, my dear, I wonder if I could trouble you to seek out Prince Thingummy and sort of see to him for a few minutes, make sure he's got a drink he fancies and all that.'

'Which is he, William?'

'To tell you the truth I'm not very clear, except that he's black or yellow or one of those. I remember he's got some kind of robes on so he's probably black or at least brown. Run along now. See you at the far end of that eating-tent affair in a brace of shakes.' The duke absently drained his glass, then he looked at Gordon and his manner sharpened. 'Drink that up and have another,' he said.

'Very kind of you, but I've —'

'If you think you don't need any more you're wrong. Don't forget you'll be meeting Louise's parents any moment. As an old friend of the family.'

'My God, I didn't —'

'At least you would have been meeting them if they'd managed to turn up. Mind you, there are plenty of other people here just as boring as they obviously are. Tell me, Gordon, did you ever meet them, Louise's parents?'

'She never even mentioned them to me.'

'Exactly. My own view is she didn't so much as tell them about this jollification taking place. Have to tip them off about the wedding, though. She can hardly hope to keep 'em in ignorance of that, what? That's if they still exist, or ever did. For all I know they blew themselves up while she was still a baby. I feel I've got to give her a bit of leeway over them. After all I get her dancing to my tune about everything else.'

'How do you do that?'

'I'm senior to her in all sorts of ways. Bigger, stronger, older, heavier and of course much, much richer. In fact I'm senior in every possible way, you name it, isn't that right? Jolly handy, that. I expect you've been wondering why I'm going to marry her, haven't you?'

'Not, not specially.'

'Haven't you? How extraordinary in your position. I'll tell you anyway. As you must have noticed, I'm rather a shy sort of chap. In my walk of life, you see, I find I'm meeting people all the time, some I've seen before and some I haven't. Well, most of them I don't care for in one way or another. Now boring old farts, well, they're one thing, after a bit you can handle them, you can put up with 'em, which is just as well. But some fellows you really take against, you want to make sure you never set eyes on 'em a second time. They're the awkward ones. I mean, a shy sort of chap like me can't quite bring himself to go up to someone and tell them in so many words to get out and stay out. Case of the spirit's willing but the flesh is weak, eh? That's where little Louise comes in. I find I can quite easily go up to someone and tell him I don't mind him myself but my wife can't stand the sight of him. Do it without turning a hair. It seems to make all the difference, saying it's her not me.'

'How does she feel about the arrangement?'

'Oh, all for it. Sometimes she does her own chucking out, there were a couple of music fellows just last week. That's really why I've got engaged to her. There are plenty of reasons for me to have a wife, but that's why I picked her, because she doesn't care for people any more than I do. You must have noticed that about her yourself.'

'I see what you mean.'

'Good.' The duke brought out a hefty timepiece at the end of a gold chain that looked sufficient to have bound Andromeda quite securely to her rock. He pressed something and the lid over the dial flew open. 'Nigger workmanship never was any good,' he said. 'There should be some grub left if we go after it now.'

There was plenty of grub left, in the shape of asparagus, gravad lax with sliced cucumber, cold chicken and ham, and potato and tomato-and-onion salads. To wash this down, magnums of château-bottled claret stood a couple of yards apart on every table. The noise, from boring old farts, fellows really taken against and perhaps others, was adequate to the occasion.

'I fancy it's a case of every man for himself here,' said the duke.

Fresh raspberries and cream, Beaumes-de-Venise, coffee, a VSOP brandy and Punch cigars followed in due course. Feeling several years older, Gordon eventually found himself in close conversation with Louise.

'Well, what do you think?' she asked him. 'You haven't really said.'

'I think you've done very well for yourself, and I don't mean that nastily.'

'I believe you. But you mean it wouldn't do for you.'

'Very likely not.'

'Obviously not. You're not seeing Joanna Fane any more, are you?'

'No. Not in the way you mean. No, I'm not.'

'I suppose it all got quite impossible, did it?'

'That would be one way of putting it.'

'I know people shouldn't inquire too closely into these sort of things, but from what I gather Jimmie was going back to one of his ex-wives or girl-friends but then he got cold feet and he stayed with Joanna on condition she dropped you, is that right?'

'More or less, on the understanding that the girl-friend in question would have given bolder men than Jimmie cold feet.'

They walked in silence for a time, out of sight of the house and towards the dilapidated remains of some habitation or chapel. Other couples or small groups were to be seen here and there, the bright colours of their clothes showing up against the surrounding greenery. The air was pleasantly warm. Louise looked at Gordon twice in quick succession.

'Don't I see a sort of fuzz on your upper lip?' she asked.

'You do. And to anticipate your next question, the answer's yes, I am growing a moustache, or re-growing my moustache, whichever you prefer.'

'Is that to show the world you're back in your old life?'

'I doubt if the world would take much notice whatever I showed it. No, it's more like a reminder to me, if it's anything more than just a moustache.'

'You needn't answer this if you don't feel like it, but you were very attached to Joanna, weren't you?'

'Yes, I was. In a way I still am.'

'Did you, you know, try to get her back at all or get her to stay with you or anything?'

'Not really. We both decided that, well, we weren't suited to a long affair. Because of the age difference and so on.'

'But much more because of the class difference and so on.' Louise spoke almost indignantly, at any rate with great vigour. Her glance flickered to and fro. 'Well wasn't it?'

'I suppose it was in a way.'

'*In a way*, Christ. William was right, of course he was, and I know you think it's comic of him to have a view about anything, but on this one he knows what he's saying, because he's done what you and Joanna couldn't face doing and is getting married outside his class. Oh, they're really there, all those distinctions are, but you shouldn't let them get out of hand and start letting them interfere with your personal feelings. It isn't class differences that keep people apart, it's thinking they bloody *matter*.'

'Is that you or William talking?'

'Take your choice. Do you mind if we go back now?'